The New York Times

CHICKEN COOKBOOK

The New York Times

CHICKEN
COOKBOOK

Edited by Linda Amster

Foreword by Julia Reed

ST. MARTIN'S PRESS ❦ NEW YORK

IN LOVING MEMORY

Steven H. Bazerman

Nika Hazelton

www.stmartins.com

Library of Congress Cataloging-in-Publication Data

The New York Times chicken cookbook / edited by Linda Amster ; foreword by Julia Reed.
   p. cm.
  ISBN 0-312-31234-2
  EAN 978-0-312-31234-3
  1. Cookery (Chicken).   I. Title: Chicken cookbook.   II. Amster, Linda.   III. New York Times.

TX750.5.C45N49 2005
641.6'65—dc22   2004065821

First Edition: August 2005

10 9 8 7 6 5 4 3 2 1

CONTENTS

FOREWORD

By Julia Reed

There is a song, recorded in 1940 by Louis Jordan and his Tympany Five, called "Chicken Ain't Nothin' But a Bird." It has a very catchy tune and funny lyrics, some of which pay homage to the chicken's long history ("It was a dish for ole Caesar, also King Henry III"), and some to its remarkable versatility ("You can boil it, roast it, broil it, put it in a pan or pot"). But in the end, the song does not treat the noble fowl with the proper respect ("Columbus was hip, he said 'Take this tip, a chicken ain't nothin' but a bird'"), so I just can't get behind it.

For one thing, chicken is far more than just a bird. It has long been a political symbol—Jordan's lyrics may rhyme, but it was actually Henry IV who said in his coronation speech that "I want there to be no peasant in my realm so poor that he will not have a chicken in his pot every Sunday," a line Herbert Hoover's campaign organizers rephrased into "A chicken in every pot and a car in every garage" almost four hundred years later. Neither man made good on his promise—as late as Hoover's day, only the affluent and people who raised chickens at home could count on a weekly poultry feast.

In the 1940's, when new production methods made chicken more readily available to the masses, chicken also became a cultural touchstone—and King Henry's vision of Sunday dinners synonymous with chicken came true. In the South, that Sunday chicken is still most likely to be fried—Colonel Sanders said his franchised

"Original Recipe" made "Sunday dinner" available "seven days a week"—but chicken and dumplings, barbecued chicken, and chicken pot pie are equally archetypal American chicken dishes, along with baked or roasted chicken with stuffing, and, most recent, beer can chicken.

Beer can—or "drunken"—chicken, featuring a whole chicken rubbed with spices and grilled while sitting upright, stuffed with a half-empty can of beer (its other name is "chicken on a throne"), could only be an American invention, but, in the words of my old *Joy of Cooking,* "the chicken is a world citizen." All the breeds of today's domestic chickens descend from the red jungle fowl that roamed the dense primeval forests of Southeast Asia, where it still exists in the wild. Domesticated chickens may have been kept in India as long ago as 3200 B.C., and they were definitely kept in China and Egypt as far back as 1400 B.C., but those early birds were primarily used for cockfights. However, by the time Columbus introduced chickens to the New World, folks all over the Old World had figured out that they were even better suited for dinner.

The scope of the recipes in this book is a testament to the culinary status of chicken throughout the globe. There is chicken cacciatore and coq au vin, of course, along with Spanish paella, Indian curries and tandoor, Chinese stir-fries, Hungarian paprikash, Morrocan tagines, Mexican tamales and Jamaican jerk. The recipes for wings alone feature those from Vietnam, Malaysia, China and Buffalo, New York. There are American recipes with foreign overtones including: Country Captain, a dish brought to the American South from India via England by, legend has it, a British sea captain who supplied its name; and Mimi Sheraton's Subgum Chicken Chow Mein, a dish that does not exactly exist in China, but to which Sheraton applies Fellini's quote about "the soft and gentle flavors of the past." It's a dish that happens to be straight out of my own past—growing up in Greenville, Mississippi, I probably ate it once a week at Henry Wong's How Joy, along with chicken egg foo young and moo goo gai pan. Henry, a Baptist and an extremely astute businessman, was as American as the fried chicken that turned up on his Sunday lunch buffet. After China was opened and a prominent local grocer made the trek, he returned to pronounce the food not nearly as delicious as that which he regularly enjoyed at How Joy.

While I am naturally a lover of fried chicken, I have to say that I think it is roast chicken that best exemplifies the bird's intrinsic greatness. The phrase "a simple roast chicken" is belied by the fact that in the first chapter of this book, there are thirty-four recipes for it, ranging from chickens roasted with tarragon, forty cloves of garlic, and even vanilla, to those fussed over by such French greats as Andre Soltner and Daniel Boulud. Roast chicken can be a masterpiece with crisp, golden skin and tender, juicy meat redolent with the flavor of whatever was stuffed in its cavity or pushed under its skin. It was what I ordered the first time I was taken to Manhattan's La Grenouille at fourteen, and I still equate it with fine French dining. It can also conjure feelings of comfort and home, but I have always found it to be a sexy dish, the perfect thing for a romantic picnic, as in Lady Wortley Montagu's "The Lover": "But when the long hours of public are past, And we meet, with champagne and a chicken, at last."

Since chicken's democratization—and thanks to such aberrations as Shake 'n Bake and Swanson's frozen dinners—I'm sometimes afraid that the perception lingers that chicken is not fancy enough for company, which couldn't be further from the truth. In the fifties, chic hostesses wowed their guests with the sophisticated-sounding Chicken Divan. My own first dinner parties featured Craig Claiborne's Chicken Breasts with Mustard Sauce (page 207) or tarragon cream, and I once watched my mother and her best friend make chicken Kiev for a seated dinner of sixty. I remember being amazed that their tedious efforts, flattening the breasts and rolling them around a dab of seasoned butter, ended up yielding the miraculous payoff that was the chicken's luxurious texture and the exciting spurt of melted butter in the mouth. Chicken Cordon Bleu, another classic company dish, is featured here, as is Chicken Pot-au-Feu. I was recently served the latter in the dining room of one of New York's most acclaimed hostesses, preceded by foie gras with Chateau D'Yquem and followed by a frozen praline soufflé—a totally elegant meal that ranks up there with an exquisite roast chicken I was once served perfumed with black truffles under the skin.

Lately chicken has been revered not just for its taste but for its nutritional content, particularly in this age of low-carbohydrate diets. A three-ounce piece of meat fulfills almost half the daily protein requirement, contains no carbs and has almost no fat (without the skin). According to the National Chicken Council, per capita consumption in 2004 was a whopping 86.3 pounds, compared to 28 pounds in 1960, while consumption of beef has been on the decline.

Whatever the reason you're buying, it's best to look for a chicken with the most elaborate pedigree possible (organic, cage-free, free-range, and so on). Birds labeled "free range" are allotted twice the one square foot of indoor space that mass-produced birds are allowed and they get to run around outside, too, a privilege that gives them a more expensive price tag but a more chicken-y taste. My friend, the amazing Jeremiah Tower (the man responsible for the truffled chicken), recommends letting the chicken dry out for about three hours if it's been wrapped in plastic, and he also gives it a lemon juice bath before cooking.

I am delighted that chicken happens to be so good for me—among its other good qualities are that it is high in the B vitamin niacin, said to be helpful in preventing

both cancer and Alzheimer's disease. But that is not the reason I eat it. I eat it because there is virtually no incarnation of it that I don't adore. I eat it because as the enormous scope of recipes in this book attest—and Louis Jordan's song aside—chicken is indeed more than just a bird. It is the most versatile of all meats, as funky as Paul Prud-homme's gumbo (page 328), as rich as a fricassee with morels and as regal as the king who wished it for his peasants.

PREFACE

No matter how you slice it—or prepare it—chicken is a canvas for infinite combinations of tastes and textures. That may be why, when I look over a menu in a restaurant or browse through a cookbook, the poultry section is invariably my first stop. And, as often as not, it's why chicken—in one form or another—is on my plate at home and when I'm dining out.

I am by no means alone in my fascination with chicken dishes. Their popularity seems as ubiquitous as the bird itself—which is understandable, given its wide availability, its moderate cost, its nutritional value and its astonishing versatility.

Check the shelves of any major bookstore and you will find cookbooks galore dedicated to the appetites of chicken lovers. There they are, lined up like hens in a coop—some devoted to a single method of preparation, like fried chicken, or even a single course, such as soup; some are compiled by noted cookbook writers or by food publications, into collections that highlight their finest chicken specialties.

But this book adopts a different approach, cutting across those categories.

The recipes that follow come from two sources—*The New York Times* and cookbooks by *Times* writers.

Those culled from the newspaper's archives showcase some of the best chicken dishes ever to appear in *The Times*'s food pages—dishes created by celebrated chefs and restaurateurs, by outstanding home cooks and, of course, by *The Times*'s own renowned food writers and columnists, as well as those reprinted from notable cookbooks and other sources.

Within each of the chapters, which are arranged by method of preparation, you will find selections from humble to haute—a balance of family and classic recipes for traditional fare and of contemporary dishes with a more innovative flair.

The "Perfect Roast Chicken" section, for example, reflects the pattern of all the chapters. There are almost three dozen mouth-watering variations on that theme— recipes ranging from the simplest preparations (designated by the word *EASY*) to more complex variations. They can be as basic as No-Hassle Roast Chicken or as sophisti-cated as Aquavit's Roasted Chicken with Spiced Apples and Onions, Daniel Boulud's Roast Chicken with Herbs and Wild Mushrooms, and even Craig Claiborne's witty Roast Chicken Stuffed with Scrambled Eggs. Essays and commentaries by *Times* writ-ers offer helpful background and handy tips about preparation.

No matter how chicken is prepared, it arguably ranks as the entrée of choice around the world—transformed in pots and woks, tandooris and tagines, over open flames and inside microwaves into dishes that reflect national cuisines and local crav-ings. I have tried to balance regional American classics like Chicken Gumbo and Buffalo Chicken Wings with recipes that underscore the bird's international appeal— dishes such as Chicken Kiev from Russia, Cacciatore from Italy, Teriyaki from Japan. In the chapter "A Meal in Itself" you'll find more than two dozen such favorites, from Indian curries to Spanish Arroz con Pollo, from Hungarian Chicken Paprika to an African stew called Hkatenkwan.

I hope the recipes that follow, with their diverse ingredients and methods of preparation, will inspire seasoned cooks who want to expand their repertoire of chicken dishes as well as novices who are just beginning to develop one.

Here's to chicken in every pot and in every way!

About the Recipes and Text

All recipes are reprinted either from *The New York Times* or from cookbooks by writers formerly affiliated with *The Times*. Restaurants and chefs are identified as they were at the time of publication and not necessarily as they are now, since some chefs have left the restaurants with which they were associated and some restaurants have closed. Similarly, personal identifications of recipe contributors are reproduced as they appeared in the paper and may have changed since their original publication.

Every recipe reprinted from the newspaper is followed by the name of the person who wrote the article in which it appeared. Recipes without that byline credit are from cookbooks written either by Craig Claiborne, the paper's renowned food editor, whose coverage profoundly influenced generations of readers and food professionals, by his frequent collaborator, food columnist Pierre Franey, or by the veteran food writer Jean Hewitt.

Cooking Methods

Roasting: The whole chicken, seasoned with herbs and/or coated with fat or moistened with wine or other liquid, is cooked uncovered in an oven and basted with juices that accumulate during the cooking process. Roasting is usually at a moderate temperature, although some recipes call for either a high-heat method or slow roasting over a low heat. Allow the roasted bird to rest when it is removed from the oven.

Baking: Pieces are cooked in a sauce, either covered or uncovered, in an oven, usually at a moderate temperature.

Braising: Pieces are browned briefly in a Dutch oven or other large pot on top of the stove, after which seasonings and liquid are added. The pot is then covered and the dish is cooked, either on top of the stove or in the oven, at low to moderate heat. The juices from the meat are released, combining with the seasoned liquid to create a flavorful sauce. This is an excellent method for cooking older, larger birds whose meat becomes tender through long cooking.

Grilling/Broiling: The chicken, whole or in pieces, is cooked using very high direct heat, either on a rack placed above the heat on a grill or in a pan below the heat in a broiler. With either method, baste the meat frequently to prevent it from drying out.

Sautéing: Pieces are patted dry and, if desired, coated with crumbs and/or seasonings, then browned over moderate heat in a small amount of fat that has been heated in a skillet or pan. If lightly browned, the meat may then be cooked in a small amount of liquid in an open pan until done.

Stir-frying: A variation of sautéing in which bite-sized pieces are browned in enough very hot fat to cover them completely. They should be completely drained and eaten as soon as possible.

Deep frying: Pieces are patted dry, dipped in beaten egg yolk and/or other liquid and then coated before being completely immersed in sizzling fat or oil and cooked until done.

Poaching: The whole bird or pieces are submerged in barely simmering liquid—usually a plain or flavored water, wine, broth or a combination of liquids, until the meat is tender.

Steaming: The whole bird or pieces, either seasoned or plain, are cooked on a rack or plate over simmering liquid—usually a plain or flavored water, wine, broth or combination of liquids. Overcooking is unlikely because the heat is indirect and gentle.

ACKNOWLEDGMENTS

First, my sincerest appreciation to the noted chefs, restaurateurs, cookbook authors and other fine cooks who graciously granted permission for their exceptional recipes to be included in this book. Each recipe, first showcased in the food pages of *The New York Times*, is an outstanding example of contemporary cooking and is a special contribution to this collection.

I am particularly grateful to my *New York Times* colleagues—especially to Mark Bittman, Florence Fabricant, Amanda Hesser, Moira Hodgson, Bryan Miller, Molly O'Neill and Mimi Sheraton—for their superb recipes and valued commentaries, which appeared under their bylines in *The Times*, and to the late Craig Claiborne, Pierre Franey and Jean Hewitt, whose classic recipes enhance this volume.

Warm thanks to Julia Reed, for her personal and evocative foreword, as well as for her essay about Southern fried chicken—the definitive word on one of America's favorite dishes.

Of the many people to whom I am indebted at St. Martin's Press, first and foremost there is my editor, Michael Flamini. He was a pleasure to work with and his knowledge of food, his astute observations and his much-appreciated enthusiasm made this a truly collaborative effort. Thanks also to Katherine Tiernan, who so skillfully assisted him, and to the rest of the St. Martin's team for their indispensable contributions: copy editor Arthur Gatti, production editor Mark Steven Long, production manager Susan Joseph, book designers Kate Nichols and Michelle McMillian, and cover designer Karen Horton.

At *The New York Times*, a special salute to Mitchel Levitas, who, as the editorial director of book development, suggested this project to me. As always, he provided essential guidance and assistance with the manuscript and in many other ways. Sincere admiration to Tomi Murata, who helped steer a steady course through the tangle of details that inevitably accompany a collection of this kind, and to Phyllis Collazo, for expertly culling the paper's photo archives to select the pictures that accompany the recipes.

My abiding thanks and love to Mort Sheinman for his wondrous editing—and for his immense importance in my life.

Finally, boundless gratitude to Judy Knipe—a superb cookbook author and editor. Her astute judgment and wise counsel, so valued in our long and cherished friendship, are evident on every page. Without her, this book would not have been possible.

A PERFECT ROAST CHICKEN

Roast Chicken: Nothing Tough About It

By Molly O'Neill

If you can roast a chicken, you can cook. Because if you can roast a chicken, you can serve a dinner for company just as easily as a satisfying family supper or a simple repast. After all, chicken can be plain, as any backyard chef who's ever waved a brush full of barbecue sauce will tell you, or it can be fancy, with truffles, compound butters and rich, delicate sauces.

In *Roasting*, Barbara Kafka praises the bird's versatility: "When in doubt, roast a chicken. When hurried, roast a chicken. Seeking simple pleasure? Roast a chicken." Hers is an easy and nearly infallible technique: Season the bird. Preheat the oven to 500 degrees. Then roast, allowing 10 minutes per pound.

Regardless of the quality or type of chicken, this method insures crisp skin and succulent meat. However, you will also have a very smoky kitchen, dining room and living room. For some, this is a small price. Others find the smoke disconcerting.

I think it is uplifting to wonder, even for a nanosecond, if a dinner guest's tears are ones of joy. Nevertheless, I trade a degree of crispness for less smoke. After a 10-minute blast of 500-degree heat, I roast at 425 degrees for the duration, allowing 12 minutes of cooking time per pound.

Either approach is simple. And if you want nothing more than a reliable, satisfying meal, read no further; just preheat the oven. If, on the other hand, you seek gastronomic heights in an uncomplicated form, consider the variables that can account for the flavor, the succulence, the crispness—the nuances—of a roasted chicken.

First, consider the bird. Since its domestication in India roughly four thousand years ago, chicken has been coaxed from a tough, muscular fellow into the tender, large-breasted fowl commonly sold in supermarkets today. The grocery-store variety is usually a battery-raised bird, which has been confined to a small wire box for anywhere from forty-five days to ten months, depending on whether it is a three-to-four-pound broiler or fryer or a large fowl or stewing hen. A free-range chicken, sold in food-specialty stores, is like the birds of yore: it is allowed to roam and may take twice the time to reach maturity as a battery-raised chicken.

The sedentary chickens tend to be more tender and meaty; they also tend to be tasteless. According to Harold McGee's *On Food and Cooking*, some seventeenth-century Frenchmen preferred chickens raised in coops or in baskets suspended from the wall. Today, toothsome chicken has become common. Too common. Free-range chicken is now all that's considered fashionable.

The fans of free-range champion the bird's wholesome diet, which generally includes no hormones or antibiotics. They also praise its old-fashioned chicken flavor and its character, which is another way of saying toughness. Such people are willing to pay up to three times more per pound for taste, nostalgia and the possibility of a more healthful meal.

But whatever your preference, each type of chicken requires particular attention. A free-range bird needs less seasoning and more basting, even marinating, to become a tender meal. Lacking distinct flavor, a commercial chicken needs help in the early stages but requires little attention once it hits the oven.

The flavor of a commercial chicken can be enhanced by rubbing it inside and out with a lemon. This creates a cleaner taste and may increase the skin's crispness. In addition to carrots and celery, aromatics, particularly chopped onions or shallots, can be stuffed in the cavity to perfume the bird. Stuffing it with cloves of garlic, branches of rosemary, tarragon leaves, parsley or thyme will also flavor the surrounding flesh.

In hedonistic moments, I also tuck a pat of butter, along with either fresh rosemary, tarragon or thyme, between the skin and the flesh of the breast. This insures moist meat and lovely flavor. Or use a variety of compound butters: butter mixed with flavorings like garlic, lemon, olives, curries, chili peppers, sun-dried tomatoes—just about anything that is compatible with chicken. Olive oil can be used to make nut pastes, olive pastes or pastes of aromatic vegetables to gently press between meat and skin. Such ministrations are critical for free-range chickens, as well as birds certified as organic. (These are raised without hormones in either cages or the free-range manner.) Without the extra moisture, you'll have stringy breast meat.

Whether you're roasting an ordinary or a free-range chicken, the skin also needs to be seasoned with salt and pepper before cooking—at least to my taste. Then again, I like salt, which may explain why I prefer roasting kosher chickens, which have been treated with salt; presumably, the kosher process leaves some residual salt in the meat.

Others observe that salting causes the skin to cook unevenly. But to me, a nearly imperceptible unevenness in the crisping of the skin is worth the additional flavor.

Today you can have your salt and crackly skin, too, by basting the bird with equal amounts of soy sauce and water. Evenly painting the surface yields even crispness and flavor. (In Chinese cuisine, the bird is sometimes submerged in a brine containing either soy sauce or salt, or both.) Or combine salt with a range of spices, like ground ginger, coriander, cumin or peppers, to name a few.

Now you're getting closer to final decisions, which include whether to truss the bird and whether to bring it to room temperature before cooking.

For battery-raised chicken, there are potentially ten thousand reasons per square centimeter to make haste between the refrigerator and the stove. According to McGee's book, a typical piece of pork contains several hundred bacteria per square centimeter, while a chicken can contain ten thousand.

This explains the importance of thoroughly cleansing hands, knives and surfaces when handling raw chicken. It also proves that unless the skin of a chicken is completely cooked, room temperature is risky.

On the other hand, rushing the bird from the refrigerator to the oven makes for dramatically uneven roasting and wildly variable cooking times. I choose to live dangerously, but I hedge my bets.

If stuffing a bird, even with simple aromatics, I bring it to room temperature and stuff both the cavity and the surface beneath the skin just before roasting. I also make sure that the skin is too crisp to support any nefarious life form.

I truss as well, but without bondage. Instead, I cut a small slit on each side of the flap of skin below the chicken's cavity, cross the bird's legs and push each one into the slit on the opposing side. It makes for a polite presentation and easy cutting.

Now come the questions of heat, position and basting. Accept the fact that roasting as we know it—in a modern, conventional oven—is really not roasting at all. Rather, it is baking and steaming, since the moisture released when a chicken is heated remains in the oven and inevitably softens the skin. The crisp skin of real roasting results from the interplay of heat and air, as in an open oven or a fireplace, preferably one equipped with a spit.

But with a modern oven there are still ways to offset the steam. Very high heat helps, as do basting and turning. One of the most laborious methods is that advocated by James Beard, who favored free-range birds. He recommended seasoning and trussing a four-to-five-pound chicken, buttering its skin, placing it on a rack in a roasting pan and cooking it on its side in a 425-degree oven for 20 minutes. The chicken is then turned on its opposite side for 20 minutes. Finally, it is roasted for 20 minutes, breast-side up.

This technique renders an extremely juicy bird, but its skin is neither crisp nor a reassuring walnut color. For a bird just as juicy, with a moderately crispy, nut-brown skin, cook it on a rack in a roasting pan in a 425-degree oven for 1 hour, basting every 10 minutes. Basting and using an even lower temperature (350 degrees for 1 hour and 30 minutes) yields a soft-skinned bird with slightly dry flesh but superb flavor. These two methods are equally appropriate for free-range and battery-raised chickens.

Barbara Kafka's blasting-the-bird technique eschews baking racks, basting and salting the chicken's skin. She simply uses a lemon to refresh the interior and exterior of the bird, then seasons the cavity lightly with salt and pepper, as well as aromatics like shallots, onion, celery leaves, sage and bay leaves.

For my own combination-temperature method, I place the bird directly in a well-seasoned cast-iron pan, which promotes a crisp skin on the chicken's underside and conducts heat more evenly than lighter roasting pans. I don't use a rack under the bird because I'm lazy and I like pan drippings. A little water or wine and a couple of scrapes and you have au jus.

I also baste. It isn't necessary, but it makes me feel that I've earned a crisp-skinned, tender bird.

I recommend testing the doneness of chicken by pricking the thickest part of the thigh. If the juices have a faint pink tinge, the bird is done. If the juices are perfectly clear, it is overdone. A thermometer can be inserted in the same place (it should register 165 degrees), but the bone often gets in the way of an accurate reading.

In practice, however, I neither prick nor prod a chicken. I know it is done by the smell, by the wiggle of the thigh, by the firmness of the breast when it is gently pressed. I guess it's a kind of instinct.

I have no idea how many chickens a cook must roast before know-how becomes instinct. Lots. However, once you can sense the second in which flesh and fire have reached the apogee of their collaboration, you can cook just about anything.

MOLLY O'NEILL'S
SIMPLE ROAST CHICKEN

1 3½- to 4-pound kosher chicken
1 teaspoon kosher salt
Freshly ground pepper to taste

1. Preheat the oven to 500 degrees. Remove the giblets and excess fat from the cavity of the chicken and allow it to come to room temperature, about 30 minutes.

2. Cut the tail off and pat the chicken dry with paper towels. Season the bird inside and out with salt and pepper. With the point of a sharp knife, cut a small slit in the flap of skin at the tail end of the bird on each side and insert the tip of each drumstick through the slit on the opposite side. (This will keep the legs secure as the chicken roasts.)

3. Place the chicken on a roasting rack in a medium-size roasting pan or heavy oven-proof skillet. Roast in the oven for 10 minutes at 500 degrees; lower the temperature to 425 and continue to roast for an additional 40 to 55 minutes. To test for doneness, use a skewer or the point of a small knife to pierce the thickest part of the thigh; if the juices are only faintly pink, the chicken is done. Or tip the bird slightly to check the juices running from the cavity; they should not be red. (A slight rosy tinge is fine, however.)

4. Remove the chicken from the oven and allow it to rest at room temperature for 10 minutes. Cut the flaps of skin that hold the legs together and carve the chicken. Serve immediately.

YIELD: 3 TO 4 SERVINGS   *Molly O'Neill*

FLORENCE FABRICANT'S
BASIC ROAST CHICKEN

1 4- to 5-pound chicken
1 lemon
1 tablespoon olive oil, vegetable oil or soft butter
Salt and freshly ground black pepper
3 to 4 sprigs parsley
2 medium onions
Water
½ cup dry white wine or chicken stock (optional)
1 teaspoon cornstarch (optional)

1. Remove the package of gizzards, heart, liver and neck from the cavity of the chicken. Except for the liver, these parts can be used to make stock. You may wish to freeze them until you have the innards of several chickens. Sauté the liver and spread on toast, or freeze it separately, adding to your supply of frozen livers as you buy whole chickens.

2. Preheat oven to 400 degrees.

3. Rinse the chicken with cold water and pat it dry on a paper towel. Pull off any excess fat from the back of the cavity near the tail. This fat can be sautéed slowly in a small skillet to use for frying or it can be frozen for future use. Pull out with tweezers or singe over an open flame any large pinfeathers on the wings. Squeeze the juice of half the lemon into the cavity and rub it in.

4. Rub the outside of the chicken with the oil or butter. Season the chicken inside and out with salt and pepper. Tuck the lemon halves and the parsley into the cavity. Peel and quarter one of the onions and tuck the quarters into the cavity.

5. The chicken will hold its shape better if it is trussed. At the very least, tuck the wing tips behind the chicken and, using butcher's cord, tie the legs together. To truss the chicken completely, first loop cord around the tail and crisscross it around the legs, pulling the legs together tightly. Then run the length of cord along the sides of the chicken, just under the drumstick and through the wing joints, pulling the ends together across the back near the neck, securing the extra flap of neck skin under the cord. Tie the cord securely, making for a tight, plump-looking bird.

6. Peel and slice the remaining onion and scatter it in the roasting pan. Position the chicken on a rack and place in the oven. Roast for 13 to 15 minutes a pound, until

the juices run clear when the meaty flesh of the upper thigh is pricked with a sharp fork. If the onions in the pan appear to be browning too rapidly while the chicken is roasting, add a little water to the pan. The onions should become dark brown but should not be allowed to blacken.

7. Remove the chicken to a platter or cutting surface and allow it to rest 10 to 15 minutes before carving.

8. Skim any excess fat from the roasting pan. Add several tablespoons of water to the roasting pan, place it on top of the stove over medium heat and stir, scraping up any browned bits clinging to the pan. Strain the pan juices into a small saucepan. These juices can be seasoned with salt and pepper and used to moisten the portions of chicken or can be used to make a gravy. Add the wine or stock to the juices and bring to a simmer. Dissolve the cornstarch in 1 tablespoon cold water and stir into the gravy mixture. Simmer until thickened, then season.

9. Carve the chicken by cutting through the joints to remove the drumsticks and wings, then slicing the breast meat and thigh meat. Arrange the meat on a platter and serve either moistened with pan juices or with the gravy on the side.

YIELD: 4 SERVINGS ⟞ *Florence Fabricant*

✦ EASY ✦
NO-HASSLE ROAST CHICKEN

(Adapted from *How to Cook Without a Book*)

Butterflying the chicken—by removing the backbone and flattening the bird—makes roasting quicker and carving much easier.

> 1 3- to 3½-pound chicken, backbone removed, rinsed, patted dry
>   and butterflied
> Salt and freshly ground black pepper
> 2 tablespoons olive oil or softened butter

1. Adjust oven rack to lower-middle position and heat oven to 450 degrees. After butterflying chicken, place it on a foil-lined 18-by-12-inch shallow roasting pan. Season under skin with salt and pepper. Pat skin back in place and drizzle with oil or rub with butter.

2. Roast chicken until golden brown and its juices run clear, about 40 minutes. Let stand 5 minutes, then cut into two breast-and-wing pieces and two leg-and-thigh pieces.

VARIATION: For roast chicken with Dijon mustard and fresh bread crumbs, remove chicken from oven after 25 minutes of roasting. Pour off and reserve pan drippings. Brush chicken with ¼ cup Dijon mustard, then sprinkle with 1 cup fresh bread crumbs. Drizzle reserved pan drippings over bread crumbs. Return chicken to oven and roast until crumbs are golden brown and juices run clear, 10 to 15 minutes longer.

YIELD: 4 SERVINGS *Amanda Hesser*

✦ EASY ✦
ELIZABETH FRINK'S ROAST LEMON CHICKEN

(Adapted from *The Artists' and Writers' Cookbook*)

Because the chicken is infused with the taste of lemon, it is perfect picnic fare—either served cold as an entrée, or as a sandwich—preferably on thin-sliced brioche with butter or a little homemade mayonnaise, salt and black pepper.

1 3-pound chicken
½ teaspoon salt
¼ teaspoon pepper
2 lemons
6 cloves garlic, peeled

2 tablespoons butter
2 tablespoons olive oil
1 tablespoon coarsely chopped
   fresh parsley

1. Preheat the oven to 325 degrees. Place the chicken in a large baking dish and season inside and out with salt and pepper. Rub the peel of one of the lemons over the outside of the chicken. Then cut the lemon into 8 pieces and squeeze juice over and into the chicken. Put the lemon pieces inside the chicken along with the garlic cloves. In a small pan, melt the butter in the olive oil and pour on top and inside the chicken. Tie the legs together with kitchen string.

2. Roast the chicken for 1½ hours, until an instant-read thermometer inserted in the thickest part of the leg registers 180 degrees or the thigh juices run clear, basting every 15 minutes with pan juices. Half an hour before taking the chicken out, pour the juice from the second lemon over the chicken and sprinkle with parsley.

YIELD: 4 SERVINGS ⟋ *Julia Reed*

✦ EASY ✦

ROAST CHICKEN WITH TARRAGON

1 3- to 4-pound chicken
About ½ cup tarragon leaves, loosely
    packed

Half a lemon
Olive oil or duck fat
Coarse sea salt and freshly ground
    pepper to taste

1. Preheat the oven to 500 degrees. Wipe the chicken dry with paper towels. Insert the tarragon leaves under chicken skin over the breast and legs. (Do this by pushing your finger underneath and gently making a pocket for the leaves without ripping the skin.) Put the lemon in the cavity of the chicken. Brush the chicken with oil and season to taste with salt and pepper, then truss it.

2. Roast without opening the oven door, if possible, for 40 minutes. The chicken is done when the juices run clear and yellow and the leg moves easily in the socket. Allow it to rest for 5 minutes before serving.

YIELD: 4 SERVINGS ⟋ *Moira Hodgson*

ROAST CHICKEN WITH THYME AND GINGER

This is a variation on a classic French recipe, in which chicken is roasted with leaves of tarragon and pieces of butter on the skin. Instead, very thin slices of ginger are placed under the skin, along with fresh leaves of thyme and a little oil, instead of butter. For those who are cutting down on fat, the skin can be removed after cooking, and the breast will retain an aroma of ginger and thyme. Ginger roots should be hard, with a smooth skin and not in the least withered or pliable. They keep for up to 2 weeks in the vegetable bin of the refrigerator.

1 3- to 3½-pound chicken
2 tablespoons ginger, sliced very thin
2 tablespoons fresh thyme leaves
Coarse salt and freshly ground pepper to taste
2 tablespoons olive oil
1 tablespoon soy sauce
6 cloves garlic, unpeeled

1. Preheat oven to 375 degrees. Using your fingers, separate the skin from the chicken breast and insert the ginger and thyme leaves, pushing them back as far as you can, to the legs if possible. Add 1 tablespoon of olive oil, pulling back the skin and pouring it in from a teaspoon.

2. Season the chicken inside and out with salt and pepper and sprinkle with olive oil and soy sauce. Place the chicken on its side on a rack in a roasting pan and arrange the garlic cloves underneath.

3. Roast the chicken for about 1 hour or until it is cooked, turning it on its other side after 20 minutes and finishing it breast-up. Allow to cool for 10 minutes before serving, so that the juices will develop.

YIELD: 4 SERVINGS   *Moira Hodgson*

✢ EASY ✢
ROASTED CHICKEN WITH ASIAN FLAVORS

A traditional way that chicken is prepared in Manhattan's Chinatown.

⅓ cup light soy sauce
¼ cup peanut oil
1 tablespoon sesame oil
1 tablespoon Sherry
1 clove garlic, peeled and crushed
½ teaspoon salt
½ teaspoon finely grated ginger
2 teaspoons five-spice powder
1 3-pound chicken

1. In a shallow dish large enough to hold the chicken, mix the soy sauce, peanut and sesame oils and Sherry. Add the garlic, salt, ginger and five-spice powder. Mix well. Rub the chicken inside and out with the mixture. Marinate, lightly covered, for at least 2 hours, and up to 24 hours, in the refrigerator, basting and turning frequently.

2. Preheat the oven to 450 degrees. Remove the chicken from the refrigerator and wipe well to remove the marinade. Place the chicken in a roasting pan. Strain the marinade through a sieve; discard the solids and spoon the liquid over the chicken. Place the pan in the oven and roast for 45 to 50 minutes, basting frequently, or until a meat thermometer registers 158 to 160 degrees when inserted in the thigh and the juices run clear. Remove from the oven and allow to rest for 3 minutes before serving.

YIELD: 4 SERVINGS ⟿ *Molly O'Neill*

ANDRE SOLTNER'S ROAST CHICKEN

When it comes to roast chicken, Andre Soltner, the original chef and owner of Lutece, prefers poussin, a young chicken that weighs about 20 ounces, over larger birds. He uses mild seasonings to emphasize the poussin's delicate and faintly gamy taste. Soltner's tenderizing rite: when the chicken thigh registers 158 to 160 degrees on a meat thermometer, he drops a teaspoon of water in the roasting pan, closes the oven door, turns off the heat and waits 3 minutes before removing the bird. "For the soft breast," he says.

2 sprigs fresh thyme

3 sprigs fresh tarragon, removing
    and reserving the leaves of
    1 sprig

2 small white onions, halved

1 poussin or small chicken
    (about 20 ounces)

1 teaspoon salt

½ teaspoon freshly ground black
    pepper

2 tablespoons peanut oil

2 sprigs fresh parsley

¼ cup white wine

¼ cup chicken broth

2 tablespoons minced Italian parsley

1 tablespoon butter

1. Preheat the oven to 450 degrees. Place the thyme, 2 of the tarragon sprigs and onions in the cavity of the chicken; season inside and out with the salt and pepper.

2. On the stove heat a roasting pan over high heat. Add the peanut oil and the chicken and brown on all sides, about 1 to 2 minutes per side. Remove from the heat and place in the oven. Roast for 20 to 25 minutes, basting frequently, or until a meat thermometer reaches between 158 and 160 degrees when inserted in the thigh and the thigh juices run clear.

3. Immediately drop 1 teaspoon of water in the roasting pan, close the oven door and turn off the heat. After 3 minutes, remove the pan from the oven and place the bird on a platter. Carefully drain the fat from the pan and place on top of the stove over medium heat. Add the wine and, using a wooden spoon, scrape the pan well. Add the chicken broth, the reserved tarragon leaves and the parsley. Simmer for 2 minutes and then remove from heat. Whisk in the butter and serve immediately over the chicken.

NOTE: Simply multiply the recipe for additional servings.

YIELD: 1 SERVING ⟜ *Molly O'Neill*

WOLFGANG PUCK'S CRISP ROASTED CHICKEN WITH PROVENÇAL VEGETABLES

At his trendy restaurant Spago, in West Hollywood, famed chef Wolfgang Puck uses a boned and flattened chicken to deliver this tasty entrée in a relative flash.

THE CHICKEN

6 tablespoons unsalted butter, softened
1 tablespoon chopped fresh rosemary
1 tablespoon chopped fresh thyme
1 teaspoon grated lemon zest
1 3½-pound chicken, deboned by the
    butcher and pounded flat
Kosher salt and freshly ground pepper
    to taste
2 tablespoons olive oil

THE VEGETABLES

2 tablespoons olive oil
1 medium onion, peeled and cut into
    ¼-inch dice
2 medium baking potatoes, peeled and
    cut into ¼-inch dice
2 Japanese eggplants, cut into ¼-inch
    dice
2 ripe tomatoes, seeded and diced
4 cloves garlic, peeled and minced
2 tablespoons chopped Italian parsley
Kosher salt and freshly ground pepper
    to taste

1. To make the chicken, preheat the oven to 450 degrees. Combine the butter, rosemary, thyme and lemon zest. Stuff the butter between the chicken skin and meat, on breasts and legs. Season the skin with salt and pepper. Heat a very large ovenproof skillet over medium-high heat and add the olive oil. Add the chicken, breast side down, and sear until browned, about 5 minutes. Turn the chicken over and cook 2 minutes. Place the skillet in the oven and roast until the chicken is cooked through, about 25 minutes.

2. Meanwhile, to make the vegetables, heat a large nonstick skillet over medium-high heat. Add the olive oil. Add the onion and potatoes and sauté for 2 minutes. Add the eggplant and sauté for 6 minutes more. Add the tomato and garlic and sauté 2 minutes. Stir in the parsley, salt and pepper.

3. Divide the vegetables among 4 plates. Quarter the chicken, place 1 piece on each plate and serve.

YIELD: 4 SERVINGS ⤝ *Molly O'Neill*

A Smart Way to Carve a Roast Chicken

There are any number of ways to carve a chicken, but the way it's done at Daniel, the highly acclaimed restaurant on Manhattan's Upper East Side, is particularly smart. No unlucky diner is left with a scrawny piece or one that requires surgical skill to eat with a fork and knife. Here's how to do it:

1. Using a medium chef's knife, cut close to the leg at the point where the leg and breast meet, peeling the leg downward as you cut. It should detach easily. At the point where it meets the backbone, make sure to cut around the oyster, a small nugget of meat at the base of the thigh (at the point of the knife above). Repeat with the other leg.

2. Remove each breast and wing by cutting along the breastbone and carefully cutting the meat from the bone. Cut through the joint where the wing meets the backbone to remove the wing and breast in one piece.

3. Cut each breast in half at an angle parallel to the wing. This will give you four breast portions, two with a wing attached.

4. Separate the thigh and drumstick. Cutting with the knife parallel to the drumstick, slice through the joint.

5. Place each thigh skin side down. Following the lines of the bone, cut alongside both sides of the thigh bone, then beneath it. Pull up the small end, cut around the thicker joint, remove the bone from the meat and discard.

DANIEL BOULUD'S ROAST CHICKEN WITH HERBS AND WILD MUSHROOMS

3 teaspoons unsalted butter, room temperature

½ small shallot, peeled and finely chopped

1½ cloves garlic, ½ finely chopped, 1 reserved whole

2 teaspoons finely chopped parsley leaves, chervil, tarragon and chives, stems reserved

¾ teaspoon Dijon mustard

1 teaspoon bread crumbs

Kosher salt

Freshly ground black pepper

1 3-pound organic chicken

Extra-virgin olive oil

2 sprigs thyme

4 tablespoons best quality butter

½ cup unsalted or low-sodium chicken broth, or water

¾ pound wild mushrooms, trimmed and washed, halved or quartered if large

Small bunch watercress, washed, large stems removed

Freshly squeezed lemon juice

1. Heat oven to 425 degrees. In a small bowl, mix together unsalted butter, shallot, ½ clove chopped garlic, chopped herbs, mustard and bread crumbs, and season generously with salt and pepper to taste.

2. Starting from the wishbone, loosen skin on chicken. Stuff butter mixture under breast skin, then roll skin back. Put garlic clove, thyme and herb sprigs into the cavity; season well with salt and pepper. Truss chicken, and brush lightly with olive oil.

3. In a small saucepan, melt the remaining butter. Put a small roasting pan into the oven to warm for 5 minutes. Add chicken, resting it on one side, and roast 20 minutes. Turn chicken to other side; cook 15 minutes, basting occasionally with butter. Pierce thigh with a small knife. If juices run clear, remove the chicken from the oven. If not, roast 5 to 10 minutes more.

4. Transfer chicken to a plate; let rest 10 minutes. Skim fat from pan juices, reserving 2 tablespoons to cook the mushrooms. Place the pan over high heat, add chicken broth and bring to a boil, stirring and scraping to incorporate caramelized bits

stuck to the pan. Add any juices that have accumulated on the plate under the chicken, and reduce to a few tablespoons.

5. Cut chicken into 6 pieces. Warm the reserved cooking fat in a medium sauté pan over high heat. Add mushrooms, season with salt and pepper, and sauté until tender.

6. Season watercress with olive oil, lemon juice, salt and pepper to taste.

7. To serve, spoon mushrooms on each serving plate. Place chicken pieces on top, drizzle with pan juices and top with watercress.

YIELD: 3 SERVINGS ⌣ *Amanda Hesser*

ALAIN DUCASSE'S
HERB-ROASTED CHICKEN

Some tips from famed chef Alain Ducasse about his method for roasting chicken, the one he devised on his first job and still uses in his four-star restaurant today: "A roast chicken can be stupidly simple, but it can also be magnificent. For the actual roasting, I didn't merely stick the chicken in the oven. I browned it on top of the stove, roasted it partway, and then bedded it on pieces of dark meat and garlic lightly browned in butter. Those extra chunks of chicken intensified the pan juices so there would be a strong, natural, thoroughly chicken-flavored base seasoned with herbs and garlic for a sauce. And I have to tell you that at home, where you don't have a ready supply of good chicken jus on hand, sacrificing a chicken leg is the easiest way to make it. I also basted the chicken every 10 minutes. . . . When the chicken was done, I set it on its end with the legs in the air so the fat from the dark meat would seep into the breast and keep it juicy. By the way, the method I like for judging whether the chicken is done is to pour out some of the juices that collect in the cavity— they should not be pink. But be sure to save them to add more flavor to your sauce. The chicken should rest for half the time it took to roast. But do not let it cool down too much. You can loosely wrap it in foil and even put it back in your oven with the heat turned off and the door slightly ajar."

13 tablespoons butter, softened

4 ounces white mushrooms, wiped clean and finely diced

1 shallot, slivered

2 tablespoons minced flat-leaf parsley leaves

2 tablespoons minced fresh chives

1 tablespoon minced fresh chervil leaves

1 branch fresh tarragon, leaves removed and minced

Salt and freshly ground black pepper

1 3½- to 4-pound chicken, at room temperature

2 tablespoons extra-virgin olive oil

1 chicken leg and thigh, chopped in 8 pieces

1 head garlic, cloves unpeeled, crushed

2 sprigs fresh thyme

1 cup chicken stock

Leaves from 8 sprigs flat-leaf parsley

1. Melt 2 tablespoons butter in medium-size skillet, add mushrooms and cook over medium-low heat, stirring, until mushrooms give up their liquid and the liquid has evaporated. Add shallot. Remove mushrooms from heat and cool to room temperature.

2. In a bowl, mix minced parsley, 1 tablespoon chives, the chervil and tarragon with 9 tablespoons butter. Mix in mushrooms. Season with salt and pepper. Place mixture in heavy self-sealing plastic sandwich bag and flatten to fill entire bag. Place in freezer until firm.

3. Rinse and dry chicken inside and out. Using your fingers, carefully separate skin from flesh of the breast and thighs. To cut thin membranes, use a paring knife or small kitchen shears, but take care not to pierce flesh or tear skin.

4. Slit bag holding herb butter and peel plastic away. Cut butter into small slabs about one by two inches. Slip slabs under chicken skin. Truss chicken or simply turn wing tips to back of chicken and tie legs.

5. Heat oven to 400 degrees. Heat oil in heavy ovenproof casserole or small roasting pan that will comfortably hold chicken. On stove top, lightly brown chicken on all sides over medium heat. Place chicken in oven breast-side up and roast 20 minutes. Remove from oven and remove chicken from casserole.

6. Add remaining butter to casserole, add leg and thigh pieces, garlic and thyme and cook over medium heat until chicken pieces start to brown. Place whole chicken on its side on top of chicken pieces, return to oven and roast 10 minutes. Turn chicken

and roast 10 minutes. Turn chicken breast-side up and roast about 15 minutes longer, until done and juices are no longer pink.

7. Remove chicken from pan, stand on end with legs pointing straight up on a rack placed over a platter. Allow to rest on an unlighted burner about 15 minutes. Wrap loosely in foil and place breast-side up on rack in turned-off oven with door slightly ajar another 15 minutes.

8. Meanwhile, pour off most of fat from casserole. Add stock to ingredients in casserole and simmer about 10 minutes. Strain contents of casserole through fine-mesh sieve into clean saucepan. Add any juices that have drained out from chicken. Reheat and season to taste with salt and pepper. Add remaining chives and parsley leaves.

9. Cut chicken into serving pieces. Spoon a little sauce over or around and serve with additional sauce on the side.

YIELD: 3 OR 4 SERVINGS ↬ *Alain Ducasse*

LA TULIPE'S ROAST CHICKEN WITH MORELS

Dried morels are almost interchangeable with fresh. In fact, there is an advantage in using dried morels and certain other varieties, especially porcini: the liquid that results when they are soaked for 30 minutes or longer, and then reduced, can be used to intensify the mushroom flavor of a beurre blanc, a red-wine sauce or a vinaigrette, for example. This delectable dish was served by Sally Darr at La Tulipe, the highly regarded restaurant that used to be in Greenwich Village.

2 ounces dried morels
3 tablespoons unsalted butter
½ cup heavy cream
Salt and freshly ground black pepper to taste
1 3½-pound chicken
¼ cup dry white wine
1 cup chicken stock
¾ cup crème fraîche
1 teaspoon lemon juice

1. Place the morels in a bowl, cover with warm water, and soak for 1 hour. Rinse, and pat dry. Preheat the oven to 450 degrees.

2. Melt 1 tablespoon of the butter in a medium-size skillet over medium heat, add the morels, and sauté 5 minutes. Add the cream, and reduce it by half. Season with salt and pepper.

3. Rub the chicken inside and out with most of the remaining butter (save a teaspoon or so), and season with salt and pepper. Spoon the morel mixture into the cavity, tuck the wing tips in back, and tie the legs together. Use the remaining butter to grease a baking dish or roasting pan just large enough to hold the chicken, one that can later be used on top of the stove. Place the chicken in it, and roast for 45 minutes. Turn the chicken breast-side down, and roast for 15 minutes more, then turn it breast-side up, and roast 5 minutes longer. The chicken is done when the pan juices run clear. Transfer the chicken to a carving board.

4. Pour most of the fat from the baking dish, and place the dish over medium-high heat. Pour in the wine and cook, stirring, until the wine is reduced to a glaze. Pour in the chicken stock, reduce the liquid by half, then strain it into a skillet. Spoon the morel mixture from the cavity of the chicken and add it to the skillet along with the crème fraîche and any chicken juices from the carving board. Simmer about 5 minutes until the sauce is smooth and creamy. Season to taste with salt and pepper and add the lemon juice.

5. Cut the chicken into serving pieces, boning the breast sections, and arrange on a warm platter. Spoon the morel sauce over it and serve.

YIELD: 4 SERVINGS   *Florence Fabricant*

DAVID LIEDERMAN'S
ROAST CHICKEN AND VEGETABLES

New York chef and restaurateur David Liederman prefers to roast a kosher chicken—which absorbs a trace of salt that boosts its flavor after it has been soaked in water, salted and washed according to kashrut, the Jewish dietary laws. He uses only 2½-to-2¾-pound chickens and marinates them in a heady herbaceous melange. "The longer they marinate," he says, "the better they taste."

1 2½- to 3-pound kosher chicken
½ cup extra-virgin olive oil
1 clove garlic, peeled and mashed
3 sprigs thyme
4 carrots, peeled, cut in half lengthwise and then across
2 teaspoons salt
1 teaspoon freshly ground black pepper
8 small roasting potatoes, scrubbed
4 small white onions, scrubbed

1. Wash and dry the chicken well. In a shallow dish big enough to hold the chicken, combine the olive oil, garlic and thyme. Add the chicken and baste with the oil, garlic and thyme. Cover and refrigerate for at least 3 hours, and up to 24 hours, basting occasionally and turning to marinate evenly.

2. Preheat the oven to 450 degrees and remove the chicken from the refrigerator. Pour the marinade in a large cast-iron pan. Line the bottom of the pan with the carrot slices. Season the chicken inside and out with the salt and pepper and place on top of the carrots. Strew the onions and potatoes around the chicken. Place the pan in the oven and roast for 50 to 55 minutes, or until a meat thermometer reaches between 158 and 160 degrees when inserted in the thigh, and the thigh juices run clear. Remove from the oven and allow the chicken to rest for 5 minutes before serving.

YIELD: 4 SERVINGS   *Molly O'Neill*

NIGELLA LAWSON'S
BUTTERMILK ROAST CHICKEN

Butterflying a chicken is a surprisingly simple task that can be done with a pair of kitchen scissors. The two immediate advantages are that the chicken takes less time to cook and it is also easier to serve since carving isn't required—you just cut the chicken into four pieces. The bird may be marinated in the refrigerator for up to two days in a freezer bag. Using buttermilk, which is usually associated with fried chicken, somehow conveys the aromatics better: you really get the full value of the rosemary, pepper and garlic. If you want to substitute maple syrup for the honey, you can. Nigella Lawson tries to remove excess buttermilk from the chicken before roasting it, but leaves some on so that the chicken browns better, even turning barbecue-black in parts.

1 4-pound chicken
2 cups buttermilk
¼ cup plus 2 tablespoons vegetable oil
2 cloves garlic, lightly crushed
1 tablespoon crushed black peppercorns
1 tablespoon Maldon or other sea salt
2 tablespoons fresh rosemary leaves, roughly chopped
1 tablespoon honey

1. Butterfly chicken by placing breast-side down and using heavy-duty kitchen shears to cut along both sides of backbone. Discard backbone, turn chicken over and open it like a book. Press gently to flatten it.

2. Place chicken in a large freezer bag. Add buttermilk, ¼ cup oil, garlic, peppercorns, salt, rosemary and honey. Seal bag securely and refrigerate overnight or up to two days.

3. Heat oven to 400 degrees. Remove chicken from marinade and place on a rack so excess can drip off. Line a roasting pan with foil and place chicken in pan. Drizzle with remaining 2 tablespoons oil. Roast for 45 minutes, then reduce heat to 325 degrees. Continue roasting until well browned and until juices run clear when chicken is pierced where leg joins thigh, about another 20 minutes.

4. Place chicken on a carving board and allow to rest for 10 minutes before cutting into serving pieces. Place a portion on each of four plates, and drizzle each serving with pan juices.

NOTE: A good coleslaw is sufficient accompaniment, but if you want potatoes, just cut some into one-inch cubes, toss them in a shallow roasting tray and pour over a tablespoon or two of oil, add a few unpeeled cloves of garlic and a sprinkling of sea salt and mix well. Roast them in the oven below the chicken. When the chicken is done, let it rest for about 15 minutes, keeping the potatoes in to crisp up.

YIELD: 4 SERVINGS ⌒ *Nigella Lawson*

✢ EASY ✢

ARGENTINE ROAST CHICKEN WITH VEGETABLES AND CHIMICHURRI SAUCE

(Adapted from Naomi Sisson)

A favorite dish from Naomi Sisson, the Argentinian wife of a former Israeli consul general in New York City.

¼ cup vinegar

1 tablespoon ground cumin

1 teaspoon sweet paprika

¼ teaspoon hot pepper flakes

1 head garlic, cloves peeled and crushed

2 teaspoons chopped fresh oregano

½ cup vegetable or olive oil

Salt and freshly ground black pepper to taste

1 3-pound roasting chicken, cut up

2 large bell peppers, cored and diced

3 large tomatoes, sliced

5 large potatoes, peeled and each cut into 6 large chunks

1. Combine vinegar, cumin, paprika, hot pepper flakes, crushed garlic and oregano in a small bowl. Whisk in oil. Season to taste with salt and pepper. Pour sauce over chicken, rubbing skin well. Cover with plastic wrap, and refrigerate overnight.

2. When ready to roast, preheat oven to 400 degrees. Grease a large baking pan. Add peppers, then tomatoes. Place chicken, bottom sides up, on top, pouring half the marinade over. Scatter potatoes around chicken.

3. Roast 20 minutes, then turn chicken pieces over, and continue roasting until the chicken is crispy on top, about 30 minutes more.

YIELD: 6 SERVINGS — *Joan Nathan*

AQUAVIT'S ROASTED CHICKEN WITH SPICED APPLES AND ONIONS

(Adapted from *Aquavit and the New Scandinavian Cuisine*)

1 3½-pound free-range chicken
1 medium sweet potato, cut into ½-inch cubes
1 onion, cut into ½-inch cubes
2 Granny Smith apples, peeled, cored and cut into ½-inch cubes
2 shallots, cut into ½-inch pieces
1 clove garlic, chopped
Leaves from 2 sprigs fresh thyme
Leaves from 2 sprigs fresh mint, chopped
1 tablespoon olive oil
½ teaspoon ground cinnamon
2 cardamom pods or ¼ teaspoon ground cardamom
2 whole star anise
2 whole cloves or ⅛ teaspoon ground cloves
4 white peppercorns
2 black peppercorns
Kosher salt
Yogurt rice (see recipe, page 26)

1. Preheat oven to 350 degrees. Rinse chicken with cool water and pat dry with paper towels. Fill a medium saucepan half full of water and bring to a boil. Add cubed sweet potato and blanch 2 minutes. Drain, rinse with cold water and drain again. In a mixing bowl, combine blanched sweet potato, onion, apples, shallots and garlic. Add thyme and chopped mint leaves. In a small bowl combine olive oil with 2 tablespoons water, and add to vegetable mixture.

2. Using a mortar and pestle, or with the base of a heavy pot on a cutting board, lightly crush together the cinnamon, cardamom, star anise, cloves, white peppercorns and black peppercorns, along with salt to taste. Add half the spice mixture to the vegetables and reserve the rest.

3. Place chicken on a rack in a medium roasting pan. Lightly stuff the bird's cavity with about half the vegetable mixture, placing the remaining vegetables around the bird in the bottom of the pan. Truss bird with kitchen string and rub with remaining spice mixture.

4. Place pan in oven and roast about 1½ hours, or until the internal temperature of the meat reaches 160 degrees and the thigh juices run clear. Check pan occasionally, adding a bit of water if it becomes completely dry. When vegetables in base of pan are tender, remove and reserve.

5. When chicken is cooked, remove vegetables from cavity and add to the reserved pan vegetables. Carve chicken, cover securely and keep warm. Add enough water to pan juices to make 1 cup, stirring well to deglaze the pan. Use vegetables and pan juices for making yogurt rice. Serve carved chicken with yogurt rice.

YIELD: 4 SERVINGS   *Marcus Samuelsson*

YOGURT RICE

1 cup basmati rice
1 cup cooking liquid from the roasted chicken with spiced apples and onions
Roasted vegetables from roasted chicken with spiced apples and onions
½ cup plain yogurt
Kosher salt
1 tablespoon sliced chives

1. In a medium saucepan combine rice with 1 cup water. Bring to a boil, and then reduce heat and simmer, covered, until rice is almost tender and liquid almost gone, about 10 minutes.

2. Add cooking liquid from the roasted chicken, and the roasted vegetables, and toss gently. Cover pan and continue cooking until the rice is tender, 5 to 10 minutes. Fold in the yogurt, and salt to taste. Stir in the chives. Serve with carved chicken.

YIELD: 4 SERVINGS　　*Marcus Samuelsson*

‍✦ EASY ✦
ROAST CHICKEN WITH 40 CLOVES OF GARLIC AND GARLIC BREAD

(Adapted from *France the Beautiful Cookbook*)

1 3½-pound chicken
Kosher salt to taste
2 sprigs fresh thyme
2 sprigs fresh rosemary
2 sprigs fresh sage
2 tender stalks celery, with their leaves
2 sprigs Italian parsley
40 cloves garlic, unpeeled
3 tablespoons olive oil
Freshly ground pepper to taste
Toasted slices of country bread

1. Preheat the oven to 400 degrees. Sprinkle the chicken with salt inside and out. Stuff the chicken with half the thyme, rosemary, sage and celery. Add the parsley and 4 cloves of garlic.

2. Place the remaining herbs and celery in an oval earthenware or enameled pot just large enough to hold the chicken. Add the oil, salt, pepper and remaining garlic cloves. Roll the chicken in the oil to coat on all sides. Cover the pot and bake for 1¾ hours.

3. Transfer the cooked chicken to a serving platter and surround it with the cloves of garlic. Skim the fat from the cooking juices and pour into a sauce boat.

4. Serve the chicken hot, accompanied by its sauce and toasted slices of bread. Each diner crushes the garlic slightly to remove the skin and spreads the puree that is left onto a slice of bread.

YIELD: 4 SERVINGS ⌁ *Molly O'Neill*

ROAST GARLIC CHICKEN WITH WATERCRESS SAUCE

1 5-pound roasting chicken
6 large cloves garlic
5 tablespoons extra-virgin olive oil
Salt and freshly ground black pepper
1 lemon, quartered
2 tablespoons pine nuts
⅓ cup, packed, watercress leaves
3 tablespoons Dijon mustard
2 tablespoons boiling water

1. Preheat oven to 425 degrees.

2. Pull any excess fat from the chicken. Cut four of the garlic cloves into slivers and poke them here and there under the skin of the chicken. Rub the chicken with a tablespoon of the olive oil and season it with salt and pepper. Put the lemon in the cavity of the chicken, then put the chicken on a rack in a roasting pan and roast it until the juices run clear, about one and a half hours.

3. Meanwhile, turn on a food processor fitted with the steel blade. With the machine running, drop the remaining two cloves of garlic through the feed tube. Then drop in the nuts and process until they are finely chopped. Stuff the watercress leaves through the feed tube and continue to process until they are chopped. Turn the machine off and scrape down the sides.

4. Turn the machine on again and slowly pour the remaining oil in through the

feed tube. Transfer this mixture to a small saucepan and stir in the mustard, then the boiling water. Season to taste with salt and pepper and set aside.

5. Remove the chicken from the oven and allow it to rest at least 15 minutes before carving or cutting it up. Skim all the fat from the roasting pan, then pour the pan juices through a strainer into the watercress sauce mixture.

6. Carve the chicken and arrange it on a warm platter. Warm the sauce briefly and serve it alongside the chicken.

YIELD: 6 SERVINGS ⟿ *Florence Fabricant*

✣ EASY ✣
CASSEROLE-ROASTED CHICKEN WITH SHALLOTS

1 3- to 4-pound chicken
½ small lemon
Coarse salt and freshly ground pepper
8 shallots, skin left on
4 cloves garlic, skin left on

1. Preheat oven to 375 degrees.

2. Wipe the chicken with paper towels. Remove loose fat from the cavity. Squeeze the juice of the lemon outside and in the cavity. Season the chicken with salt and pepper and place half the lemon in the cavity.

3. Place the chicken in a lightly oiled casserole and arrange the shallots and garlic around it, along with the gizzards and liver. Cover and roast, breast-down, for 20 minutes.

4. Remove the cover, turn the chicken and finish cooking uncovered for about 40 minutes, or until the juices run yellow when the chicken is pricked with a skewer. Allow it to rest 15 minutes before serving. Serve on a platter, surrounded with the shallots and garlic.

YIELD: 4 SERVINGS ⟿ *Moira Hodgson*

LE CIRQUE'S FREE-RANGE CHICKEN WITH SWISS CHARD AND MARROW GRATIN

(Adapted from Le Cirque, New York City)

For a leaner meal, replace the butter with olive oil in the gratin and eliminate the marrow bones.

THE CHICKEN

3 slices good-quality white bread, cut in ½-inch cubes

2 teaspoons unsalted butter

3 ounces sliced bacon, cut across into ½-inch pieces

4 ounces chicken livers, cleaned and chopped

1 3½-pound free-range chicken

1½ ounces black truffles, thinly sliced

½ teaspoon salt, plus more to taste

Freshly ground black pepper to taste

THE GRATIN

2 teaspoons unsalted butter

6 cups Swiss chard stems, peeled and cut into 1-inch pieces

½ cup chicken broth, homemade or low-sodium canned

2 pounds marrow bones, cut in 2-inch pieces, optional

½ teaspoon salt, plus more to taste

Freshly ground pepper to taste

¼ cup grated Parmesan

1. To make the chicken: Preheat the oven to 375 degrees. Toss the bread cubes with the butter and place them on a baking sheet. Bake until lightly toasted, about 6 minutes. Remove from oven and set aside.

2. Turn oven up to 450 degrees. Place the bacon in a medium sauté pan over medium heat. Cook, stirring, until bacon is almost done, pouring off most of the fat as it is released. Add the chicken livers and cook, stirring constantly until browned, about 2 minutes. Drain and toss with the bread cubes. Season with salt and pepper. Set aside.

3. Carefully slip your hand between the chicken breasts and chicken skin to form a pocket. Place truffle slices between the breasts and skin. Fill the chicken cavity with the liver mixture. With a trussing needle and twine sew the cavity closed. Sprinkle the chicken with salt and pepper. Place in a roasting pan. Roast the chicken until juices run clear when pricked in the thickest part of the leg, about 1 hour and 10 minutes.

4. Meanwhile, make the gratin: Melt butter in a large skillet over medium heat. Add the Swiss chard stems and cook for 5 minutes. Add the chicken broth and simmer slowly until tender, about 25 minutes.

5. If using marrow bones, while chard is cooking, fill a medium saucepan with salted water. Bring to a boil. Reduce to a simmer and add the marrow bones. Simmer for 6 minutes. Drain. Extract the marrow from the bones and cut across into ¼-inch slices.

6. Season chard with salt and pepper. Place half of the chard in the bottom of a medium-size gratin dish. Place the marrow, if using, evenly over the chard. Top with remaining chard. Sprinkle with Parmesan cheese.

7. Broil until top is browned, about 3 minutes. Serve immediately with chicken and stuffing.

YIELD: 4 SERVINGS ⁓ *Molly O'Neill*

BARBARA KAFKA'S ROAST CHICKEN WITH POMEGRANATE GLAZE AND FRESH MINT

(Adapted from *Roasting: A Simple Art*)

Brilliant red pomegranate and green mint combine in this tasty and unusually colorful dish.

1 bunch (1 ounce) fresh mint
1 5- to 6-pound chicken, excess fat trimmed; wingtips, neck and giblets
   reserved for stock
2 to 3 teaspoons kosher salt
Freshly ground black pepper, to taste
4 whole cloves garlic, unpeeled
Seeds from 1 large or 2 small pomegranates (1½ cups) (see Note)
Juice from 1 large or 2 small ripe pomegranates (½ cup) (see Note)
½ cup chicken stock

1. Place rack on second level from bottom of oven. Preheat oven to 500 degrees. Remove leaves from half the mint, reserving stems. Stack the leaves, roll and cut them across into thin strips, and set aside.

2. Place the chicken, breast-side up, in a 12-by-8-by-1½-inch heavy roasting pan. Sprinkle chicken cavity with some of the salt and pepper, and stuff it with garlic, ½ cup pomegranate seeds, the reserved mint stems and the remaining half bunch of mint with leaves attached. Pour ¼ cup pomegranate juice over chicken. Sprinkle with 1 teaspoon salt.

3. Place chicken in oven, legs first. Roast for 50 minutes. Move chicken once after the first 10 minutes with wooden spatula to keep it from sticking. The chicken should not burn. (If chicken smells as if it is burning, reduce heat to 400 degrees, and open oven door for a minute to lower the temperature quickly. Continue roasting at lower temperature.)

4. The chicken will be a beautiful mahogany brown and the thigh juices will run clear. Tilt chicken over pan to drain juices, and then remove chicken to a platter.

5. Tilt roasting pan, and spoon out fat, leaving any juices. Place pan over medium-high heat. Pour in chicken stock and remaining ¼ cup pomegranate juice. Bring liquid to a boil, scraping up any browned bits from bottom of pan with a wooden spoon. Stir in remaining mint leaves. Lower heat, and simmer for 1 minute. Season with salt and pepper. Add any juices that have collected on the platter. Simmer for 30 seconds.

6. Pour about half the pan juices over the bird, taking care that the platter does not overflow. Top with a few remaining seeds. Combine the rest of the juices into a sauce boat with remaining seeds, and serve with chicken.

NOTE ABOUT POMEGRANATES: The word *pomegranate* comes from the Latin *pomum granatum*, or "apple of many seeds." The flavor, as Andre Gide described it, is tart and somewhat lemony, "like the juice of unripe raspberries." Pomegranate juice and seeds are easy to extract. *But beware: Pomegranate juice stains like a red dye.*

FOR THE JUICE: Cut the pomegranate in half horizontally. Holding one half at a time over a bowl, use a citrus juicer, electric is easier, to extract as much juice as possible. If necessary, transfer to a mesh strainer and press down hard with the back of a spoon to get out as much juice as possible. One large pomegranate will yield ½ to 1 cup of juice. A small pomegranate may yield as little as ¼ cup.

FOR THE SEEDS: Cut the pomegranate in half horizontally. Then cut each piece in half to produce quarters. Bend each quarter back on itself, so that the seed sacs loosen. Use your fingers or a demitasse spoon to pluck out the seeds.

YIELD: 3 OR 4 SERVINGS *Barbara Kafka*

NIGELLA LAWSON'S GEORGIAN STUFFED CHICKEN

Nigella Lawson: "This recipe was inspired by the cuisine of Georgia, on the Black Sea. The stuffing is a simple affair of rice cooked with onions, garlic and dried sour cherries. Parsley is forked through before spooning the rice into the chickens. And yes, chickens: I take the view that one bird is a meal, two is a feast. You could turn this into a Christmas feast by stuffing a turkey with a version of the rice, with dried cranberries replacing the cherries. Just double the quantities: for one turkey think four chickens' worth of stuffing.

2 5-pound chickens
6 tablespoons butter
2 onions, peeled and finely chopped
2 cloves garlic, finely chopped
1 cup basmati rice
½ cup dried sour cherries, roughly chopped
Salt and freshly ground black pepper
¼ cup chopped parsley

1. Remove any fat from cavities of chickens, and place fat in a wide saucepan. Add 4 tablespoons of the butter and place over medium heat. When butter melts, add onions and garlic. Sauté until onions soften and begin to brown, about 5 minutes.

2. Discard any remaining hard bits of chicken fat. Add rice and chopped cherries to pan. Stir well, and add 2 cups water and salt to taste. Bring to a boil, cover and reduce heat to as low as possible. Cook for 15 minutes. Meanwhile, heat oven to 425 degrees.

3. Season rice mixture with salt and pepper to taste and stir in parsley. Spoon rice into cavities of both chickens, and secure openings with toothpicks.

4. Place chickens in a roasting pan and rub with remaining 2 tablespoons butter. Place in oven and roast until skin is crisp and golden and juices run clear when pierced near the thigh with a knife, 1½ to 2 hours. Discard toothpicks and allow chicken to rest before carving. Serve each portion of chicken with some stuffing.

YIELD: 8 SERVINGS 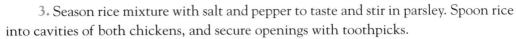 *Nigella Lawson*

WALDY MALOUF'S ROAST CHICKEN WITH MAPLE WALNUT GLAZE

(Adapted from *The Hudson River Valley Cookbook*)

1 3-pound chicken
3 tablespoons olive oil
Coarse sea salt and freshly ground pepper to taste
5 shallots, sliced thin
3 cloves garlic, sliced thin
3 sprigs fresh thyme

FOR THE GLAZE
½ cup chopped walnuts
⅓ cup maple syrup
1 tablespoon red wine vinegar

FOR THE SAUCE
1 cup chicken stock
1 tablespoon unsalted butter
1 tablespoon flour
2 tablespoons red wine vinegar

1. Preheat the oven to 400 degrees. Rub the chicken all over with the olive oil, season it inside and out with salt and pepper and put about one-fourth of the shallots, garlic and thyme in the cavity. Truss the chicken and roast it for 15 minutes. Add the remaining shallots, garlic and thyme to the pan and roast for 15 minutes more. Turn the oven down to 300 degrees and pour off any fat that has accumulated in the pan.

2. Make the glaze: In a small bowl, combine the walnuts, maple syrup and vinegar. Spoon half the glaze over the chicken.

3. Add the stock to the roasting pan and return the chicken to the oven. After 20 minutes baste with the remaining glaze and continue to roast the chicken for 25 minutes more, or until the thigh juices run clear. Turn the oven off, remove the chicken to a platter and return it to the oven while you make the sauce.

4. Melt the butter in a small saucepan, whisk in the flour and cook, whisking frequently over low heat for a minute or two until the mixture is tinged with color. Strain the pan juices into the saucepan and stir the sauce over medium low heat until it is smooth and slightly thickened. Let it simmer gently for 5 minutes, stirring frequently. Season the sauce with salt and pepper and stir in the vinegar. Serve in a heated sauce boat on the side.

YIELD: 4 SERVINGS ⌒ *Moira Hodgson*

LYNNE ROSETTO KASPER'S
BALSAMIC ROAST CHICKEN

(Adapted from *The Splendid Table*)

1 4- to 4½-pound frying or roasting chicken

1 tablespoon fresh rosemary leaves

1 large clove garlic

¼ teaspoon salt

2 tablespoons extra-virgin olive oil

Freshly ground black pepper to taste

8 sprigs fresh rosemary

3 to 4 tablespoons of balsamic vinegar blended with ½ teaspoon brown sugar

1. Rinse the chicken under cold running water and dry thoroughly inside and out. Set on a dinner plate. Mince together the rosemary leaves and garlic in the salt. Rub the olive oil over the chicken, then rub in the herb mixture. Sprinkle with pepper. Put two rosemary sprigs in the bird's cavity and refrigerate several hours lightly covered with plastic wrap. Keep remaining rosemary sprigs for garnishing.

2. When ready to cook, preheat oven to 350 degrees. Truss the chicken if desired. Rub into the chicken any seasoning that may haven fallen onto the dinner plate. Place chicken breast-side down in a small, heavy roasting pan. Roast 20 to 25 minutes per pound (about 1¼ to 1¾ hours), or until a thermometer tucked into the thickest part of the thigh or leg reads 170 degrees and the thigh juices run clear. Baste every 15 minutes or so with pan juices. During the last 30 minutes of roasting, turn the chicken over to brown the breast. If the chicken is not deep golden brown when the cooking time is up, turn up the heat to 475 degrees and brown it for about 10 minutes, turning once.

3. Transfer chicken to a heated serving platter. Present it whole, drizzled with the balsamic vinegar and garnished with rosemary sprigs, and carve at the table. Or cut into eight pieces with poultry shears, spoon the vinegar over the pieces and scatter with remaining sprigs. Serve immediately.

YIELD: 6 SERVINGS ᜱ *Nancy Harmon Jenkins*

CHICKEN BAKED IN SALT

Molly O'Neil: *"The large, flaky grains of kosher salt can be used as a fairly economical substitute for the more expensive sea salt. It is impossible to prescribe how much salt a cook should use, since what pleases one person is as intimate and private as that person's tongue. The salt called for in any recipe is a suggestion. Always take it with a grain of salt."*

About 4 pounds kosher salt
1 4-pound chicken

1. Preheat the oven to 350 degrees. Put the salt in a heavy pot with a lid, slightly larger than the chicken. Place the pot, uncovered, over medium heat until the salt is very hot, stirring from time to time, about 30 minutes.

2. Scoop most of the salt into a large bowl, leaving a 1½- to 2-inch layer of salt in the bottom of the pot. Place the chicken over the salt layer, breast-side up. Spoon the remaining salt over and around the chicken so that it is completely buried in salt.

3. Cover the pot with the lid. Bake until the chicken is cooked through, about 1½ hours. Scrape the salt from the chicken and remove from the pot. Wipe off as much of the salt as possible and let stand for 10 minutes. Carve the chicken and serve.

YIELD: 4 SERVINGS   *Molly O'Neill*

✤ EASY ✤
MADELEINE KAMMAN'S BRINED AND ROASTED CHICKEN

(Adapted from *The New Making of a Cook*)

Brining adds flavor and makes skin crispier. Blood orange adds subtle flavor to final sauce.

1 3- to 4-pound chicken, organic if possible
3 tablespoons salt
½ lemon

2 branches of rosemary
Juice from one medium blood orange

1. Soak chicken overnight in a brine made of 2 quarts of water and 3 tablespoons of salt. Remove, rinse and pat dry. Preheat oven to 375 degrees.

2. Trim wing tips off chicken and reserve. Squeeze half a lemon in the cavity, then place the squeezed lemon and the rosemary in the cavity and truss the chicken.

3. Place chicken in a roasting pan and roast for 1 hour 10 minutes, spooning its juices over it every 15 minutes or so. Meanwhile, place wing tips in a small saucepan with 2 cups of water, bring to a boil and reduce to simmer for 1 hour. Strain and set aside.

4. When juices of chicken run clear at joints, remove chicken from oven to warm platter. In roasting pan, spoon off fat from drippings. Place roasting pan on stove top over high heat. Add chicken broth and, scraping and stirring constantly, boil until half a cup of liquid remains, about 10 minutes.

5. Add the orange juice to broth. Drizzle over the carved chicken, which goes well with braised endive and browned potatoes.

YIELD: 4 SERVINGS ⌒ *Molly O'Neill*

✦ EASY ✦

WINTER CHICKEN À LA JUDY RODGERS

(Adapted from *The Zuni Café Cookbook*)

When Judy Rodgers became the head chef at Zuni Café in San Francisco, she began to experiment with presalting, which led to the idea of seasoning chickens 48 hours or so in advance of cooking. "And if you add spices or aromatics when you presalt," she says, "those flavors permeate whatever you have salted, and that does stunningly good things to flavor, texture and moistness." Those techniques inspired this variation of her signature dish.

1 4-pound chicken, preferably organic, not kosher	⅛ teaspoon ground cinnamon
2 teaspoons salt	⅛ teaspoon ground allspice
1 teaspoon sugar	⅛ teaspoon ground cloves
	⅛ teaspoon ground nutmeg

1. Rinse chicken and pat dry. In a small bowl combine salt, sugar and spices. Coat chicken evenly with seasoning, sprinkling a little in cavity and rubbing the rest into skin.

2. Set chicken uncovered on a rack above a plate. Let chicken stand for 48 hours in refrigerator, preferably on top shelf for maximum air circulation.

3. Heat oven to 500 degrees. In a small roasting pan, place chicken breast-side down on a rack. After 15 minutes, reduce heat to 450 degrees, turn bird breast-side up,

and roast 15 minutes more. Reduce heat to 425 degrees, baste chicken with released juices, and cook 30 minutes more, or until temperature at leg reads 160 degrees.

4. Remove chicken from oven and let stand 15 minutes before carving. Serve warm.

YIELD: 4 SERVINGS ⌒ *Emily Kaiser*

PATRICK O'CONNELL'S SPICE-BRINED CHICKEN

(Adapted from the Inn at Little Washington, Washington, Va.)

Patrick O'Connell: The sugar in the brine helps a turkey or chicken take on a rich amber color as it cooks, and the combination of salt water and herbs and spices cures and flavors the bird. The salt draws out fluid from the tissues and concentrates the flavor. The liquid in the brine replaces the moisture drawn out by the salt, so the meat is much juicier. Any spices in the brine also penetrate all the way through the meat. The result is a tender and succulent bird that needs no additional seasoning. Salt alone could be used, but the brining liquid works much faster.

FOR THE BRINE

½ cup kosher salt

1¾ cups sugar

1 cup honey

3 sprigs each fresh parsley, dill,
   thyme, tarragon, sage

1 sprig fresh rosemary

1 tablespoon mustard seeds

1 tablespoon fennel seeds

1 cinnamon stick

2 large bay leaves

4 cloves

½ tablespoon juniper berries

½ tablespoon cardamom pods

1 tablespoon black peppercorns

1 lemon, halved and squeezed lightly

3 star anise

½ tablespoon whole allspice

FOR THE CHICKEN

1 3- to 4-pound chicken

1 cup sliced carrots

1 cup sliced celery

1 cup sliced onion

2 tablespoons unsalted butter,
   melted

1. In a large stockpot or roasting pan large enough to hold chicken, place 1 gallon of water. Bring to a boil and remove from heat. Add all ingredients for brine and stir. Cool to room temperature.

2. Add chicken to pan. Cover and refrigerate overnight.

3. Drain chicken well and discard brine. Cut off and discard wing tips. Preheat oven to 350 degrees. In a roasting pan, place carrots, celery and onion. Place chicken on top of vegetables. Brush chicken with melted butter.

4. Roast chicken until thigh joint temperature reaches 150 degrees or until the thigh juices run clear, about 1 hour. Baste with pan juices at least every 15 minutes. Watch carefully to avoid burning; if parts become well browned cover with foil. When chicken is done remove from oven and allow it to rest 10 minutes before carving.

NOTE: The brine can be made well in advance. Be sure to cool it to room temperature before adding the bird, and keep it refrigerated or in a very cool place to prevent bacterial growth.

YIELD: 4 TO 5 SERVINGS   *Marian Burros*

Begging for Crumbs

By Molly O'Neill

Be honest. Isn't stuffing a bird its raison d'etre? I've heard people say they wouldn't bother with the fat and mess of a goose, if it weren't for what a goose can hold. I've heard the same thing said about ducks, pheasants and capons. I've also wondered if modern poultry techniques would have survived given the sacrifices in flavor, if not for the larger, sturdier cavity that science has devised.

Considering the universal popularity of stuffing, and the prevailing tide of nutritional thought, you would think we would abandon the bird altogether and bake as much stuffing as we like, en casserole. Yet the bird remains, harboring its precious cargo like an egg. Not out of sentiment, especially, but out of utility, because a properly made stuffing is, at once, a perfume and a moisturizer that improves its host by the mere act of filling space.

The simplest stuffing—carrots, onions and thyme, roughly chopped—lends a faintly sweet and herbaceous taste to the fowl. This same mixture, when chopped fine along with celery, becomes that most potent of vegetable aromatics—a *mirepoix*—so popular in French and Italian kitchens alike. Stuffings made with chili on the other hand add a delicious, piquant fire.

Since bread stuffings absorb drippings, they change character during the roasting, mellowing the bird while becoming more unctuous in the process. A rye bread stuffing with caraway seeds, for example, is a wonderful sponge for a rich dish like goose. Corn bread stuffings lend nuttiness to the bird, while sourdough ones insure a tart and subtle flavor.

There are probably as many options for stuffings as there are personal preferences in the matter. The only caveats in making them are first, to err on the dry side (stuffing gets wetter as it cooks) and, second, to season the mixture liberally beforehand since it will inevitably be eaten alone, surreptitious bite upon bite.

Though the meat of a stuffed bird is moister and more flavorful than that of an unstuffed bird, it is often soggier, too—a disadvantage the cook might want to consider. Also, a stuffed bird takes longer to cook. A 3½-pound chicken, for example, roasted at 375 degrees, requires 20 minutes per pound, rather than 15.

Since the American Revolution, stuffing has gradually grown lighter, and more in keeping with the times. Fruits and vegetables have slowly replaced butter and pork, while salt has dwindled and so have eggs. Indeed, quick stuffings have upstaged slow-simmered ones, as the definition of sumptuousness has changed. Still, eternal stuffing questions remain for which there are no simple answers. For example, what is the correct proportion of fat to bread? Should you use cubed bread or bread crumbs? Are packaged crumbs an affront? These questions, like those of religion and politics, are best resolved within the privacy of one's own home.

How to Roast a Stuffed Bird

Bring the bird to room temperature and sprinkle with salt, inside and out. Fill the cavity with stuffing, and tie the legs together with string. Place the bird in a large roasting pan and bake until it reaches an internal temperature of 180 degrees at the inner thigh. A 3½-pound chicken requires 20 minutes per pound at 375 degrees; a 10-pound capon 25 minutes per pound at 350 degrees. Should the bird begin to brown too soon, cover it loosely with aluminum foil. Let stand for 15 minutes before carving.

Molly O'Neill

BREAD STUFFING WITH MUSHROOMS, MADEIRA AND HERBS

(Adapted from *The New York Times Cook Book*)

½ cup butter
¾ pound mushrooms, thinly sliced
1½ tablespoons finely chopped shallots
1 chicken liver, coarsely chopped
¼ cup Madeira
¼ cup chopped celery
½ cup dry white bread crumbs
2 tablespoons chopped flat-leaf parsley
½ teaspoon dried tarragon
¼ teaspoon salt
⅛ teaspoon freshly ground black pepper

1. Melt half of the butter. Add the mushrooms and shallots and sauté for about eight minutes, until tender. Place in a bowl.

2. Melt the remaining butter and sauté the chopped chicken liver for 2 minutes. Add it to the mushroom mixture.

3. Pour the wine into the skillet and bring to a boil, scraping to loosen the drippings. Reduce the liquid to one tablespoon and scrape all into the bowl.

4. Add the remaining ingredients and toss lightly. Allow to cool before stuffing the chicken.

YIELD: ENOUGH FOR A FOUR-POUND CHICKEN

SAUSAGE STUFFING

(Adapted from The New New York Times Cookbook)

1 chicken liver, finely chopped

¼ pound fresh sausage meat

1 tablespoon finely chopped shallots
   or green onion

1 tablespoon chopped onion

2 tablespoons chopped flat-leaf
   parsley

1 clove garlic, finely minced

¾ cup soft fresh bread crumbs

1 egg

3 tablespoons dry white wine

Salt and freshly ground black pepper

Combine the chicken liver and sausage meat and cook until meat loses color. Mix in the remaining ingredients.

YIELD: 1½ TO 2 CUPS, ENOUGH FOR A 3 TO 4 POUND CHICKEN

SAUSAGE-AND-APPLE STUFFING

1 pound pork sausage meat

1 tablespoon butter

1 large onion, finely chopped

1 stalk celery, finely chopped

1 clove garlic, minced

3 cooking apples, peeled, cored and
   diced

1 cup fresh homemade-type bread
   crumbs

½ cup milk

Dash dried thyme

1 fresh sage leaf, chopped

1 egg, lightly beaten

Coarse salt and freshly ground
   pepper to taste

1. Cook the sausage meat in a skillet and drain off the fat. Set aside.

2. Melt the butter in the skillet and soften the onion, celery and garlic. Add the apple and cook for 3 minutes, stirring.

3. Meanwhile, put the bread crumbs in a large bowl and add the milk. Mix well.

4. Add all the ingredients to the bread crumbs and mix thoroughly. Stuff into the bird cavity.

YIELD: 3 CUPS STUFFING, ENOUGH FOR A 6-POUND BIRD ⌐ *Moira Hodgson*

CHESTNUT STUFFING

2 pounds chestnuts (see Note)

2 cups chicken stock

2 tablespoons butter

3 shallots, minced

2 stalks celery, minced

2 tablespoons parsley, chopped

1 large egg, lightly beaten

Coarse salt and freshly ground
    pepper to taste

1. Make an incision in each chestnut with a knife. Drop the chestnuts into boiling water and simmer for 10 minutes. Drain and peel the chestnuts, using rubber gloves to protect your fingers.

2. Coarsely chop the chestnuts and simmer in the chicken stock until tender. Set aside.

3. Melt the butter in a frying pan and sauté the shallots with the celery until soft. Mix with the chestnuts, parsley and egg. Season and stuff into the bird cavity.

NOTE: Unsweetened canned chestnuts or those in jars can be used instead of fresh ones. They do not have to be cooked, so omit steps 1 and 2. In step 3, add 1 cup of chicken stock to the stuffing mixture or it will be dry.

YIELD: 2 CUPS STUFFING OR ENOUGH FOR A 4-POUND BIRD ⌐ *Moira Hodgson*

LAURIE COLWIN'S SIMPLE STUFFED ROAST CHICKEN

(Adapted from *More Home Cooking*)

In her fiction and her short stories, as well as in her life, the late Laurie Colwin celebrated food like this—simple, unpretentious, heartwarming and delicious.

> 1 3- to 3½-pound chicken
> 3 to 4 cups cubed whole wheat bread
> ½ cup porcini mushrooms
> ¼ to ⅓ cup broth
> Salt and freshly ground pepper
> Paprika
> 1 tablespoon olive oil
> 1 tablespoon melted butter or water or broth for basting

1. Preheat oven to 300 degrees. Rinse chicken and pat dry. Combine bread and mushrooms in a bowl and toss with broth. Season to taste. Stuff chicken and secure with poultry pin or toothpick. Place in roasting pan and sprinkle with salt, pepper and paprika. (If desired, surround it with carrots, potatoes, onions, garlic and a red pepper.)

2. Roast for about 2 hours, basting frequently with melted butter and pan juices. The chicken is done when the leg bone wiggles, the thigh juices run clear and the skin is the color of teak.

YIELD: 4 SERVINGS   *Pilar Viladas*

ROASTED CHICKEN WITH
SIMPLE OYSTER DRESSING

(Adapted from Susan McGowan, Hall Tavern, Deerfield, Mass.)

At the Hall Tavern on Main Street in Deerfield, Mass., Susan McGowan fires up a brick oven and roasts the chicken over an open hearth, the way that it was prepared more than two hundred years ago. Here is the version better suited to contemporary kitchens.

> 1 roasting chicken, 3 to 4 pounds
> 1 teaspoon coarse salt, or to taste
> 7 slices day-old bread
> Approximately 8 tablespoons unsalted butter
> ¼ cup (packed) fresh sage leaves, stems removed
> 12 to 14 fresh shucked oysters
> ¼ cup white wine
> 1 tablespoon Worcestershire sauce

1. Preheat oven to 450 degrees.

2. Wash and dry chicken and salt the cavity. Using about half the butter, liberally butter each slice of bread and cover with sage leaves, pressing leaves into butter. Add 1 or 2 oysters to each slice, roll slices up and thrust into cavity, packing tightly.

3. Truss the bird and place on a rack in a shallow roasting pan. Melt remaining butter in wine. Place bird in oven and cook 45 minutes, basting three times with butter and wine mixture. Reduce heat to 350 degrees and continue roasting an additional 15 minutes. Remove bird from oven and set aside to rest for 15 minutes or so before serving. Cooking time will vary depending on size of bird. Count on an hour or more. Chicken is done when leg juices run clear yellow when pierced with a fork.

4. Collect juices in the roasting pan. Skim off excess fat. Just before serving, bring juices to a boil and add Worcestershire sauce. Serve the bird on a platter and pass juices separately in a gravy boat.

YIELD: 2 TO 4 SERVINGS, DEPENDING ON SIZE OF BIRD
↳ *Nancy Harmon Jenkins*

ROAST CHICKEN WITH PECAN STUFFING

1 3½-pound roasting chicken, with giblets
2 tablespoons unsalted butter (or use the fat rendered from the inner chicken fat)
½ pound bulk sausage
1 cup finely chopped onion
1 tablespoon loosely packed leaf sage
¼ cup finely chopped parsley
1 cup fine, fresh bread crumbs
1 large egg, lightly beaten
Salt and freshly ground pepper
1 cup toasted pecans
1 onion, peeled and quartered
¼ cup water

1. Preheat oven to 400 degrees.

2. Remove the gizzard, heart and liver from the chicken. Cut away and discard the tough outer membrane of the gizzard. Chop the soft, fleshy part of the gizzard, the heart and liver.

3. Heat the butter in a saucepan and add the sausage, breaking it up with the flat side of a metal kitchen spoon. Add the liver mixture and chopped onion. Cook, stirring, about three minutes and add the sage.

4. Cook about 3 minutes, stirring, or until the sausage is cooked. Add the parsley, bread crumbs, egg, salt and pepper to taste and the pecans. Blend well and let cool.

5. Sprinkle the chicken inside and out with salt and pepper to taste. Stuff the chicken with the pecan mixture and truss. Place the chicken on its side in a shallow baking dish and scatter the quartered onion around it.

6. Roast the chicken 20 minutes. Turn the chicken to the other side and continue roasting, basting often, about 20 minutes.

7. Turn the chicken on its back and continue roasting, basting often, about 20 minutes.

8. Ten minutes before the chicken is done add the water and continue baking.

9. Remove from the oven and let stand 10 minutes before carving.

YIELD: 4 OR MORE SERVINGS *Craig Claiborne and Pierre Franey*

CHICKEN STUFFED WITH RICE, PROSCIUTTO AND BLACK OLIVES

1 3- to 4-pound chicken
Coarse salt and freshly ground pepper
1 small onion, chopped
1 clove garlic, minced
1 tablespoon butter
1½ cups cooked rice
¼ pound prosciutto, diced (see Note)
⅓ cup black oil-cured olives, pitted and chopped
1 tablespoon fresh sage leaves, minced, or 1 teaspoon dried sage, crumbled

1. Preheat oven to 375 degrees.

2. Wipe the chicken inside and out with paper towels. Remove loose fat from cavity. Season the bird with salt and pepper.

3. Soften the onion and the garlic in the butter. Chop the chicken liver, heart and gizzard, add to the onion and sauté briefly over medium heat for a minute.

4. Off the heat, stir in the rice, prosciutto, olives and sage leaves. Season to taste and mix well. Stuff the mixture into the chicken and truss or secure the cavity with skewers.

5. Roast for about 1 hour, or until the chicken is tender and the thigh juices run clear, basting frequently. Allow to rest at room temperature before serving.

NOTE: Proscuitto ends, sold more cheaply than regular sliced prosciutto, may be used in the stuffing.

YIELD: 4 SERVINGS ⌁ *Moira Hodgson*

CARMELLA QUATTROCIOCCHI'S ROAST CHICKEN WITH ITALIAN STUFFING

½ pound unsalted butter

3 cups chopped onions

2 cups chopped giblets

½ pound Italian sweet sausage

3 cups crumbled day-old bread

¼ cup grated Romano cheese

3 large eggs, beaten slightly

1 tablespoon sage

Pinch tarragon

Salt and pepper to taste

1 4- to 5-pound chicken

1. Melt ¼ pound of the butter. Sauté onions until lightly colored. Set onions aside and add 6 tablespoons butter to pan and lightly brown giblets and sausage. In large bowl thoroughly combine all other stuffing ingredients.

2. Stuff bird lightly and truss. (Bake any additional stuffing separately in baking dish.)

3. Roast chicken in covered pan at 350 degrees, allowing 20 to 25 minutes per pound, basting occasionally with remaining 2 tablespoons butter. During last 15 minutes remove cover so skin will brown. Before carving allow chicken to stand 15 to 20 minutes.

YIELD: 4 TO 5 SERVINGS   *Marian Burros*

CRAIG CLAIBORNE'S ROAST CHICKEN STUFFED WITH SCRAMBLED EGGS

Well-seasoned scrambled eggs, when cooked in a chicken, produce a custard-like stuffing with a delicate flavor and tender, gossamerlike texture.

> 5 eggs
> ¼ cup heavy cream
> ½ teaspoon chopped tarragon
> Salt and freshly ground black pepper
> 3½ tablespoons unsalted butter
> 1 2½-pound chicken
> 1 small onion, peeled and quartered

1. Preheat the oven to 450 degrees.

2. Beat the eggs in a mixing bowl until well blended. Add the cream, tarragon, and salt and pepper to taste.

3. Heat 1 tablespoon butter in a skillet and add the egg mixture. Cook over low heat, stirring with a rubber spatula, until the eggs are almost set. Do not overcook. Remove from the heat. Stir in ½ tablespoon of butter. Cool.

4. Sprinkle the inside of the chicken with salt and pepper and stuff the chicken with the egg mixture. Truss the chicken. Sprinkle the outside with salt and pepper to taste.

5. Melt 2 tablespoons of butter in a shallow roasting pan and turn the chicken around in it until coated. Add the onion to the pan. Rest the chicken on one side and place it in the oven. Bake 15 minutes, basting occasionally.

6. Turn the chicken to the other side and continue baking about 15 minutes, basting occasionally. Turn the chicken once again and bake 15 minutes, basting often.

7. Untruss the chicken and carve it. Serve the stuffing on the side.

YIELD: 4 SERVINGS ✒ *Craig Claiborne*

MOIRA HODGSON'S ROAST CHICKEN STUFFED WITH APRICOTS AND BULGUR

1 3- to 4-pound chicken
1 lemon
¾ cup bulgur
1½ cups cold water
½ cup dried apricots
Port wine to cover (about ¾ cup)
2 tablespoons unsalted butter
1 small onion, chopped
1 clove garlic, minced
2 stalks celery, chopped
Coarse salt and freshly ground pepper to taste
¼ teaspoon dried thyme

1. Wipe the chicken inside and out with paper towels. Remove the loose fat from inside the cavity. Squeeze the juice of the lemon on the skin and inside the chicken cavity. Set the chicken aside.

2. Put the bulgur in a small bowl and add the cold water. Put the apricots in a small saucepan and cover with the port. Let stand for 1 hour.

3. Bring the apricots to a boil, cover, and simmer gently over low heat for 30 minutes, or until tender.

4. Preheat the oven to 375 degrees. Drain the water from the cracked wheat. Melt the butter in a frying pan and gently soften the onion with the garlic and celery. Add the cracked wheat, salt, pepper and thyme. Mix well and cook for 5 minutes. Add the apricots, whole or chopped, with their juice. Mix thoroughly and cook for another 5 minutes.

5. Stuff the mixture into the chicken and truss with needle and thread or skewers.

6. Roast the chicken for 40 minutes to 1 hour, or until the thigh juices run clear. Let rest at room temperature before serving.

YIELD: 4 SERVINGS ⤳ *Moira Hodgson*

GREAT BAKED CHICKEN

TOM COLICCHIO'S
ROAST CHICKEN

For crispness, acclaimed New York City chef-restaurateur Tom Colicchio browns the chicken parts in a skillet before placing them in the oven.

1 3- to 3½-pound free-range chicken, cut into 6 pieces
Kosher salt
Freshly ground black pepper
1 tablespoon peanut oil
2 tablespoons unsalted butter
2 sprigs rosemary
2 sprigs thyme

1. Heat oven to 400 degrees. Rinse chicken pieces and dry thoroughly with paper towels. Cut off the last joint of each wing and discard. Season chicken liberally inside and out with salt and pepper.

2. Heat the oil over medium heat in a large skillet. Place the chicken pieces skin-side down in the skillet and brown about 7 minutes. Turn, and brown other side, about 4 minutes. Transfer pan to oven, and roast, basting occasionally, about 20 minutes. Add butter, rosemary and thyme, and cook, spooning butter over chicken every 5 minutes, until thigh juices run clear, 15 to 20 minutes more. Remove chicken pieces from pan as they are cooked; the breasts will finish first.

3. Cover pieces loosely with foil, and allow to rest 10 to 15 minutes before serving.

YIELD: 3 SERVINGS ⤶ *Amanda Hesser*

SOTTA KHUNN'S CHICKEN WITH GINGER

(Adapted from Le Cirque, New York City)

1 frying chicken, about 3 pounds, cut into 8 pieces
Salt and freshly ground black pepper
4 tablespoons corn oil
¾ cup minced red onion
1 medium-size sweet red pepper, cored and julienned
2 bunches scallions, white part only, chopped
2 medium-size leeks, white part only, in fine julienne strips
2 tablespoons fresh ginger in fine julienne strips
1 clove garlic, minced
¼ cup sherry wine vinegar
1 tablespoon honey

1. Preheat oven to 350 degrees.

2. Dry chicken pieces and season them to taste with salt and pepper. Heat half the oil in a large skillet, add chicken and cook over medium-high heat until golden, about 10 minutes. Do not crowd chicken in the pan. As pieces are browned, remove them to a platter.

3. Add red onion, red pepper, scallions, leeks, 1 teaspoon of the ginger and the garlic to pan. Place chicken over vegetables and put pan in oven, uncovered, to wilt vegetables, about 15 minutes.

4. Remove pan from oven and remove chicken, leaving the vegetables. Stir in vinegar and cook, stirring over medium-high heat until there is just a film of liquid left in pan. Stir in honey. Return chicken to pan, baste with vegetable and sauce mixture and bake another 10 to 15 minutes, until chicken is done.

5. While chicken is finishing its cooking, heat remaining oil in a small saucepan, add remaining ginger and fry ginger until it is golden. Drain.

6. Arrange chicken and vegetables, moistened with pan juices, on a platter, scatter fried ginger over top and serve.

YIELD: 4 SERVINGS ⌒ *Florence Fabricant*

NIKA HAZELTON'S
BRAZILIAN CHICKEN WITH ORANGE

1 2½- to 3-pound chicken, cut into pieces
½ cup olive oil
1 cup fresh orange juice
1 cup dry white wine
½ cup raisins
½ cup blanched almonds, ground fine
½ cup orange pulp
½ teaspoon ground ginger
Salt and freshly ground black pepper

1. Preheat oven to 350 degrees.

2. Remove all the fat and the skin from the chicken.

3. Heat the olive oil in a frying pan. Over medium heat, brown the chicken pieces in it on all sides. Transfer to a shallow baking pan.

4. Combine all the other ingredients in a bowl and mix well. Pour over the chicken pieces.

5. Bake for about 45 minutes or until tender. Baste frequently. Serve with rice.

YIELD: 3 TO 4 SERVINGS ⌒ *Craig Claiborne*

CHICKEN WITH ARTICHOKES

(Adapted from The New York Times Heritage Cook Book)

3 tablespoons unsalted butter

1 3½-pound chicken, cut into serving pieces

1 tablespoon finely chopped shallot or scallion, including green part

½ tablespoon flour

1 tablespoon tomato paste

1 cup chicken broth

¾ cup dry white wine

¼ cup Italian parsley

1 sprig fresh rosemary or one half teaspoon dried rosemary

Salt and freshly ground black pepper to taste

6 small artichokes, trimmed, cut in half and "choke" removed, or one package
    frozen artichoke hearts, defrosted

1. Preheat oven to 350 degrees.

2. Heat the butter in an ovenproof skillet and brown the chicken on all sides. Remove chicken to a warm place. Add the shallot or scallion to skillet. Cook, stirring 1 minute longer.

3. Add the tomato paste, stir it around in the skillet and add the broth and wine. Simmer five minutes. Return the chicken to the skillet and sprinkle with the parsley, rosemary, salt and pepper. If fresh artichokes are used, add them now. If frozen artichokes are used, add them for the last fifteen minutes of cooking.

4. Cover the skillet and bake 30 to 45 minutes.

YIELD: 4 SERVINGS

CHICKEN WITH
END-OF-SEASON TOMATOES

Brining the chicken before cooking results in a juicy bird. For a successful dish, use only very ripe tomatoes.

3 teaspoons sea salt, more for
    seasoning
1 4-pound chicken, cut into 6 pieces
¾ cup flour, for dusting
Freshly ground black pepper
1 tablespoon olive oil
I tablespoon butter

3 sprigs thyme
1 shallot, finely chopped
½ cup fino sherry (see Note)
3 very ripe tomatoes (from a
    farmstand, if possible),
    coarsely chopped
1 teaspoon aged sherry wine vinegar

1. In the morning, pour salt into a bowl large enough to fit chicken. Add a cup of tepid water and dissolve salt. Add chicken pieces, then cover with water. Refrigerate 8 to 12 hours, until ready to cook.

2. Preheat oven to 375 degrees. Remove chicken from water and pat it dry. Place flour and more salt and pepper in a plastic bag. Add chicken pieces, two at a time, and shake to lightly coat them. Vigorously shake off excess flour and repeat with remaining chicken.

3. Place a deep, ovenproof sauté pan over medium-high heat. Add oil and butter. When foam subsides, add chicken pieces, skin-side down. Brown well, adjusting heat as needed, then turn and cook for 3 minutes. Add thyme sprigs and transfer pan to oven. Roast chicken, basting every few minutes.

4. When chicken is cooked (20 to 30 minutes), transfer it to a platter and keep warm. Place pan back on stove, over medium heat. Add shallot and sauté 1 minute. Pour in sherry and boil, scraping up any pan drippings. Reduce until pan is almost dry, then add tomatoes and increase heat to high. Cook until tomatoes have broken down and juices have condensed, 10 minutes. The sauce should be pulpy, not drippy. Taste and adjust seasoning, sprinkle with vinegar, then spoon sauce over chicken. Serve.

NOTE: Fino is a pale, very dry Spanish sherry.

YIELD: 4 SERVINGS   *Amanda Hesser*

JEAN-GEORGES'S
CHICKEN WITH FIGS

(Adapted from *Jean-Georges: Cooking at Home with a Four-Star Chef*)

1 3-pound chicken, cut into 8 pieces
Coarse sea salt and freshly ground black pepper
2 teaspoons sugar
1 tablespoon unsalted butter
2 tablespoons olive oil
1 4-inch piece of cinnamon stick or ½ teaspoon ground cardamom
2 large shallots, minced (about ½ cup)
¼ cup red wine vinegar
½ cup port wine
4 ripe figs, left whole
½ cup chicken stock

1. Preheat the oven to 500 degrees. Season the chicken well on both sides with salt and pepper, then sprinkle the skin side with a teaspoon of sugar.

2. Combine the butter and olive oil in a large casserole or Dutch oven and turn the heat to high. When the butter foam subsides, put the chicken, skin-side down, in the pot. Sprinkle the other side with the remaining teaspoon of sugar. Brown the chicken on one side—this will happen faster than usual because of the sugar—then turn over and cook for another minute. Add the cinnamon or cardamom and shallots and cook, stirring a little, for 2 minutes.

3. Add the vinegar. When it has almost evaporated, add the port wine and the figs. Cook for 2 more minutes, then add the chicken stock and put the uncovered pot in the oven.

4. Roast for 5 minutes, then remove the wing-breast and breast pieces to a warm platter. Roast for another 10 minutes, then return the breast meat to the pot on top of the stove over medium heat. Stir, then adjust the seasoning by adding more vinegar, salt and/or pepper as necessary.

YIELD: 4 SERVINGS   *Moira Hodgson*

PORCH CHICKEN

Marinating the chicken overnight deepens the citrus-rosemary flavor. Because this dish can be prepared ahead of time and served cold, it is ideal picnic fare.

2 3½- to 4-pound chickens, each cut into 8 to 10 pieces, or 6 to 7 pounds of
    chicken parts with bones in and skin on
8 to 10 cloves garlic, peeled and coarsely chopped
⅓ cup extra-virgin olive oil
¼ cup freshly squeezed lemon juice
3 tablespoons dry white table wine or white vermouth
1 teaspoon kosher salt
½ teaspoon freshly ground pepper
6 to 8 sprigs fresh rosemary

1. Rinse the chicken under cold running water and pat dry with paper towels. Place in a large, shallow baking dish.

2. In a smaller bowl, combine garlic, oil, lemon juice, wine, salt and pepper. Whisk until blended; stir in rosemary sprigs. Pour mixture over chicken, turning the parts to coat evenly. Cover with plastic wrap and marinate in the refrigerator at least 2 hours or overnight, if possible. Turn chicken pieces in marinade at least once during this time.

3. To cook, preheat oven to 350 degrees. Line a large baking pan with heavy-duty aluminum foil.

4. Place chicken pieces in the pan. With a rubber spatula, scrape out every bit of marinade and spread it onto the chicken, evenly distributing garlic and rosemary. Arrange pieces skin-side down in a single layer.

5. Bake for 45 minutes, turn the pieces over every 20 minutes and baste with pan juices. Bake until a deep golden brown, at least 50 to 60 minutes more. Cool chicken to room temperature, cover and refrigerate until ready to serve. Serve chilled or at room temperature.

YIELD: 8 SERVINGS   *Marialisa Calta*

DONNA HAY'S BAKED CHICKEN WITH GREEN OLIVES AND TOMATOES

(Adapted from *Off the Shelf*)

Donna Hay's recipes are simple and deliver maximum flavor for a minimum of effort.

¾ cup pitted green olives, halved
1 3½- to 4-pound chicken, cut into 8 pieces
4 cloves garlic, peeled and halved
½ cup chopped flat-leaf parsley
2 tablespoons grated lemon zest
8 ounces cherry tomatoes
2 tablespoons extra virgin olive oil
Sea salt and cracked black pepper

1. Heat oven to 400 degrees. Soak olives in cold water for 5 minutes; drain.

2. Place chicken in a 9-by-12-inch baking dish, skin-side up, with half a garlic clove under each piece. In a small bowl, combine olives, parsley, lemon zest, tomatoes, olive oil, and salt and pepper to taste. Spoon mixture over chicken to cover evenly.

3. Bake until golden, 45 to 55 minutes. Place on serving plates, drizzle with juices, serve.

YIELD: 4 SERVINGS ⟿ *R. W. Apple Jr.*

MAMA ROMANO'S
BAKED LEMON CHICKEN

(Adapted from Michael Romano of Union Square Cafe, New York City)

3½ pounds chicken breasts and thighs, skinned
¼ teaspoon salt
Freshly ground black pepper
⅓ cup flour for dredging
2 tablespoons olive oil
3 cups thinly sliced onions
1½ tablespoons thinly sliced garlic
8 sprigs fresh thyme
1½ cups chicken stock
2 lemons

1. Preheat the oven to 400 degrees.

2. Cut the chicken breasts in half, and season all chicken pieces with salt and pepper. Dredge in the flour.

3. Heat 1 tablespoon of olive oil in large ovenproof skillet or Dutch oven over medium heat. Sauté the chicken pieces until golden brown. Transfer to a plate, and reserve.

4. Discard the fat from the skillet, and add the remaining olive oil. Add the onions and garlic, and cook over low heat for 15 minutes, stirring occasionally, until the onions are very soft and lightly browned. Remove from heat.

5. Spread the thyme over the onions and garlic. Arrange the browned chicken pieces side by side over the onions in the skillet. Add the chicken stock.

6. Cut one lemon into thin slices, remove the seeds, and place one slice atop each piece of chicken. Cut other lemon in half and squeeze through a strainer over the chicken. Return the skillet to the heat, and bring the stock to a simmer. Cover the pot, and bake in the oven for 5 to 15 minutes, basting the chicken with the cooking liquid.

YIELD: 4 SERVINGS   *Marian Burros*

JO JO'S ROAST CHICKEN
WITH GREEN OLIVES AND CILANTRO

This dish, served at Jo Jo, one of Jean-Georges Vongerichten's Manhattan restaurants, is redolent with flavors of green olives, ginger, cinnamon, saffron and cilantro.

2 tablespoons plus 1 teaspoon extra-virgin olive oil
¼ cup minced onion
2 teaspoons minced ginger
2-inch piece cinnamon
Pinch saffron or ½ teaspoon turmeric
Kosher salt
2 cups rich chicken stock
2 tablespoons peanut oil
1 3- to 4-pound chicken, cut into 4 pieces
Freshly ground black pepper
2 tablespoons minced green olives
2 teaspoons lemon juice
1 tablespoon coarsely chopped cilantro

1. Heat oven to 500 degrees. Place 2 tablespoons olive oil in a small saucepan over medium heat. Add the onion, ginger, cinnamon, saffron and a pinch of salt, and cook, stirring occasionally, for about 5 minutes. Add the stock, and increase the heat to high. Cook, stirring occasionally, while you prepare the chicken. When the liquid has reduced by about three-quarters and becomes syrupy, turn off the heat.

2. Heat peanut oil in a large, ovenproof skillet, preferably nonstick, over medium-high heat for a minute or two. Season chicken on both sides with salt and pepper. Place it in the skillet, skin-side down, and cook undisturbed until lightly browned, 5 to 8 minutes. Turn it over, and cook the other side for about 2 minutes. Turn it over, skin-side down again, and place the skillet in the oven. Check chicken after 15 minutes, and remove pieces as they are cooked through. (Breasts will finish cooking before legs. Keep them warm.)

3. To finish the sauce, whisk in the remaining teaspoon olive oil and olives, and season to taste with salt and pepper. Cook about 2 minutes over medium-high heat, stirring once or twice. Turn off the heat, and add the lemon juice and cilantro. Remove the cinnamon stick.

4. To serve, arrange chicken on 4 plates. Spoon sauce around it, not over it, so that the chicken stays crunchy.

YIELD: 4 SERVINGS *Amanda Hesser*

ORSO'S CHICKEN WITH BLACK OLIVES AND SAUSAGE

A dish with classic Italian ingredients—sausage, olives, tomatoes, wine, Parmesan cheese—from the famed restaurant in Manhattan's theater district.

> 2 2½-pound frying chickens
> 3 cloves garlic
> 4 tablespoons olive oil
> Juice of 1 lemon, or more to taste
> Salt to taste
> Freshly ground pepper to taste
> 1 bunch fresh rosemary, coarsely chopped
> 1½ pounds sweet Italian sausage
> 1 cup Ligurian or niçoise olives, pitted
> 8 to 10 plum tomatoes, seeded and cut lengthwise into wedges
> 1 splash red or white wine (optional)
> 2 tablespoons butter
> 3 tablespoons grated Parmesan cheese

1. Preheat the oven to 375 degrees.

2. Cut the chickens in half lengthwise. Separate the legs and thighs from the breasts. Smash 2 of the garlic cloves and rub them over the chicken pieces. Sprinkle with 2 tablespoons of the olive oil, the lemon juice, salt, pepper and half of the rosemary. Place the chicken in an ungreased baking pan and bake for 45 minutes, or until the juice runs clear when the chicken's skin is pricked.

3. Meanwhile, place the sausage and 1 tablespoon of the olive oil in a sauté pan.

Sauté over medium heat for 15 to 20 minutes, or until the sausage is well-browned and cooked through. Remove the skin and slice into 2-inch pieces. Set aside.

4. When the chicken is done, smash the remaining garlic clove and place it in the sauté pan. Add the remaining oil and cook the garlic until it begins to brown, about 1 minute. Remove the garlic and discard.

5. In the same pan, add the sautéed sausage and the olives to the oil. Cook for 1 minute over high heat. Add the tomatoes, the remaining rosemary and the salt and pepper. Sauté for another 2 minutes, or until the tomatoes begin to soften. Stir in the wine, if desired. Add the butter and Parmesan cheese and stir briskly until the sauce becomes creamy. Pour the sauce over the chicken and serve.

YIELD: 4 SERVINGS 	*Alex Witchel*

CHICKEN BREASTS IN FOIL WITH SUN-DRIED TOMATOES AND OLIVES

(Adapted from *The New Joy of Cooking*)

10 kalamata or other black olives, pitted and minced

8 sun-dried tomato halves in oil, cut into thin strips

3 tablespoons oil from sun-dried tomato jar, or olive oil

2 tablespoons shredded fresh basil or minced parsley

4 teaspoons vegetable or olive oil

Salt and freshly ground black pepper

4 boneless, skinless chicken breast halves, trimmed of fat, rinsed and patted dry
   (about 1½ pounds)

1. Place rack in center of oven, and preheat to 450 degrees. Combine olives, sun-dried tomatoes, their oil and fresh herbs in bowl.

2. Fold 4 12-inch squares of aluminum foil in half to make creases at center, unfold, and lightly coat shiny sides with teaspoon of vegetable oil on each. Lightly salt

and pepper chicken breasts on both sides. Place each breast on shiny side of a piece of foil, just to one side of crease. Spoon tomato mixture over each breast, leaving ¼-inch border around edges.

3. Loosely fold foil over chicken, then crimp edges of packet to seal it tightly. Place packets on baking sheet, and bake on center rack for 20 minutes. Remove from oven, and let stand for 5 minutes. To avoid possibility of burning by steam, cut slit in packets before opening them.

YIELD: 4 SERVINGS   *Molly O'Neill*

CHICKEN, CHILIES AND CORN

2 tablespoons olive oil
1 frying chicken, cut up and patted dry
1 medium-size onion, chopped
1 small sweet red pepper, seeded and chopped
1 jalapeño pepper, seeded and chopped
2 cloves garlic, chopped
1 tablespoon pine nuts
1 teaspoon ground cumin
1 cup fresh, frozen or canned corn kernels, well drained
1 cup finely chopped fresh or canned tomatoes
Juice of 1 lime
Salt and freshly ground black pepper
2 tablespoons chopped fresh coriander

1. Heat the oil in a large, heavy, ovenproof skillet. Add the chicken pieces and cook over high heat until they are nicely browned. Do not crowd them in the pan, and remove them to a bowl as they brown. You may have to brown the chicken in several shifts.

2. Preheat oven to 350 degrees.

3. Lower the heat and add the onion and red pepper to the pan. Sauté until tender. Add the jalapeño pepper, garlic and pine nuts and sauté for a minute or so, then stir in the cumin. Add the corn, increase the heat to medium-high and sauté a few minutes longer. Stir in the tomatoes and the lime juice.

4. Return the chicken to the pan along with any juices that may have been released by the chicken as it cooled. Baste the chicken with the pan juices and season with salt and pepper.

5. Cover and bake 40 minutes. Sprinkle with coriander before serving.

YIELD: 4 SERVINGS *Florence Fabricant*

✤ EASY ✤

LEMON CHICKEN WITH CRÈME FRAÎCHE

(Adapted from *The Crème Fraîche Cookbook*)

A good crème fraîche is a thick, cloudlike cream that is a little nutty, yet still fresh and creamy. It will stay fresh for at least a month. As it ages, it gets thicker and acquires a more pronounced cheesy flavor, so it is best to use it fresh, when it seems bright and lively on your palate. Crème fraîche can be approximated at home by combining a couple of teaspoons of either buttermilk or yogurt to one cup of cream and letting it thicken at room temperature. Sometimes it takes just a few hours to achieve the right consistency; sometimes more than a day. It can be quite good, but real crème fraîche is truly superior.

1½ tablespoons unsalted butter
1½ tablespoons olive oil
4 whole chicken legs (with thighs attached)
Coarse sea salt or kosher salt
Freshly ground black pepper or ground multicolored peppercorns
Juice and grated zest of 1 lemon
½ cup crème fraîche

1. Heat oven to 375 degrees. Heat a large, deep sauté pan over medium heat. After 3 minutes add butter and oil. Season chicken generously with salt, and very generously with pepper. Place chicken, skin-side down, in sauté pan and brown well on both sides, turning once.

2. Turn chicken skin-side down in pan, and transfer pan to oven to finish cooking, about 15 minutes. (Chicken is done when juices run clear when pierced with a knife.)

3. Return pan to top of stove. Transfer chicken to a platter and keep warm. Remove all but about 1 tablespoon of fat from pan. Place over medium heat, add lemon juice and stir to scrape up any pan drippings. Simmer for 1 minute, then add crème fraîche and stir until melted and bubbling. If mixture is too thick, add a few tablespoons of water. Pour sauce over chicken, and sprinkle with lemon zest and additional ground pepper. Serve hot.

YIELD: 4 SERVINGS   *Amanda Hesser*

✦ EASY ✦
TRIXIE'S SESAME-BAKED CHICKEN

(Adapted from *Home-Cooking Sampler*)

1 tablespoon vegetable oil

⅓ cup dry, unseasoned bread crumbs

1 teaspoon salt

½ teaspoon paprika

¼ teaspoon freshly ground black pepper

2 tablespoons sesame seeds

1 3-pound chicken, well trimmed and cut into 8 pieces

2 tablespoons unsalted butter

1. Preheat the oven to 375 degrees. Lightly oil a 9-by-13-inch baking pan.

2. On a large plate, combine the bread crumbs, salt, paprika, pepper and sesame

seeds. Coat the chicken pieces with the bread crumb mixture and place in the baking dish, skin-side down.

3. Dot the chicken with the butter and bake for 30 minutes. Turn the chicken over, skin-side up, and baste with any accumulated juices. Bake an additional 30 minutes, basting occasionally, until the chicken is brown and crisp. Transfer to a platter and serve.

YIELD: 4 SERVINGS ⟑ *Marialisa Calta*

✦ EASY ✦

MADHUR JAFFREY'S SPICY INDIAN CHICKEN

(Adapted from *Madhur Jaffrey's Indian Cooking*)

1 tablespoon ground cumin seeds
1 tablespoon paprika
1½ teaspoons cayenne pepper, or to taste (if you use less, increase paprika to make up for it)
1 tablespoon ground turmeric
1 to 1½ teaspoons pepper
2 teaspoons salt, or to taste
2 to 3 cloves garlic, minced
6 tablespoons lemon juice
6 leg-thigh pieces of chicken, skinned and cut apart
3 tablespoons vegetable oil
Indian-Style Pilaf (see recipe, page 71)

1. Combine cumin seeds, paprika, cayenne pepper, turmeric, pepper, salt, garlic and lemon juice and mix into a paste.

2. Rub chicken pieces with the paste until well coated and allow to stand, covered with plastic wrap, for 3 hours or longer.

3. Preheat oven to 400 degrees. Arrange the chicken pieces in a baking pan, brush with the oil and bake 20 minutes. Turn the pieces over and bake 20 to 25 minutes more, basting occasionally.

4. Remove chicken pieces to a warm serving platter. Add water, if necessary, to the baking pan and stir over a high heat until the sauce is somewhat reduced. Pour sauce over chicken and serve with rice pilaf.

YIELD: 6 SERVINGS

INDIAN-STYLE PILAF

1 cup long-grain rice

1 medium onion, chopped

2 tablespoons unsalted butter or vegetable oil

4 whole cardamom pods

1 piece stick cinnamon

5 whole cloves

½ teaspoon ground turmeric

4 bay leaves

2 cups water

1 teaspoon salt, or to taste

1. If desired, wash rice and let stand in cold water for 30 minutes. Drain.

2. Sauté onion in butter in a pot until golden. Add cardamom pods, cinnamon, cloves, turmeric and bay leaves and sauté 2 minutes. Add rice and sauté 2 minutes, stirring to color all grains. Add water and salt, bring to a boil, cover and simmer over very low heat 15 to 20 minutes. Turn off heat and allow to stand, covered and undisturbed, until needed. Fluff before serving. (The whole spices are not meant to be eaten.)

YIELD: 6 SMALL SERVINGS ✑ *Robert Farrar Capon*

MATT LEE AND TED LEE'S
BAKED CHICKEN THIGHS WITH
GINGER, THYME AND YOGURT

Matt Lee and Ted Lee: "The lowly thigh is our absolute favorite cut of chicken for picnic fare. Like wings or drumsticks, thighs can be brandished with one hand, but more important they offer the perfect mix of light and dark meat in about four or five good bites. Once they have been skinned and trimmed, the thigh's fatty crevices seem to hold sauces and glazes better than any other piece except for wings. We let the thighs sit for an hour in a marinade of yogurt, pureed ginger and shallot, and give them a quick bake, uncovered, either the morning of the picnic or the night before. Fresh, flowery thyme rounds out the seasonings in the recipe but a teaspoon of garam masala works beautifully, too, with the ginger and shallot. The marinade bakes down to an aromatic, tangy glaze that somehow takes the edge off oppressive heat."

2 large shallots, or 6 small shallots

6 tablespoons fresh ginger, minced

¼ cup lemon juice

2 teaspoons lemon zest

1¾ cups plain yogurt

1½ teaspoons salt

2 tablespoons fresh thyme leaves,
  stripped from the stalk and rubbed
  between fingers

12 chicken thighs

1. Puree shallots, ginger, lemon juice and lemon zest in a blender or a food processor. Gently fold yogurt into puree with a wooden spoon. Stir in salt and thyme.

2. Skin chicken thighs, trimming excess fat, and place them in a shallow baking dish that is large enough to hold them in a single layer. Pour the yogurt mixture over chicken thighs, turning the chicken pieces to coat them on all sides, and marinate in refrigerator for an hour.

3. Heat oven to 425 degrees. Bake chicken uncovered for 55 minutes, until corners of chicken just begin to brown and marinade has thickened to a paste. Chicken may be served hot or cold. If taking to a picnic, remove to a container and refrigerate until departure.

YIELD: 6 SERVINGS ⟍ *Matt Lee and Ted Lee*

CHICKEN WITH SOUR CREAM, LEMON JUICE AND MANGO CHUTNEY

(Adapted from *Fifteen-Minute Meals*)

2 whole boneless, skinless chicken breasts, cut in half, 4 ounces each
½ cup Hellmann's mayonnaise
½ cup sour cream
2 tablespoons Major Grey's mango chutney
1 teaspoon curry powder
Juice of 1 Meyer lemon or 1 regular lemon
Freshly ground black pepper

1. Preheat the oven to 450 degrees. Lay the chicken flat in a medium roasting dish (either Pyrex or enamel). In a small bowl, whisk together the mayonnaise and sour cream. Add the chutney and curry powder and whisk until smooth. Add the lemon juice a little at a time and taste as you go. It should taste quite tangy. Stop when it is to your liking.

2. Spoon the sauce evenly over the chicken. Place in the oven and roast until the chicken is just cooked through, about 15 minutes. Remove from the oven, season with freshly ground black pepper and serve.

YIELD: 2 SERVINGS   *Amanda Hesser*

SERENA BASS'S
TANDOORI CHICKEN FINGERS

6 tablespoons tandoori masala (see Note)

3 tablespoons Patak's Tandoori (see Note)

Curry paste (see Note)

¼ cup peeled, finely grated ginger

2 cloves garlic

1½ cups heavy cream

½ teaspoon salt

¼ teaspoon freshly ground black pepper

2 pounds boneless, skinless chicken breasts, cut into ½-inch-wide strips

Cilantro, chopped for garnish

1. In a large nonreactive bowl, combine all the ingredients except the chicken and cilantro and stir until well mixed.

2. Add the chicken, toss to coat and cover the bowl. Refrigerate overnight.

3. Preheat the oven to 375 degrees. Cover the bottom of two large sheet pans with parchment paper and lay the strips of chicken on top of the paper. Discard excess marinade.

4. Bake the chicken, turning once, for 10 minutes, or until just cooked through. Garnish with cilantro and serve.

NOTE: See "Selected Sources for Ingredients," page 352.

YIELD: 8 APPETIZER SERVINGS ⌐ Molly O'Neill

EASY

DEVILED CHICKEN LEGS

A mild heat emanates from these chicken legs, which are coated with a mixture of mustard and chicken broth, then with shallots, garlic, bread crumbs and parsley.

4 chicken legs with thighs attached
Salt and freshly ground pepper to taste
1 tablespoon butter
2 tablespoons olive oil
2 tablespoons Dijon mustard
4 tablespoons fresh or canned chicken broth
2 tablespoons finely chopped shallots
2 teaspoons finely chopped garlic
4 tablespoons fresh fine bread crumbs
4 tablespoons finely chopped parsley

1. Preheat the oven to 425 degrees.
2. Sprinkle the chicken legs with salt and pepper.
3. In a baking dish large enough to hold the legs in one layer, melt the butter, and add the olive oil. Add the chicken legs, and turn them in the butter mixture until well coated. Place the legs, skin-side down, in the oven. Bake for 15 minutes.
4. Meanwhile, blend the mustard and chicken broth in a small bowl with a whisk. In another small bowl blend well the shallots, garlic and bread crumbs, plus 2 tablespoons parsley. Set aside.
5. Loosen the chicken from the pan with a fork or spatula. Then with a pastry brush, brush the chicken on both sides with the mustard mixture. Arrange the legs skin-side up, return them to the oven, and bake for 10 minutes more.
6. Sprinkle the chicken evenly with the shallot mixture. Reduce the heat to 400 degrees, and bake for 10 minutes longer or until lightly browned. Sprinkle with the remaining parsley. Serve immediately.

YIELD: 4 SERVINGS   *Pierre Franey*

OLIVER CLARK'S
BUFFALO CHICKEN WINGS

Buffalo chicken wings were said to have originated at Frank and Teressa's Anchor Bar on Main Street in Buffalo, N.Y.

FOR THE DRESSING

1 cup mayonnaise
½ cup sour cream
2 tablespoons fresh lemon juice
½ teaspoon Worcestershire sauce
¼ teaspoon sugar
¼ teaspoon cayenne pepper
¼ teaspoon onion powder
¼ teaspoon garlic powder
8 ounces blue cheese, crumbled

FOR THE WINGS

12 chicken wings (about 2 pounds),
    cut in two at joints, tips discarded
3 tablespoons Louisiana hot sauce
2 tablespoons olive oil
2 tablespoons Cajun seasoning mix
1 teaspoon onion powder
½ teaspoon garlic powder
½ teaspoon dried dill weed
½ teaspoon salt
¼ teaspoon black pepper
4 to 6 large celery stalks, trimmed,
    cut into 3-inch lengths

1. Preheat oven to 375 degrees and line a large roasting pan with foil.

2. To make the dressing, combine all ingredients except cheese in blender or food processor and blend well. Add ¾ of the cheese and blend until just mixed. Stir in remaining cheese and refrigerate for an hour.

3. To make wings, coat with 2 tablespoons hot sauce and oil. Sprinkle remaining ingredients over wings and toss. (Wings can marinate in the refrigerator for up to a day.) Spread wings in a pan, and, in a single layer, roast them about 50 minutes, turning halfway through. Cover and set aside.

4. Preheat broiler. Line a baking sheet with foil. Using tongs, remove wings from pan, place on baking sheet and pour on remaining hot sauce. Place them onto the baking sheet and, watching closely, broil till they are crisp but don't burn, about 1 to 3 minutes. Serve immediately with ice-cold dressing and celery.

YIELD: 2 TO 3 SERVINGS ⌒ *Jonathan Reynolds*

SUVIR SARAN'S SPICY
ROASTED CHICKEN THIGHS

(Adapted from Devi, New York City)

Suvir Saran, the Indian chef at Devi, in the Gramercy Park area of Manhattan, tosses chicken thighs with spices up to one day before roasting them. The result is a dish as flavorful as it is easy.

> 8 chicken thighs, with skin, pierced all over with a small knife
> 5 cloves garlic, peeled
> 1 2-inch piece fresh ginger root, peeled
> 1 small jalapeño pepper, seeded, or cayenne to taste
> Juice and zest of 1 whole lemon
> 2 tablespoons tomato paste
> ½ teaspoon salt, or to taste
> 1 teaspoon cumin powder
> 1 teaspoon coriander seeds or ground coriander

1. Heat oven to 400 degrees. Put chicken thighs in a bowl. Mince garlic, ginger and pepper. Toss with all remaining ingredients or put in a small food processor, and grind to a paste. (It is okay if the coriander seeds are not fully pulverized. They will add a little crunch.)

2. Rub mixture thoroughly into chicken. At this point you can cover and refrigerate for up to a day.

3. Put thighs, skin-side up, in a roasting pan. Roast for 25 to 35 minutes or until done.

YIELD: 4 SERVINGS 〰 *Mark Bittman*

CHINESE CHICKEN WINGS

(Adapted from *The Calico Pantry Cookbook*)

24 chicken wings
3 tablespoons hoisin sauce
3 tablespoons dry sherry
3 tablespoons soy sauce
1 tablespoon dry mustard
3 tablespoons grated fresh ginger root

1. Separate the chicken wings at the joints. Set wing tips aside to use in soup or stock.
2. Combine remaining ingredients.
3. Marinate the rest of the chicken wing parts in this mixture overnight.
4. Preheat oven to 350 degrees. Arrange chicken wings on foil-lined baking sheets and roast for about 45 minutes, until well glazed.

YIELD: 10 OR MORE APPETIZER SERVINGS ⤜ *Florence Fabricant*

OVEN-BARBECUED CHICKEN WINGS

24 chicken wings, about 4 to 5 pounds

Salt to taste, if desired

2 teaspoons medium-grind black pepper

3 teaspoons paprika

½ cup corn, peanut or vegetable oil

1 cup tomato ketchup

¼ cup honey

3 tablespoons red wine vinegar

3 tablespoons white vinegar

2 tablespoons Worcestershire sauce

1 teaspoon Tabasco sauce

1 tablespoon imported mustard

1 tablespoon finely minced garlic

4 tablespoons butter

1 bay leaf

1. Preheat oven to 400 degrees.

2. Fold the small tips of the chicken wings under the main wing bones so that the wings remain "flat."

3. Arrange the wings in one layer in a baking dish so that they bake comfortably close together without crowding.

4. Sprinkle with salt, pepper and two teaspoons of the paprika. Pour half of the oil over all and turn the wings in the mixture so that they are evenly coated. Arrange them in one layer with the small-wing side down.

5. Place in the oven and bake 15 minutes.

6. Meanwhile, combine the ketchup, remaining oil, honey, vinegars, Worcestershire sauce, Tabasco sauce, mustard, garlic, butter, bay leaf and remaining paprika. Bring to a boil.

7. Brush the wings lightly with sauce and turn them to the other side. Brush that side with sauce and continue baking 15 minutes.

8. Brush the wings once more. Turn the pieces and brush this side once more. Continue baking 15 minutes.

9. Continue turning, brushing and baking the chicken for 15 minutes longer or a total of about 1 hour.

YIELD: 6 OR MORE SERVINGS ⌒ *Craig Claiborne with Pierre Franey*

TURNING UP THE HEAT

IGOR'S TUSCAN GRILLED CHICKEN

6 cloves garlic, crushed
2 tablespoons fresh or dried rosemary
Juice of 2 limes
½ cup olive oil
½ teaspoon salt
¼ teaspoon freshly ground black pepper
1 3- to 3½-pound chicken, split and butterflied

1. In a stainless steel or ceramic bowl, combine the crushed garlic, rosemary, lime juice, olive oil, salt and pepper. Place the chicken in the mixture, making sure that it is well covered with the marinade. Cover the bowl and refrigerate overnight.

2. Preheat the oven to 400 degrees, or if using a grill, light the coals.

3. Place a cast-iron skillet over high heat until it smokes. Remove the chicken from the marinade, pat it dry with paper towels and reserve the marinade. Place the chicken, skin-side down, in the hot pan. Press a weight on the bird and sear for 5 minutes. Remove the pan from heat; remove weight.

4. If using the oven, roast the chicken, still in the skillet and skin-side down, for 15 minutes, basting twice with the excess marinade. Turn over, rebaste and roast an additional 20 minutes.

5. If using a grill, sear the chicken on the top of the stove as above. Remove from the skillet and place on a grill very close to the white coals, skin-side down, for 20 minutes. Turn over, cover the grill and continue cooking for 20 to 30 minutes, or until the thigh juices run clear when pricked with a fork. Baste the chicken frequently with the extra marinade.

YIELD: 4 SERVINGS ↝ *Molly O'Neill*

GRILLED BUTTERFLIED
CHICKEN DIJONAISE

Chicken roasted with a glaze made from Dijon mustard is a classic French dish, but it can also be cooked on the grill whole. (Do it over moderate heat and make sure the inside of the legs are properly cooked.) It can be prepared in advance and served at room temperature.

> 2 3-pound chickens
> 4 tablespoons extra-virgin olive oil
> Juice of 1 lemon
> 2 cloves garlic, minced
> 2 tablespoons fresh rosemary leaves
> Coarse salt and freshly ground pepper to taste
> ½ cup imported Dijon mustard

1. Cut the chickens down the backbone and remove the backbone and wing tips. (If you wish, save them in the freezer for making stock.)

2. Combine the olive oil, lemon juice, garlic and a tablespoon of rosemary leaves and coat the chickens with the mixture. Leave them to marinate for at least an hour, turning occasionally.

3. Preheat the grill. Season the chickens with salt and pepper and spread the skin liberally with the mustard. Put them underside-down on the coals and cook for 15 to 20 minutes, or until they are well browned.

4. Turn the chickens over and finish cooking them skin-side down until they are charred and the juices run a clear golden yellow (about 15 minutes). Sprinkle with the remaining rosemary and serve hot or at room temperature.

NOTE: Instead of a charcoal grill, you can use a preheated broiler. Begin broiling the chicken with the skin side down and cook for 15 to 20 minutes, then turn and broil another 10 or 15 minutes.

YIELD: 6 TO 8 SERVINGS ⌒ *Moira Hodgson*

CHRISTOPER IDONE'S GRILLED CHICKEN WITH ORANGE-BALSAMIC MARINADE

3 2½-pound broilers, halved or quartered
Zest of 1 orange
2 cups orange juice
½ cup balsamic vinegar
¼ cup oil
1 teaspoon fresh thyme leaves, crushed
2 garlic cloves, peeled and crushed
Vegetable oil to brush the grill
Kosher salt and freshly ground pepper to taste

1. Cut away the chicken wings and reserve for another use. Wash and pat dry the chicken pieces and place them in a large baking dish.

2. In a medium bowl, mix the orange zest, orange juice, vinegar, oil, thyme and garlic and pour over the chicken pieces. Cover and refrigerate for two hours, turning once.

3. Prepare the charcoal fire 45 minutes before cooking time. Remove the chicken pieces from the refrigerator 30 minutes before cooking time. When the coals are ash-covered and glowing, lightly brush the grill with vegetable oil. Remove the chicken from the marinade and season with salt and pepper. Place the chicken cavity-side down on the grill and cook for 10 minutes. Turn and baste the chicken with the marinade and continue to cook for another 10 minutes. Baste and turn the chicken every five minutes for an additional 15 to 20 minutes or until fork tender.

YIELD: 6 SERVINGS   *Christopher Idone*

FIVE POINTS'S GRILLED
CITRUS-MARINATED POUSSIN

(Adapted from Five Points, New York City)

1 juice orange, diced (skin on)
1 lemon, rinsed and diced (skin on)
1 tablespoon chopped fresh oregano
½ cup dry white wine
½ cup fresh orange juice

½ cup extra-virgin olive oil
Salt and freshly ground black pepper
6 poussins (baby chickens) or
   6 Cornish game hens, halved
1 lemon, cut in 6 wedges

1. Combine orange, lemon, oregano and wine in food processor, and puree. Add orange juice and olive oil. Season with salt and pepper. Transfer to large bowl.

2. Place poussins in marinade, turning to coat well. Cover; refrigerate 3 to 4 hours.

3. Preheat grill. Grill poussins, turning once, until evenly browned and cooked through, about 45 minutes. Arrange on platter, garnish with lemon wedges and serve.

YIELD: 6 TO 8 SERVINGS   *Florence Fabricant*

‡ EASY ‡

SPICY MARINATED CHICKEN

1 3½-pound chicken
1 medium onion chopped coarse
Juice of 1 lemon
1 1-inch piece of fresh ginger, grated
3 tablespoons sun-dried tomato paste

1½ tablespoons medium-hot curry
   powder
½ teaspoon red pepper flakes,
   or to taste
1 to 2 tablespoons peanut or
   vegetable oil

1. Cut the chicken into eighths and remove the skin, except from the wings. Set aside.

2. Combine the remaining ingredients in a food processor and puree. Coat the chicken pieces thoroughly with the mixture and allow them to marinate for 2 to 3 hours, or overnight.

3. Preheat broiler or grill. Place the chicken pieces on a rack and cook until done (about 20 minutes), turning occasionally.

YIELD: 4 SERVINGS ⟿ *Moira Hodgson*

✤ EASY ✤

CHICKEN WITH SPICE RUB

1 tablespoon ground cumin	4 baby chickens or Cornish hens,
½ teaspoon ground allspice	each about 1¼ pounds, split in
½ teaspoon ground ginger	half
¼ teaspoon ground cloves	Juice of 2 limes
¼ teaspoon cayenne pepper,	Lime wedges and cilantro sprigs for
or to taste	garnish
Salt to taste	

1. Combine the cumin, allspice, ginger, cloves, pepper and salt. Rub the chicken with this mixture and set aside for 30 minutes.

2. Preheat a grill or broiler.

3. Rub the chickens with the lime juice to moisten the spice coating. Grill or broil the chickens, turning them frequently, until cooked through and nicely browned but not charred.

4. Serve, garnished with lime wedges and cilantro.

YIELD: 4 SERVINGS ⟿ *Florence Fabricant*

SAFFRON'S
THAI-GRILLED CHICKEN

The flavors of Southeast Asia are immediately apparent in this grilled chicken dish that was served at the now-closed Saffron restaurant in La Jolla, California. A little bit of coconut milk in the marinade adds a sweet moisture to the meat, as well as a kind of protective insulation.

2 whole boneless, skinless chicken breasts, split
1 tablespoon white peppercorns
1 tablespoon coriander seeds
1 teaspoon fennel seeds
1 teaspoon New Mexico Chili powder
1 teaspoon turmeric
1 tablespoon sea salt
6 or 7 cloves garlic, peeled and minced
¼ cup cilantro leaves and stems, finely chopped
1 cup unsweetened coconut milk
2 tablespoons vegetable oil

1. Poke holes in the chicken with the tines of a fork and set aside.
2. Toast the white peppercorns, coriander seeds and fennel seeds in a small frying pan over medium heat until they are aromatic, about 2 minutes. Grind the spices in an electric coffee grinder or with a mortar and pestle. In a large bowl, combine the ground spices with the remaining ingredients. Add the chicken and marinate for 1 hour at room temperature or longer in the refrigerator.
3. Heat the grill. Remove the chicken from the marinade. Brush the grill with oil. Grill the chicken for 5 minutes. Turn and baste with sauce. Continue to turn and baste, using as much sauce as desired, until the juices run clear when pricked with a knife, about 12 to 15 minutes.

YIELD: 4 SERVINGS ⌒ *Molly O'Neill*

✦ EASY ✦

KANEEZ'S TANDOORI CHICKEN

(Adapted from Kaneez Fatima)

A tandoor is a cylindrical clay oven, fired to a high heat by wood or charcoal, in which food is grilled and bread is baked. Kaneez Fatima, born in Pakistan into the Machi caste of tandoori cooks, seems to have this cooking in her blood. Here is her traditional recipe for this classic dish featuring chicken that has absorbed the flavors of a spicy marinade. Instead of a tandoor oven, a charcoal grill or regular oven will yield excellent results.

> 1 chicken, 2½ pounds, quartered
> 1 teaspoon salt, or to taste
> 1 cup plain yogurt
> 1 tablespoon lemon juice
> 1 tablespoon white vinegar
> 2 teaspoons garlic paste or 2 teaspoons minced garlic
> 2 teaspoons fresh ginger paste or 2 teaspoons minced ginger root
> 1½ teaspoons garam masala (see Note)
> 3 tablespoons vegetable oil

1. Remove skin from chicken and trim fat. Using a sharp knife, make diagonal slashes ½ inch deep and about ½ inch apart, along the grain (6 on each leg and 4 on each half breast). Rub salt in slashes and put the chicken in a ceramic bowl.

2. Mix in all other ingredients, except oil, and pour over chicken. Mix well, cover and marinate chicken for 8 hours or overnight in refrigerator. Take chicken from the refrigerator at least 1 hour before cooking.

3. Light a tandoor or prepare a covered charcoal grill or preheat an oven to 550 degrees. Remove chicken from marinade; coat lightly with oil.

4. For tandoori cooking, thread chicken pieces on long tandoor skewers and roast in a tandoor for 10 minutes or until cooked. For charcoal grilling, place chicken pieces on the rack and barbecue, covered, with the vents open, turning 3 to 4 times, without basting, for 25 minutes, or until juices run clear when pierced at the joint. For oven roasting, set chicken pieces over racks in a baking dish and roast for 20 to 25 minutes, until done.

NOTE: Garam masala, a blend of spices, is widely available in Indian grocery stores or from "Selected Sources for Ingredients," page 352. To make your own, combine 1½ teaspoons ground cumin, 1 teaspoon each ground coriander, ground cardamom and ground black pepper, ¼ teaspoon each ground cloves and ground bay leaf.

YIELD: 2 TO 4 SERVINGS *Molly O'Neill*

NOBU'S CHICKEN TERIYAKI

(Adapted from Nobu, New York City)

The Nobu restaurant in Manhattan is rightly famous for its teriyaki grilled chicken, marinated with soy sauce, sugar and homemade chicken stock.

1 cup chicken stock (see recipe, page 91)
½ cup Japanese soy sauce
7 tablespoons sugar
1 tablespoon cornstarch
1 tablespoon water
2 whole boneless, skinless chicken breasts
2 tablespoons vegetable oil

1. Bring the stock, soy sauce and sugar to a boil in a small saucepan. Lower the heat and simmer for 2 minutes. Mix together the cornstarch and the water and whisk into the teriyaki base. Bring back to a boil and simmer for 2 more minutes. Remove from the heat.

2. Prick holes in the chicken with the tines of a fork. Pour the sauce over the chicken breasts and marinate, turning occasionally, for 6 hours, or overnight.

3. Heat the grill. Scrape the excess sauce off the chicken and reserve. Brush the grill with oil. Grill the chicken for 5 minutes. Turn and baste with the sauce. Continue to turn and baste, using as much sauce as desired, until the juices run clear when the bird is pricked with a knife, about 12 to 15 minutes.

YIELD: 4 SERVINGS

Nobu's Chicken Stock

Back and neck from a 3-pound chicken
1 medium carrot, cut into ½-inch pieces
1 medium onion, cut into ½-inch pieces
1 bulb garlic, cut in half, skin on
1 2-inch piece of ginger, cut into ¼-inch pieces
6 cups water

1. Heat the oven to 425 degrees. Roast the back and neck in a shallow roasting pan until lightly browned, about 20 minutes. Lower the heat to 375 and add the remaining ingredients, except the water. Roast for another 35 to 40 minutes.

2. Transfer the mixture to a small stockpot. Place the roasting pan on top of the stove over high heat. Add 1 cup of water. Bring to a boil, scraping vigorously to get the browned bits from the bottom of the pan. Pour this over the bones and vegetables. Add the remaining water. Bring to a boil. Lower the heat and simmer for 2 hours. Strain through a fine sieve.

YIELD: 3½ CUPS   *Molly O'Neill*

KEN HOM'S GRILLED
SOY-MUSTARD CHICKEN

12 skinless, boneless chicken thighs, about 1½ pounds

3 tablespoons Japanese soy sauce

3 tablespoons Dijon mustard

1 tablespoon chopped garlic

1 tablespoon chopped cilantro

1 tablespoon chopped Italian parsley

1 tablespoon Chinese or Japanese sesame oil

1 tablespoon olive oil

2 teaspoons chopped orange zest

1 teaspoon chopped fresh ginger

1. With a sharp knife trim all the fat from the chicken. Place the pieces on a platter.

2. In a blender or a small-capacity food processor mix the soy sauce, mustard, garlic, fresh cilantro, parsley, sesame oil, olive oil, orange zest and ginger to make a rough paste. With a spatula spread this paste evenly over the surface of each chicken thigh. Cover with plastic wrap, refrigerate and marinate 1½ hours.

3. A half hour before you are ready to grill the chicken, remove it from the refrigerator. Preheat a grill or broiler.

4. Grill the chicken, turning it once, until it is brown and fairly firm to the touch, 15 to 20 minutes total cooking time. Alternatively, the chicken can be broiled in a preheated oven broiler. Serve at once.

YIELD: 6 SERVINGS   *Florence Fabricant*

SUSANNA FOO'S CANTONESE-GRILLED CHICKEN BREASTS

2 whole boneless, skinless chicken breasts, split

4 tablespoons, plus 1 teaspoon, corn oil

7 medium cloves garlic, minced

1 1½-inch piece ginger, peeled and minced

3 scallions, coarsely chopped

4 tablespoons plus 1 teaspoon brandy

4 tablespoons plus 1 teaspoon yellow bean paste

3 tablespoons honey

3 tablespoons soy sauce

2 tablespoons vegetable oil.

1. Poke holes in the chicken with the tines of a fork. In a large bowl, mix together the remaining ingredients. Add the chicken and marinate, covered, overnight in the refrigerator, turning occasionally.

2. Heat the grill. Remove the chicken from the marinade, scrape off excess sauce and reserve. Brush the grill with oil. Grill the chicken for 5 minutes. Turn and baste with sauce. Continue to turn and baste, using as much sauce as desired, until the juices run clear when chicken is pricked with a knife, about 12 to 15 minutes.

YIELD: 4 SERVINGS　　*Molly O'Neill*

JULIE SAHNI'S EASY
TANDOORI CHICKEN

Julie Sahni, the cookbook author, has devised a marinade for grilled chicken that duplicates the taste of tandoori chicken without the drying aspects of the tandoori oven.

2 whole skinless, boneless chicken
    breasts, split

FOR THE MARINADE

1½ cups plain yogurt

4 tablespoons lemon juice

8 medium cloves garlic minced

1 2-inch piece ginger, peeled and
    minced

2 tablespoons ground cumin

2 teaspoons ground coriander

½ teaspoon ground cardamom

¼ teaspoon ground cloves

1 teaspoon cayenne pepper

½ teaspoon freshly ground black
    pepper

Kosher salt to taste

2 tablespoons vegetable oil

FOR THE GARNISH

2 medium tomatoes, thinly sliced

1 medium cucumber, thinly sliced

1 medium red onion, thinly sliced

2 lemons quartered

½ small bunch cilantro, leaves only

1. Prick holes in the chicken with the tines of a fork. In a large bowl, mix together the marinade ingredients. Add the chicken and marinate, covered, overnight in the refrigerator, turning occasionally.

2. Heat the grill. Remove the chicken from the marinade. Scrape off excess and reserve. Brush the grill with oil. Grill the chicken for 5 minutes. Turn and baste with sauce. Continue to turn and baste, using as much sauce as desired, until the juices run clear when pricked with a knife, about 12 to 15 minutes.

3. Serve garnished with slices of tomato, cucumber, onion, lemon and cilantro sprigs.

YIELD: 4 SERVINGS   *Molly O'Neill*

BADEMIYA'S JUSTLY FAMOUS BOMBAY CHILI-AND-CORIANDER CHICKEN

(Adapted from *The Barbecue Bible*)

1½ tablespoons coriander seeds
2 teaspoons peppercorns
1 teaspoon cumin seeds
6 cloves garlic
1 2-inch piece ginger, peeled and thinly sliced
3 tablespoons vegetable oil
¼ cup water, or as needed
1 tablespoon cayenne pepper or hot paprika
2 tablespoons lemon juice
1½ teaspoons kosher salt
½ cup cilantro, chopped
4 chicken legs (2¼ pounds), skinned, or 1 whole chicken, cut into
    8 pieces skinned, washed and dried

THE GARNISH
Thinly sliced red onion, limes and lemons
Cilantro Sauce (see recipe, page 96) and tamarind sauce (see Note, page 96)

1. In a skillet over medium heat, toast the coriander seeds, peppercorns and cumin seeds until fragrant, 1 to 2 minutes. Transfer to a spice mill or mortar and pestle and grind to a fine powder.

2. Puree the ground spices in a blender with the garlic, ginger, oil, water, cayenne, lemon juice and salt. Transfer this paste to a bowl and stir in the coriander. Add the chicken and thoroughly coat with the spice paste. Marinate in the refrigerator for 4 to 6 hours.

3. When ready to cook, start a charcoal fire. When the coals are white, grill the chicken until done, 10 to 15 minutes per side. Serve immediately with the onions, limes and lemons, cilantro and tamarind sauces and Indian bread.

YIELD: 2 TO 4 SERVINGS

CILANTRO SAUCE

1 cup fresh chopped cilantro
3 cloves garlic, peeled
1 jalapeño, seeded or not
½ cup shelled walnuts
⅓ cup fresh lemon juice
1 teaspoon kosher salt
½ teaspoon freshly ground pepper
¼ teaspoon ground cumin
¼ cup water

Puree the cilantro, garlic, jalapeño, walnuts, lemon juice, salt, pepper and cumin in a blender or food processor. Add the water and pour into a serving container. Add salt or lemon juice to taste.

NOTE: Tamarind sauce is available from the Oriental Pantry (see "Selected Sources for Ingredients," page 352).

YIELD: 1 CUP   Molly O'Neill

STEVEN RAICHLEN'S PERSIAN-GRILLED CHICKEN WITH SAFFRON

(Adapted from *The Barbecue Bible*)

The gentle acidity of yogurt pervades this recipe.

2 chickens, about 3½ pounds each, cut into 8 pieces

THE MARINADE
½ teaspoon saffron
1 tablespoon warm water
1½ cups plain yogurt, preferably from whole milk
½ cup lemon juice
1 large onion, finely chopped, about 2 cups
2 teaspoons kosher salt
1 teaspoon freshly ground pepper

THE BASTING MIXTURE
1 tablespoon fresh lemon juice
½ teaspoon saffron
6 tablespoons salted butter

1. Wash the chicken and blot dry. Cut off any lumps of fat.

2. For the marinade, place the saffron in the bottom of a large nonreactive bowl and pulverize it with a wooden spoon. Add the water and allow to stand 5 minutes.

3. Stir in the yogurt, lemon juice, onion, salt and pepper. Add the chicken and refrigerate, covered, overnight or for at least 6 hours.

4. For the basting, warm the lemon juice over low heat in a small pot. Pulverize the saffron in a bowl with a wooden spoon, add it to the juice and remove from heat. After 5 minutes, add the butter and gently warm the mixture until it is melted.

5. When ready to cook, start a charcoal fire. When the coals are white, grill the chicken until tender, 8 to 10 minutes per side, basting with the butter mixture. Move the chicken around as needed to keep it from burning. Season with salt and pepper. When cooked, the juices will run clear and an inserted skewer will come out very hot to the touch. Serve immediately.

YIELD: 4 TO 8 SERVINGS   *Molly O'Neill*

STEVEN RAICHLEN'S GARLIC-LEMON ROTISSERIE CHICKEN WITH MOROCCAN SPICES

(Adapted from *Raichlen's Indoor Grilling*)

Steven Raichlen: "Rotisserie grilling offers the advantages of direct grilling without the drawbacks of most setups, where the food is next to the fire, not on it, so the exterior is browned and crisped without flare-ups and charring. The steady rotation bastes the meat internally and externally, producing exceptional moistness and succulence. The dripping fat collects in a drip pan, making rotisserie grilling cleaner than direct grilling or oven roasting. And it is easy, when spit-roasting on a grill, to add smoke flavor by putting wood chips on the fire. Rotisserie grilling is especially well suited to poultry. The skin of a chicken or a game hen will be even more crackling crisp than that of a bird roasted in the oven."

FOR THE CHICKEN

1 3½- to 4-pound chicken
1 head garlic, cut in half
1 lemon, cut in half
1 tablespoon olive oil

FOR THE RUB

2 teaspoons sea salt
2 teaspoons sweet paprika
1 teaspoon ground coriander
1 teaspoon ground cumin
1 teaspoon ground ginger
1 teaspoon freshly ground black pepper

1. Set up the grill for rotisserie cooking and preheat to high.

2. Remove any lumps of fat in chicken cavity; wash inside and out, and blot dry. Rub chicken all over with half the cut head of garlic, then with half the cut lemon.

3. Mix ingredients for rub together. Sprinkle some rub into chicken and place re-

maining garlic and lemon halves inside. Truss chicken, brush outside with oil, and rub with remaining spice mix. Thread chicken onto spit and secure with prongs.

4. Cook chicken until skin is crisp and a deep golden brown and meat is cooked through, 1¼ to 1½ hours. When cooked, internal temperature in thigh will be 175 degrees. Transfer chicken to a platter, let rest for 5 minutes and untruss. Carve or cut in half, and serve.

YIELD: 2 SERVINGS ⟿ *Steven Raichlen*

JIMBOJEAN'S
JAMAICAN JERK CHICKEN

In Jamaican cuisine, jerk refers to a marinade and also a method of barbecuing—preferably outdoors in an oil-drum grill. The jerk sauce is a bit of fire laced with chilies. At the Jimbojean restaurant in Brooklyn, Hernel Fraser bastes the chicken with a jerk flavored with beer and ketchup.

3 medium cloves garlic, chopped

2 bunches green onions, chopped

1 medium white onion, chopped

1 green, yellow or red Scotch bonnet pepper, stemmed and chopped (with seeds)

3 tablespoons fresh thyme, chopped, or 1 tablespoon dried thyme

1 tablespoon ground allspice

10 whole cloves

1 tablespoon molasses

1 tablespoon white or cider vinegar

1 teaspoon salt

Pinch of Accent, optional

1 5-pound chicken, quartered

½ cup beer

½ cup ketchup

Oil for greasing the rack

1. Blend the garlic, onions, pepper, thyme, allspice, cloves, molasses, vinegar, salt and Accent in a food processor until smooth.

2. Place the chicken in a glass baking dish. Coat with marinade over and under the skin. Cover and marinate in the refrigerator at least 4 hours but preferably overnight, turning the pieces occasionally.

3. Remove and discard the marinade from under the chicken's skin. Pour remaining juices and marinade from baking dish into a bowl. Add beer and ketchup; mix.

4. Cut chicken quarters at the joints to make 8 pieces. Brush with basting sauce and place skin-side down on a hot, oiled grill rack or skin-side up on an oiled rack in a broiler pan lined with heavy-duty foil. Cook until the skin is crisp and the meat is cooked through, 30 to 40 minutes, turning and basting every 10 minutes.

NOTE: Charcoal grilling is as close as you'll come to an authentic jerk experience, but jerk also may be cooked on top of the stove or baked in an oven.

YIELD: 6 SERVINGS ✒ *Dulcie Leimbach*

GRILLED CHICKEN WITH QUICK APPLE CHUTNEY

2 cups fresh apple cider

⅓ cup plus 2 tablespoons cider vinegar

1 teaspoon crushed black peppercorns

2 tablespoons minced fresh ginger

3 shallots, minced

6 sprigs fresh thyme

6 baby chickens or Cornish hens, quartered

1 tablespoon vegetable oil

4 tart apples, peeled, cored and diced

½ cup raisins

1. Combine cider, the ⅓ cup of vinegar, peppercorns, a tablespoon of ginger, a shallot and two thyme sprigs in a dish. Add chicken quarters, turn in marinade, cover and marinate 3 hours.

2. Remove chicken from marinade and pat dry. Reserve marinade, discarding thyme.

3. Preheat grill.

4. To make chutney, heat oil in a skillet, add remaining shallots and ginger and sauté until soft. Add reserved marinade. Increase heat and cook until liquid just films pan. Add apples and raisins and cook just until apples are tender but still hold their shape. Stir in remaining vinegar. Remove from heat.

5. Grill chicken, turning frequently, until browned and cooked through, about 30 minutes. Arrange on a platter, garnish with remaining thyme sprigs and serve with apple chutney on the side.

YIELD: 6 SERVINGS ⟶ *Florence Fabricant*

✦ EASY ✦
CHICKEN PUTANESCA

Putanesca is a well-known, vibrant Neapolitan sauce for spaghetti, but it also does a fine job as a flavoring for grilled chicken.

¼ cup extra-virgin olive oil

1 tablespoon lemon juice

2 pounds skinless and boneless
    chicken breasts

Freshly ground black pepper

3 large garlic cloves, sliced

4 anchovies, mashed

1 pound ripe tomatoes, peeled, cored
    and finely chopped, or substitute
    well-drained canned tomatoes,
    chopped

1 tablespoon drained capers

Red pepper flakes to taste

1. Combine 2 tablespoons of the oil with the lemon juice. Brush over the chicken breasts, season with pepper and set aside to marinate about 30 minutes.

2. Meanwhile, heat 2 tablespoons of the oil in a large, heavy skillet. Add the garlic and cook until it just begins to color, then stir in the anchovies.

3. Add the tomatoes and cook over medium heat for 10 to 15 minutes, until the sauce begins to thicken. Stir in the capers and season with red pepper flakes. Set aside.

4. Preheat grill or broiler. Grill or broil the chicken breasts until they are just cooked through and lightly browned, about 6 minutes on each side. Transfer to a serving platter.

5. Reheat the sauce, spoon over the chicken and serve.

YIELD: 6 SERVINGS   *Florence Fabricant*

✦ EASY ✦

GRILLED MEXICAN CHICKEN WITH SALSA CRUDA

(Adapted from *The Best of Craig Claiborne*)

3 chicken breasts, split in half and boned, with skin left on
1 teaspoon dried oregano
Salt and freshly ground pepper to taste
2 tablespoons lime juice
2 tablespoons peanut, vegetable or corn oil
2 tablespoons finely chopped parsley
Salsa cruda (see recipe, page 103)

1. Cut each chicken breast half crosswise into 4 pieces. This will yield 24 cubes.

2. Place the chicken in a dish and add the remaining ingredients except the salsa cruda. Turn the chicken pieces occasionally so that they are well seasoned. Let stand until ready to cook.

3. Arrange the pieces on 4 to 6 skewers. If wooden skewers are used, let them soak for an hour or so in water. Cover the tips with foil to prevent burning.

4. Prepare a charcoal fire in a grill. When the coals and grill are properly hot, brush the grill lightly with oil. Grill the chicken, turning as necessary, until done, 20 minutes or longer. Serve with salsa cruda.

YIELD: 4 TO 6 SERVINGS

SALSA CRUDA
(RAW TOMATO AND CHILI SAUCE)

2 cups drained, canned tomatoes or fresh cubed tomatoes
2 tablespoon red wine vinegar
½ cup finely chopped onion
Salt and freshly ground pepper to taste
1 or 2 fresh or canned serrano chilies, finely chopped
1 ice cube
1 tablespoon or more chopped cilantro

Chop the tomatoes and combine with the remaining ingredients. Stir until the ice melts.

YIELD: ABOUT 2 CUPS

GRILLED CHICKEN BREASTS
TOPPED WITH MIXED MELON SALSA

Before they ripen, all melons resemble cucumbers, to which they are related. When ripe, they are sweet, with varying degrees of spice. Since a melon has no starch reserves, it will never grow sweeter than at the moment it is picked. A ripe melon should feel heavier than it appears, it should smell like a melon and it should have no scar at its stem. Unless you find a melon with a sharp herb or musk flavor, its inherent sweetness is one-dimensional. This is why, when combined with something salty or pungent—a squeeze of lime, a wafer of salty ham, briny seafood—a melon quickly becomes more intriguing.

1 cup ripe honeydew melon, cut into ¼-inch dice
1 cup ripe cantaloupe, cut into ¼-inch dice
1 teaspoon grated fresh ginger
3 tablespoons minced scallion
1 teaspoon seeded and minced jalapeño pepper
1 tablespoon fresh lime juice
¾ teaspoon salt
2 chicken breasts, boned, skinned and split
Freshly ground pepper to taste

1. In a medium bowl, toss together the melons, ginger, scallion and jalapeño. Mix in the lime juice and ¼ teaspoon of salt. Refrigerate until cold.

2. Heat a grill or broiler. Season the chicken breasts with the remaining salt and pepper to taste. Grill or broil until cooked through, about 4 minutes per side. Divide among 4 plates and top with the salsa. Serve immediately.

YIELD: 4 SERVINGS   *Molly O'Neill*

SIMPLE SMOKE-ROASTED WHOLE CHICKEN

⅔ cup mixed herbs: parsley, sage, rosemary and thyme or
   any combination, all roughly chopped
2 tablespoons minced garlic
3 tablespoons olive oil
1 teaspoon red pepper flakes
1 tablespoon kosher salt
1 tablespoon freshly ground black pepper
2 whole chickens, 3 to 3½ pounds each
Salt and freshly ground black pepper to taste

1. In a small bowl, combine the herbs, garlic, oil, pepper flakes, salt and pepper, and mix well. Starting at the tip of the breastbone, loosen the skin from the breasts of the chickens, being careful not to tear the skin. Gently rub the herb mixture under the skin. Rub the outside of the chickens with any remaining mixture and sprinkle with additional salt and pepper if desired.

2. In a covered grill, build a small fire to one side, making sure that all the wood or charcoal becomes engulfed in flames. When the flames die down and you are left with flickering coals, place the chickens on the grill over the side without fire. It is important that the chickens do not come in contact with the flames at any time during cooking.

3. Cover the grill, vent slightly and cook, checking the fire every 20 minutes or so and adding a bit more fuel as necessary to keep the fire going, for about 2 hours. Check the chickens for doneness by piercing a thigh with a fork. When the juices run clear, the birds are done.

YIELD: 6 SERVINGS   *Craig Claiborne*

STEVEN RAICHLEN'S
BEER CAN CHICKEN

(Adapted from *Beer Can Chicken*)

Steven Raichlen: "Beer can chicken, also known as drunken chicken or chicken on a throne, is a modern classic on the American competition barbecue circuit. The meat is unbelievably moist and tender, the bite of the spice mix accenting the perfume of wood smoke. The use of the beer can turned out to be a brilliant, if crude, tactic: the bird is steamed and infused with aromatics from the inside on what amounts to a vertical roaster. And because the steaming takes place inside the chicken, it accomplishes all this without making the skin soggy. Beer can chicken is always cooked with wood or wood chips. To reinforce the beer flavor, many pit masters will actually soak their wood chips in beer. There's a final benefit: the fact that the chicken is roasted upright. This vertical position allows the fat to drain off and the skin to roast quickly, crisply and evenly. Indeed, cookware shops sell special vertical chicken roasting stands for this purpose. But these devices lack the allure of steaming beer. To cook beer can chicken on a backyard grill, you need to use the indirect method. This means that you configure your fire so that it is hottest away from the food. On a charcoal kettle grill, light the charcoal or Charwood in a chimney starter. When it glows red, dump it in two piles at opposite sides of the grill. Place a foil drip pan in the center of the grill, between the mounds of embers. Place the grate on the grill, and cook the chicken in the center over the drip pan. Toss soaked wood chips on the coals to generate smoke. Keep the grill covered, adjusting the vents to keep the temperature at 350 degrees. After cooking the chicken for an hour, add 10 fresh briquettes or an equal amount of Charwood. Leave the grill uncovered for a few minutes until the coals ignite. On a gas grill, if it has two burners, light one side on high, and cook the chicken on the other. On a three-burner grill, light the front and rear or outside burners, and cook the chicken in the center. On a four-burner grill, light the outside burners, and cook in the center. Many gas grills come with smoker boxes, in which you can put the wood chips. If you don't have a smoker box, loosely wrap the chips in heavy-duty foil, make a few holes on top, and place the foil package under the grate over one of the burners."

2 cups hickory or oak chips, soaked in beer or water to cover for
    1 hour and then drained

2 12-ounce cans beer

½ cup of your favorite barbecue rub

2 3½- to 4-pound chickens, fat removed, washed and blotted dry

1. Place wood chips in bowl. Pop tab of each beer can, and make 2 additional holes in each top, using a "church key" opener. Pour half the beer from each can over the chips. Add additional beer or water to cover chips, soak them for 1 hour, and drain.

2. Set up grill for indirect grilling.

3. Sprinkle 1 teaspoon barbecue rub in neck cavity and 2 teaspoons in main cavity of each chicken. Add 1 tablespoon rub to each open, half-full can of beer. (Don't worry if it foams up.) Season outside of each bird with 2 tablespoons rub.

4. Stand beer cans on work surface. Holding each chicken upright, lower it over can so that can goes into main cavity. Pull chicken legs forward to form a sort of tripod: the chicken should sit upright over can. Carefully transfer chickens to grill in this position, placing them in center over drip pan, away from heat.

5. If using charcoal, toss half the wood chips on each mound of coals. If using gas, place chips in smoker box. Barbecue chickens until nicely browned and cooked through, about 1½ hours, keeping temperature about 350 degrees. (If using charcoal, replenish coals as needed.) The internal temperature of the birds (taken in thickest part of thigh) should be at least 165 degrees.

6. Carefully transfer birds to platter in same position. To carve, lift bird off can, and discard can.

YIELD: 4 SERVINGS   *Steven Raichlen*

JACQUES PEPIN'S GRILLED TABASCO CHICKEN

A tablespoon of Tabasco sauce in the marinade may seem like a lot, but by the time it is exposed to direct heat, much of the hotness disappears, and you are left with the sauce's great flavor. Ketchup lends a little sweetness and helps the chicken brown beautifully. Always grill the chicken skin-side down to start, turning it after a nice crusty exterior has formed. Most of the marinade should cling to the chicken; any left in the container can be brushed onto the chicken as it cooks. The chicken can be grilled ahead and kept in a warm oven or on the corner of the grill. It is good served hot or at room temperature.

6 chicken legs (about 3½ pounds)
1 tablespoon soy sauce
1 tablespoon ketchup
1 tablespoon cider vinegar
1 tablespoon Tabasco sauce

1. Cut halfway through the joint that connects the thigh and the drumstick of each leg (to make cooking easier).

2. Mix the soy sauce, ketchup, vinegar and Tabasco together in a tray and roll the chicken legs in the marinade.

3. Place the legs skin-side down on the rack of a hot grill about 10 inches from the heat, and cook for about 10 minutes. Turn the legs over, and cook for about 10 minutes on the other side. Turn them again, and cook them skin-side down for 10 minutes more.

4. Take the legs off the heat to rest for 5 minutes before serving.

NOTE: If you don't have access to a grill, broil the chicken in a conventional oven. Arrange the chicken pieces skin-side up on a foil-lined cookie sheet and place them 3 to 4 inches from the heat source. Cook for 10 to 12 minutes, turn them over and cook for 8 to 10 minutes on the other side. Turn again, move the tray so that the chicken is 6 to 8 inches from the heat, and continue to cook it skin-side up for another 12 to 14 minutes before serving.

YIELD: 6 SERVINGS ⚊ *Jacques Pepin*

MARK BITTMAN'S GRILLED CHICKEN THIGHS WITH SAUCE AU CHIEN

(Adapted from *The Minimalist Cooks Dinner*)

This thin, powerful sauce made of lime juice, scallions, chili, garlic and loads of allspice comes from the Caribbean island of Martinique, where it accompanies almost everything that is grilled.

Mark Bittman: "It was the allspice that made the sauce unusual; similar sauces without it are quite common, all over the world. But there was more to the mixture than that: the garlic and scallions looked raw but had lost their harshness and become easily digestible, and the base of the sauce was not oil but water. It's called sauce au chien, which translates roughly as dog sauce. And the strong elements are tamed by pouring boiling water over the solid ingredients. Lime juice is added at the last moment, so the sauce retains its freshness. If you can get a Scotch bonnet pepper, its fierce heat and distinctive flavor will make the sauce more authentic, but I used a small amount of Asian chili paste instead and thought the results fine. Jalapeños or just hot red pepper flakes will also work. If you have the patience to grind whole allspice, the sauce will taste fresher, and I thought it was worth the effort, but ground allspice will do, as long as it is fresh. Sauce au chien is a spectacular accompaniment to any hearty grilled food.

1 tablespoon peeled and slivered or minced garlic

6 scallions, trimmed and minced

1 Scotch bonnet or jalapeño pepper, stemmed, seeded and minced, or chili
    paste or crushed red pepper flakes to taste (start with ½ teaspoon)

Salt and fresh black pepper

½ teaspoon ground allspice, or to taste

1 tablespoon peanut or canola oil

8 chicken thighs, about 2 pounds

Juice of 1 lime

1. Prepare a charcoal or gas grill, or preheat the broiler. While it is heating, prepare the sauce: In a small bowl, combine the garlic, scallions, chili, salt, allspice and oil. Add ½ cup boiling water; stir and set aside.

2. Sprinkle the chicken with salt and pepper, and grill or broil, turning 2 or 3 times, until it is cooked through, about 15 minutes. Taste the sauce, and add more chili, salt, pepper or allspice if needed. Stir in the lime juice. Serve the chicken hot or at room temperature, passing the sauce at the table.

YIELD: 4 SERVINGS ⟋ *Mark Bittman*

✤ EASY ✤
STEVEN RAICHLEN'S MALAYSIAN CHICKEN WINGS

(Adapted from *The Barbecue Bible*)

12 whole chicken wings (2 pounds)

THE MARINADE

⅓ cup soy sauce

⅓ cup sweet soy sauce
(or 3 tablespoons soy sauce
and 3 tablespoons molasses)

⅓ cup sake (rice wine)

⅓ cup sugar

5 star anises

2 cinnamon sticks

2 teaspoons freshly ground pepper

2 tablespoons sesame oil for basting

1. Wash and dry the chicken wings. Make 2 to 3 slashes in the meaty part of each wing to the bone.

2. For the marinade, whisk the soy sauces, sake and sugar in a mixing bowl until the sugar is dissolved. Add the remaining marinade ingredients and stir.

3. Put the wings in a large Ziploc bag and pour the marinade over them. Refrigerate for 24 hours, turning several times.

4. When ready to cook, start a charcoal fire. When the coals are white, grill the wings until they are very crisp, about 4 to 6 minutes per side, basting frequently with the oil. Hack into bite-size pieces with a cleaver and serve.

YIELD: 4 TO 6 APPETIZER SERVINGS ⟋ *Molly O'Neill*

Skewered Chicken

By Mark Bittman

The skewer is one of the most efficient tools in a cook's arsenal: once all the cutting is done, you can grill a lot of food in a short time, and take it right to the table with no further fuss.

One of my favorite foods to cook this way is chicken, but it presents a challenge: small chunks of chicken, especially breast meat, cook through before they have a chance to brown. Keep them on the fire any longer and you end up with dry, stringy meat. This summer, I decided to solve the problem.

My basic idea was to protect the chicken, to insulate it with foods that would give up moisture as they cooked. First I tried sausage, thinking that the fat would do the trick; it made a good flavor combination, but most of today's sausage is too lean to help the moisture problem.

So I turned to vegetables, specifically eggplant and zucchini, both quite watery but with enough integrity to stand up to skewering and grilling. This helped, but the chicken was still too dry. So I focused on it: I used only thighs, which are more moist and stand up better to grilling than breasts, and I cut them into larger chunks.

Better still. But the skewers needed a bit more moisture. I didn't want to use olive oil (I wanted to reduce flare-ups, not encourage them). So I tried some pieces of lemon on the skewers, and that really did the trick. The results were moist and flavorful, and the hot lemon juice squeezed over everything else at the table was lovely.

A few words about the actual skewers. Branches of rosemary are ideal: slide the food right onto them and they will flavor it brilliantly. With wood or metal, turning is easier if you use two parallel sticks for each skewer, separated by about half an inch.

MARK BITTMAN'S SKEWERED CHICKEN, SAUSAGE AND EGGPLANT

(Adapted from *The Minimalist Entertains*)

8 chicken thighs, boned and skinned, small thighs cut in half, larger ones in
   thirds or quarters
1 pound sweet or hot Italian sausage (optional), cut into 1- to 2-inch lengths
1 pound eggplant, zucchini or baby pattypan squash, cut into 1-inch pieces
2 bell peppers, preferably one each red and yellow, cut into 2-inch sections
2 lemons, cut into eighths
Salt and pepper to taste
Several sprigs fresh rosemary

1. Start a gas or charcoal grill (or preheat the broiler); the fire should be moderately hot. If you're using wooden skewers, soak them in water to cover while you prepare the food. Using 8 skewers, alternate the ingredients, but generally, surround both chicken and sausage with the moister lemon and eggplant. Pack the food fairly tightly together on each skewer, and sprinkle with salt and pepper. If you're not using rosemary skewers, tuck some rosemary among the chicken and vegetables.

2. Grill over moderate heat, covered or not, turning the skewers 3 or 4 times to brown evenly. Total cooking time will be 10 to 15 minutes, depending on the heat of the grill and the distance from the heat source. When the chicken and sausage are browned, the eggplant will be tender; do not overcook.

3. Serve, squeezing hot juice from skewered lemons over all.

YIELD: 4 TO 8 SERVINGS   *Mark Bittman*

MARK BITTMAN'S
HERBED CHICKEN KEBABS

Mark Bittman's chicken kebab recipe is heavily flavored with onion, lemon and herb. "When you try it, you may never grill breast meat again," he says.

2 large onions, peeled

2 tablespoons extra-virgin olive oil

Juice of 1 lemon

1 tablespoon minced garlic

Salt and pepper to taste

3 bay leaves, crumbled

1 tablespoon fresh marjoram or oregano leaves, or 1 teaspoon dried oregano

1½ pounds boneless chicken thighs or legs, cut into 1½-inch chunks

Lemon wedges or ground sumac (see Note)

1. Start a charcoal or wood fire or heat a gas grill. The fire should be moderately hot and the rack about 4 inches from the heat source. Mince one onion, and combine it in a large bowl with oil, lemon juice, garlic, salt, pepper, bay leaves and marjoram or oregano. Taste, and adjust seasoning. Marinate chicken in this mixture for at least a few minutes or overnight in refrigerator.

2. If using wooden skewers, soak them in water to cover for a few minutes. Cut remaining onion into quarters, then separate it into large pieces. Thread chicken and onion alternately onto skewers, leaving a little space between pieces.

3. Grill, turning as each side browns, and brushing with remaining marinade, for about 12 to 15 minutes or until chicken is cooked through. Serve with lemon wedges or sprinkle with a bit of sumac.

NOTE: For sumac, see "Selected Sources for Ingredients," page 352.

YIELD: 4 SERVINGS ⌒ *Mark Bittman*

VONG'S CHICKEN SATAY WITH PEANUT SAUCE

¼ cup white wine
¼ cup nuoc mam (Thai fish sauce) (see Note)
1 tablespoon peanut oil
1 tablespoon fresh lime juice
2 large cloves garlic, peeled and chopped
1 pound boneless, skinless chicken breasts (see Note)
About 3 dozen bamboo skewers, soaked in water
1 recipe Vong's Peanut Sauce (see recipe, page 115)

1. Combine the white wine, nuoc mam, peanut oil, lime juice and garlic and put in a nonreactive shallow dish.

2. Cut the chicken on the diagonal into thin strips.

3. Place the meat in the dish and toss with the marinade. Refrigerate for 1 to 2 hours.

4. Preheat a grill or broiler. Thread each piece of chicken onto a skewer, making an S pattern. Grill or broil, turning the skewers once, until chicken is just cooked through. Place on a platter and serve hot with peanut sauce for dipping.

NOTE: Boneless pork loin or flank steak can be substituted for the chicken. See "Selected Sources for Ingredients," page *352*.

YIELD: ABOUT 36 SKEWERS

VONG'S PEANUT SAUCE

(Adapted from Vong, New York City)

In general, peanut sauce—a Thai mixture of nuts, curry, coconut, soy and lime—is rich and sweet and therefore marries well with acidic flavors like lemon and lime, or even aromatics like lemongrass. It can also stand alone, as it does at Vong restaurant in Manhattan, where it is served with rice crackers before the meal, or as part of a larger dish like cold noodles with shrimp and scallions.

½ cup shelled, unsalted, roasted peanuts
1 tablespoon peanut oil
2 teaspoons red curry paste (see Note)
1 teaspoon sugar
1 cup unsweetened coconut milk
2 teaspoons soy sauce
1 tablespoon fresh lime juice

Grind the peanuts in a food processor. Set aside. Heat the oil in a medium saucepan over low heat. Add the curry paste and stir for about 1 minute. Whisk in the sugar, coconut milk and peanuts. Bring to a boil, whisking constantly. Remove from heat and whisk in the soy sauce and lime juice. Serve warm.

NOTE: Peanut sauce in a jar varies from fiery hot to sweet and sour, from a thick paste to a smooth consistency. Of the fifteen commercial brands that Molly O'Neill sampled, four were quite distinctive; of these, Thai Kitchen Spicy Thai Peanut Satay Sauce, with its thick, chunky texture and mahogany color, is perhaps closest to home-made. Available in specialty groceries and by mail through Mo Hotta-Mo Betta, its initial sweet taste gives way to a pleasant fire. It is, however, rather oily and the oil tends to separate. Ho Tai's Spicy Peanut Sauce, which can be ordered through Williams-Sonoma, has a semichunky consistency with a bold, acidic flavor, medium-hot spice and understated sweetness. Fire House Thai Peanut Sauce, on the other hand, is aptly named. It is roaring hot and delicious, a highly complicated blend of aromatic herbs and spices, rich in coconut and peanut flavor, slightly chunky, though not as thick as other commercial brands. See "Selected Sources for Ingredients," page 352.

YIELD: 1⅓ CUPS *Molly O'Neill*

NIGELLA LAWSON'S
HERB-NUT CHICKEN SATAY

4 skinless, boneless chicken breast halves

½ teaspoon ground cinnamon

½ teaspoon turmeric

1 teaspoon ground cumin

1 teaspoon ground coriander

1 teaspoon sugar

2 tablespoons salted, roasted peanuts

¼ cup peanut oil

6 scallions, trimmed

Zest of 1 lemon, removed in strips

1. Cut chicken breast halves lengthwise into long strips, about 5 from each. Place in a freezer storage bag, and set aside.

2. In a food processor, combine all remaining ingredients. Process to make a smooth paste. Add to bag of chicken, seal bag, and mix well so that chicken is well coated. Refrigerate for at least 2 hours, preferably overnight.

3. About an hour before cooking, soak 10 bamboo skewers in water. Heat a grill or broiler. Thread two long strips of chicken onto each skewer. Grill or broil until lightly browned and crisp on edges.

YIELD: 10 SKEWERS   *Nigella Lawson*

FIERY CHICKEN SATE

1½ tablespoons dark brown sugar

¼ cup panang curry paste (see Note)

1 cup unsweetened coconut milk

2 tablespoons fish sauce (see Note)

1 teaspoon lime juice

1½ tablespoons ground coriander

1½ pounds boneless, skinless chicken breasts, cut into 24 ½-inch wide and
    4-inch long strips

24 12-inch wooden or bamboo skewers, soaked in hot water for 10 minutes

1. In a large nonreactive bowl, whisk together the sugar, curry paste, coconut milk, fish sauce, lime juice and coriander. Add the chicken and toss until well coated. Transfer the mixture to a resealable plastic bag and refrigerate for at least 3 hours and up to 12.

2. Preheat the broiler or grill. Remove the chicken from the marinade and thread each strip onto a skewer. Grill or broil the skewers, turning once, until cooked through, about 3 minutes per side. Serve immediately.

NOTE: Available at Asian markets, or see "Selected Sources for Ingredients," page 352.

YIELD: 4 SERVINGS ⤸ *Molly O'Neill*

Magic With Quick Marinades

By Mark Bittman

As far as I'm concerned, there are only two goals in marinating before grilling: to add flavor and to promote browning and crispness. Neither of these requires long soaking, although dunking the meat or fish while the grill heats contributes to a slightly greater penetration of flavor. (If you really have no time, simply smear the food with the sauce as it is going on the grill.)

Which flavor to add is a matter of taste. My favorite is soy sauce, complemented with garlic and ginger; for best flavor, each of these should be fresh, rather than powdered.

It's easy to promote browning. Anything with sugar browns quickly—often too quickly, as you know if you've ever slathered a piece of chicken with barbecue sauce before grilling it. That's why ketchup forms the basis of so many commercial barbecue sauces; it contains so much sugar (or, more likely, corn syrup), that it browns in a flash. Honey works better in my sauce. It has a clean sweetness and contributes stickiness and heft, allowing the sauce to adhere better to the food. Molasses is also good, and so is hoisin sauce, a kind of Chinese ketchup that contains a great deal of sugar but also soy.

The final ingredient is acid, not to tenderize the meat but to balance sweetness. Lime goes best with soy, but almost any acidic liquid will do, from lemon juice to white vinegar.

That's it: soy and spices for flavor, honey for browning, body and sweetness, and lime for acidity. There are ways to make this sauce more complex, as listed below. But even in its simple form, it perfectly enhances naturally tender meats like steak, burgers, boneless chicken breasts or thighs, tuna and swordfish, all of which can be turned in the sauce before putting them on the grill. Longer-cooking meats, like bone-in chicken, should be cooked within 10 minutes of doneness before basting with the sauce.

Finally, a safety tip: To avoid bacterial contamination, marinade that was applied to raw food should not be brushed on again during the last few minutes of cooking, nor should it be used as a sauce unless it is boiled for a few minutes. And, as always, marinade brushes and other utensils that are used with raw food should not be used again near the end of cooking.

How to Make a Good Thing Even Better

Many ingredients can be added to this basic marinade to heighten its flavor. Add too many at once, however, and you run the risk of muddying the taste. Some possible additions:

- Mustard: 1 teaspoon to 1 tablespoon.
- Sesame or other roasted nut oil: about a teaspoon.
- Peanut butter or tahini (sesame paste): about a tablespoon. (Some sesame seeds or finely chopped peanuts are good, too.)
- Minced onion, chopped scallion or shallots.
- Prepared horseradish (about 1 tablespoon) or wasabi powder (about 1 teaspoon).
- Minced zest of a lemon, lime or orange.
- Minced cilantro or shiso: about 1 tablespoon, plus more for garnish.
- Ground cumin (up to a tablespoon) or coriander (up to a teaspoon) or a combination of the two.
- Minced jalapeño, crushed red chilies or Tabasco or other hot sauce.
- Worcestershire or fish-sauce (nuoc mam or nam pla, sold in most Asian markets): about a tablespoon.

Barbecue Basting Sauces

By Craig Claiborne

The three most popular sauces for basting are based on vinaigrette, ketchup and soy sauce. The vinaigrette may be made of oil and vinegar or oil and lemon juice. It may contain red or white wine. You can vary the flavors of this marinade by adding herbs and spices such as chopped garlic, parsley, rosemary, tarragon, bay leaf, thyme and so on, according to taste and inspiration.

The classic Southern barbecue sauce is one based on ketchup blended with Worcestershire sauce, Tabasco sauce, lemon juice, chopped garlic and honey or brown sugar.

The soy baste is of Japanese inspiration and generally contains ginger, Sherry (or better yet, the Japanese mirin) plus sugar. Here are four basic recipes for the season:

⊹ EASY ⊹
SOY BASTING SAUCE
FOR BARBECUES

½ cup soy sauce
¼ cup Japanese Mirin or sherry wine
1 tablespoon finely chopped fresh ginger
2 teaspoons finely minced garlic
2 teaspoons sugar
¼ teaspoon hot dried red pepper flakes

Combine all the ingredients in a mixing bowl. Stir until the sugar dissolves. Use to baste charcoal-grilled chicken when it is almost done.

YIELD: ABOUT ¾ CUP

KETCHUP BASTING SAUCE
FOR BARBECUES

1 cup ketchup
3 tablespoons lemon juice
2 tablespoons honey
1 tablespoon finely minced garlic
1 tablespoon Worcestershire sauce
Tabasco sauce to taste
4 tablespoons unsalted butter
Salt and freshly ground pepper to taste
4 thin, seeded lemon slices

Combine all the ingredients in a saucepan and bring to a boil, stirring. Use to baste charcoal-grilled chicken when it is almost done.

YIELD: ABOUT 1½ CUPS

+ EASY +

LEMON VINAIGRETTE BASTING SAUCE
FOR BARBECUES

⅓ cup fresh lemon juice
½ cup olive oil
1 teaspoon finely minced garlic
Salt and freshly ground pepper to taste
1 teaspoon oregano
6 very thin, seeded lemon slices

Put the lemon juice in a small mixing bowl. Add the oil while stirring vigorously with a whisk. Add the remaining ingredients and blend well. Use to baste charcoal-grilled chicken.

YIELD: ABOUT 1 CUP

✣ EASY ✣
Tarragon-Wine Basting Sauce for Barbecues

¼ cup red wine vinegar
½ cup peanut, vegetable or corn oil
2 teaspoons chopped fresh tarragon
Salt and freshly ground pepper to taste

Put the vinegar in a small mixing bowl and add the oil, beating with a wire whisk. Add the tarragon and salt and pepper to taste. Blend well. Use to baste charcoal-grilled chicken.

YIELD: ABOUT ¾ CUP

MOLLY O'NEILL'S
MARINADES AND SPICE RUB FOR
GRILLED CHICKEN

✦ EASY ✦
CHICKEN PAILLARD

Pound four 6- to 8-ounce boneless chicken breasts until they are ¼-inch thick. Marinate breasts in the refrigerator. Grill over hot coals until tender, about 2 to 3 minutes per side.

✦ EASY ✦
TUSCAN MARINADE

This marinade is especially good with chicken paillard.

⅓ cup red wine
⅓ cup olive oil
2 cloves garlic, peeled and minced
1 tablespoon grated orange rind
½ cup minced sage leaves
¼ cup minced rosemary leaves
1 tablespoon black peppercorns, crushed

Combine all ingredients in a glass or ceramic bowl. Refrigerate in an airtight container for up to 3 days.

YIELD: 1 CUP

⚜ EASY ⚜
KOREAN BARBECUE

This marinade is wonderful with chicken wings.

1 tablespoon grated ginger
1 medium papaya, peeled and coarsely chopped
1 small pear, peeled and chopped
1 small onion, peeled and chopped
1 small clove garlic, peeled and minced
1 tablespoon honey
¼ cup soy sauce
⅓ cup pineapple juice
1 tablespoon Korean rice wine or sake
½ teaspoon freshly ground pepper
½ teaspoon sugar
2 tablespoons sesame oil
½ teaspoon sesame seeds
¼ cup minced scallions

Put all ingredients, except sesame seeds and scallions, in a blender. Puree until smooth. Pour the marinade into a glass or ceramic bowl. Add the sesame seeds and scallions. Refrigerate in an airtight container for up to 3 days.

YIELD: 2 CUPS

SPICE ISLAND MARINADE

This marinade imparts a pungent, Indian flavor.

1 ripe papaya, ¾ pound, peeled and diced
½ pound fresh, ripe apricots, pitted and finely chopped
¼ cup fresh lime juice
2 cloves garlic, peeled and minced
2 small Thai or jalapeño chilies, seeded, deveined and minced
1 tablespoon grated ginger
1 tablespoon cardamom pods, crushed
2 tablespoons coriander seeds, crushed

Combine all ingredients in a glass or ceramic bowl. Refrigerate in an airtight container for up to 2 days.

YIELD: 2 CUPS

PROVENÇAL SPICE RUB

This rub from the south of France is particularly delectable with chicken. Marinate two 3-pound chickens, split in half, in the refrigerator for 6 hours. Place the chicken on the grill, skin-side down. Cook over hot coals until the skin is charred, about 5 minutes. Turn the chicken and cover the grill. Continue cooking slowly until the meat is opaque at the bone, about 20 to 25 minutes.

1 teaspoon juniper berries

1 whole clove

1 teaspoon white peppercorns

1¼-inch cinnamon stick

¼ teaspoon grated nutmeg

2 teaspoons dried savory

1 tablespoon dried thyme

1 red onion, peeled and minced

2 cloves garlic, peeled and minced

½ cup fresh mint leaves

¼ cup olive oil

1 teaspoon grated orange rind

¼ cup red wine

Grind all dried spices and herbs together in a spice mill or coffee grinder until finely ground. Place the spice powder in a large glass or ceramic bowl. Add the onion, garlic, mint, orange rind, olive oil and red wine. Mix well. Refrigerate in an airtight container for up to 2 days.

YIELD: I CUP  *Molly O'Neill*

FRIED CHICKEN

Bird Song

By Julia Reed

To the Southerner, there is simply no other food that possesses the stature of fried chicken. It cuts across class lines. (When I was growing up, if we were dressed in church clothes, we'd eat it at the country club; if not, we'd stand in line at KFC and take home a bucket from the Colonel.) It cuts across regional lines (unlike say, gumbo, which is enjoyed in other states but does not retain the same exalted rank outside Louisiana, or pilau, which is relatively unheard of beyond South Carolina). It can also be the subject of intense debate. For example, should the chicken be marinated overnight in milk and seasonings before being coated with flour, or simply washed and dried and coated with seasoned flour? And what should the seasonings be? Also, what should the chicken be fried in, lard or oil? Most cooks I know have passionate, unequivocal answers to these questions. And just about everybody I know has his or her own highly personal benchmark, the standard against which all other fried chicken must be measured.

For my friend Rick Smythe, it's the chicken at Fratesi's, a store on Highway 82 near Tribbett, Mississippi, where they've been frying chicken at least as long as Rick has been alive. There the chicken is soaked in a mixture of milk and water, coated in flour seasoned with onion salt, garlic salt, Season-All and black pepper and fried in oil. Last time I was home, Rick insisted I try it, so I sampled four pieces until there was nothing left but bones. When I told our mutual friend Ralph McGee that I thought Fratesi's chicken was indeed pretty good, Ralph looked at me as if I was crazy. "It ain't nothing like Lola Belle's," he said, and so it goes.

Lola Belle was the McGee family cook. Lottie Martin was ours, and she really did cook the best fried chicken in the world. And even though I conservatively estimate that I ate more than a thousand pieces of it before she died, I cannot tell you what made it so good. Great fried chicken has an ineffable quality. The cook's hand probably has at least as much to do with it as black pepper versus cayenne; when everything somehow comes together just right, there is nothing better in this world.

The only person I know who has accurately articulated the feelings that good fried chicken inspires is my friend Jimmy Phillips. Like Ralph and Rick and me, he grew up in the Mississippi Delta, and for a while he was a songwriter in Nashville, where he wrote "Fried Chicken" and recorded it as a single. He also recorded a really great album that boasted liner notes from no less a personage than Peter Guralnick, but Jimmy left Music City behind and currently hides his light under a bushel by running a ski lodge in Telluride, Colorado. None of us can understand this since Telluride is about 10,000 feet above sea level and not, to my knowledge, remotely famous for fried chicken. Fortunately, Ralph still lives in the Delta, below sea level, where he farms and plays a mean guitar. Pretty much every time I go to see him, he plays "Fried Chicken" for me, preferably after we've just eaten some.

Since I've always thought the song deserves a wider public, I'm offering the lyrics here, with Jimmy's permission, of course, along with a few notes of my own:

> It was high noon, Arcola,
> Mississippi, another Sunday feast
> Popped my head into the kitchen
> and I heard that gurgling grease
> I said, Georgie, what you cooking?
> She said, Jimmy, what you think?
> You better come on in this kitchen
> and wash your hands up in
> the sink
> 'Cause we having
> Fried chicken. Wing takes a breast,
> leg takes a thigh
> Rice and gravy, black-eyed peas,
> and corn bread on the side
> It's a Southern institution
> Black skillet is preferred
> Fried chicken: a most delightful
> bird

Well, first of all, the "gurgling grease" line is a genius stroke. People's hearts skip beats when they hear that sound. It is also useful. When the grease is at the right temperature, a little corner of the chicken dipped into it will get that grease gurgling like crazy. That's how you know it's time to slide the pieces in. Second, "black skillet" is definitely preferred, if not required. A heavy cast-iron skillet that has been cured over the years, developing that almost menacing blackness (Ralph named his black Labrador "Skillet"), will cook the chicken more evenly and lend it a deeper color and flavor. Properly seasoned skillets are so valuable that they are handed down from generation to generation.

When we sat down at the table,
it was glorious to see
All that knuckle-sucking goodness
just looking back at me
Grandmama said the blessing but
I could not concentrate
For I had visions of drumsticks
dancing in my plate
Thinking 'bout that
Fried chicken
If you have not been enlightened
May I hasten to explain:
Full awareness is heightened
When the grease goes to your brain
Fighting over white meat, loser gets
the wing
I declare I love that chicken more
than anything
Pass the fresh tomatoes, man, I just
can't stop
And don't forget the sweet potatoes
with marshmallows on the top
To complement that
Fried chicken

These side dishes, as well as those in the chorus, are typical accompaniments, although there is very little that doesn't go well with fried chicken. I love it with potato salad and green beans cooked with ham hocks, and I'm in Jimmy's camp where the sliced tomatoes are concerned. Lottie always served her fried chicken with mashed potatoes and yeast rolls, but some people are more partial to biscuits (hence the greasy and extremely tasty examples available at Popeyes and KFC). The other night I served it with corn pudding, but anything equally sweet and starchy—Jimmy's sweet potatoes, summer squash casserole—is a good counterpoint to the chicken's saltiness.

I would be remiss here if I didn't address some of the subjects that cause disputes among fried chicken cooks. In recent taste tests I conducted on some willing participants, we all agreed that the chicken that had been soaked overnight in buttermilk was by far the tenderest. Some people don't dry the milk off and dip the pieces into the flour wet, which makes a crunchier batter that holds up better cold. I dry mine off. I also stick with the basic seasonings of plain old salt, black pepper and red pepper (with a bit of paprika for color). For frying, I know old-timers and sticklers who won't use anything but lard. I'm sure it is superior, but vegetable oil and shortening are a heck of a lot easier to find. Melted vegetable shortening, which is what Lottie used, is more refined so that it leaves less odor.

All that said, I don't think I've ever had a piece of bad fried chicken. You just have to be brave that first time at the stove. Or you can go out. Among my favorites are Sherman's in Greenville, Mississippi, a former grocery store where I ate the great majority of my chicken after Lottie died and where it is still mighty delicious, and Jacques-Imo's in New Orleans. Last year I ordered 150 pieces from Jacques-Imo's for my friend Anne McGee's surprise birthday party. (She is Ralph's first cousin, and her favorite food is fried chicken—and yes, he sang the song.) The restaurant received a high compliment when many of the guests assumed the chicken had come from my own kitchen. It's not that I'm a particularly great fried chicken cook, it's just that home-cooked chicken nearly always trumps a restaurant's. Especially a restaurant where the chicken, of necessity, is cooked in a deep fat fryer. As Calvin Trillin has observed, "A fried chicken cook with a deep fryer is a sculptor working with mittens."

Which leads me to another of my fine chicken establishments, Prince Hot Chicken Shack in Nashville. My friend Joe Ledbetter (who founded the Houston's restaurant chain with George Biel and knows a thing or two about excellent food) turned me on to Prince's one night by forcing me to try each of their three flavors, regular, hot and extra hot. The extra hot will kill a normal person—at least a half a bottle of cayenne pepper must coat each piece. But the regular (still plenty hot enough, believe me) is a truly superlative example of what fried chicken should be. After the first bite I said, "This was fried in a skillet." Joe assured me that it had been. Then we all got quiet and went to work eating. It was the closest to Lottie Martin I had felt in twenty-six years. That ineffable something had happened, that thing that makes fried chicken, as Jimmy Phillips always ad libs when he sings the last chorus to his song, "a most delightful, quite exciteful bird."

JULIA REED'S
SOUTHERN FRIED CHICKEN

1 frying chicken, about 3 to 3½ pounds, cut into 8 pieces
2 teaspoons salt plus more for seasoning chicken pieces
Black pepper
1½ cups all-purpose flour
1 teaspoon cayenne pepper
1 teaspoon hot paprika
Lard, vegetable shortening or vegetable oil for frying

1. Place chicken in bowl of cold water and soak for a few minutes. Drain chicken and dry well with paper towels. Season chicken with salt and black pepper.

2. Mix flour, 2 teaspoons of salt, cayenne and paprika in a brown paper or Ziploc bag. Add a few chicken pieces at a time and shake until well coated. Remove and shake off excess flour mixture.

3. Over medium-high heat, melt lard, vegetable shortening or oil to a depth of about 1½ inches in cast-iron skillet. When fat has reached about 350 degrees, slip in chicken pieces, dark meat first, being careful not to crowd them. (To test temperature, use a candy thermometer or dip a corner of a chicken piece into the fat; if vigorous bubbling ensues, the temperature is right.) Turn heat down and cook chicken for 10 minutes. Turn pieces with tongs. Cook until other side is browned, another 10 to 12 minutes. Drain on a wire rack over paper towels.

NOTE: To season a skillet: Preheat oven to 200 degrees. Wash new cast-iron skillet with soap. (This will be the first and last time skillet will be touched by soap.) Rinse and dry thoroughly. Rub inside generously with lard, olive oil or vegetable oil. Place in oven for one hour. Turn off oven and leave overnight. The next morning, wipe skillet out. Repeat process. The skillet is ready for cooking. After each use, wipe it out, rinse if necessary and wipe dry. If food sticks to pan, use a nonabrasive plastic scrubber or salt to get rid of it. Rub spot with olive oil.

YIELD: 4 SERVINGS *Julia Reed*

MARK BITTMAN'S
CINNAMON-SCENTED FRIED CHICKEN

Lard and butter combined, or vegetable oil
2 cups all-purpose flour
1 tablespoon coarse salt
2 tablespoons ground cinnamon
1 teaspoon freshly ground black pepper
1 good chicken, cut into serving pieces, or use 8 to 10 leg pieces (drumsticks
 and thighs), trimmed of excess fat

1. Choose a skillet or casserole at least 12 inches in diameter that can be covered. Add enough fat to come to a depth of about ½ inch, and turn heat to medium-high. If you are using butter, skim any foam as it rises to the surface.

2. While fat heats, mix together the flour and seasonings in a plastic bag. Toss chicken in bag, 2 or 3 pieces at a time, until well coated. Put pieces on a rack as you finish.

3. When oil is hot (a pinch of flour will sizzle) raise heat to high. Slowly add chicken pieces to skillet (if you add them all at once, temperature will plummet). Cover skillet, reduce heat to medium-high, and cook for 7 minutes.

4. Uncover skillet, turn chicken and continue to cook, uncovered, for another 7 minutes. Turn chicken again and cook for about 5 minutes more, turning as necessary to ensure that both sides are golden brown.

5. Remove chicken from skillet and drain on paper towels. Serve hot, warm or at room temperature.

YIELD: 4 SERVINGS   *Mark Bittman*

EDNA LEWIS'S VIRGINIA
FRIED CHICKEN

(Adapted from Edna Lewis)

One of the many recipes for fried chicken that have been created by Edna Lewis, the doyenne of Southern cuisine. Born in 1916 in Freetown, Virginia, a community established by former slaves, one of whom was her grandfather, she moved to New York City and eventually became chef at Gage & Tollner, one of Brooklyn's most-famous restaurants. Although her ingredients of choice in-cluded buttermilk and lard, she became just as celebrated as more worldly chefs; in 1999 she was named Grande Dame of Les Dames d'Escoffier International, and in 2003 she was inducted into the James Beard Foundation's Cookbook Hall of Fame.

> 1 cup unbleached flour
> 1 cup whole-wheat flour
> 3 teaspoons salt
> 1 teaspoon freshly ground black pepper
> 2 2¼- to 2½-pound chickens, cut into 8 pieces each
> ½ cup lard at room temperature
> ½ cup butter at room temperature

1. In a wide, flat dish, combine flours, salt and pepper, and mix well. Roll chicken in the mixture and put on a tray lined with wax paper. Let rest an hour, so flour will ad-here to chicken.

2. In a large skillet over medium-high heat, warm lard until nearly smoking and add butter. When butter is melted, add the chicken. The cooking fat should come halfway up the sides of the chicken, so that when the pieces are turned, they brown evenly. Each side should take 10 to 12 minutes. After cooking, drain on a paper towel and serve.

YIELD: 6 SERVINGS   *Molly O'Neill*

MARK BITTMAN'S SPICY SUPERCRUNCHY FRIED CHICKEN

1 good chicken, cut into serving pieces, or use 8 to 10 leg pieces (drumsticks
    and thighs) trimmed of excess fat

Salt and pepper to taste

1 tablespoon curry powder

½ teaspoon ground allspice

2 tablespoons minced garlic

1 Scotch bonnet (habanero), or other fresh chili, stemmed, seeded and
    minced, or cayenne to taste, optional

1 large egg, lightly beaten

1 cup flour

Lard and butter combined, or vegetable oil

Lemon or lime wedges for garnish

1. In a bowl, toss chicken with salt, pepper, curry, allspice, garlic, chili, egg and 2 tablespoons water. When thoroughly combined, blend in flour, using your hands. Keep mixing until most of the flour is blended with other ingredients and chicken is coated (add more water or flour if mixture is too thin or too dry; it should be dry but not powdery). Let sit while you heat fat; at this point chicken can marinate, refrigerated, for up to a day.

2. Choose a skillet or casserole at least 12 inches in diameter that can be covered. Add enough fat to come to a depth of about ½ inch and turn heat to medium-high. If you are using butter, skim any foam as it rises to the surface.

3. When oil is hot (a pinch of flour will sizzle) raise heat to high. Slowly add chicken pieces to skillet (if you add them all at once, temperature will plummet). Cover skillet, reduce heat to medium-high and cook for 7 minutes.

4. Uncover skillet, turn chicken and continue to cook, uncovered, for another 7 minutes. Turn chicken again and cook for about 5 minutes more, turning as necessary to ensure that both sides are golden brown.

5. Remove chicken from skillet and drain on paper towels. Serve chicken at any temperature, with lemon or lime wedges.

YIELD: 4 SERVINGS   *Mark Bittman*

✦ EASY ✦
CRAIG CLAIBORNE'S FAVORITE
SOUTHERN FRIED CHICKEN

(Adapted from *The New York Times Cook Book*)

This is Craig Claiborne's family recipe, which he said "has a crisp, crunchy crust because the chicken pieces are soaked in milk before coating with flour . . . good cold to carry along in a picnic basket."

> 1 2½- to 3-pound chicken, cut into serving pieces
> Milk to cover
> ¼ teaspoon Tabasco sauce
> 1 cup flour
> 1½ to 2 teaspoons salt
> 2 teaspoons freshly ground black pepper
> 1 pound lard or corn oil, for frying
> ½ cup butter

1. Put the chicken pieces in a bowl and add milk to cover. Add the Tabasco sauce and stir. Refrigerate for 1 hour or longer.

2. Combine the flour, salt and pepper (the flavor of pepper is important) in a flat baking dish. Blend well. Remove the chicken pieces, two or three at a time, and dip them into the flour mixture, turning to coat well.

3. Heat the lard and butter in a skillet, preferably a black iron skillet, large enough to hold the chicken pieces in one layer without touching. Heat the fat over high heat. Add the chicken pieces, skin-side down, and cook until golden brown on one side. Turn the pieces and reduce the heat to medium low. Continue cooking until golden brown and cooked through. The total cooking time should be 20 to 30 minutes. As the pieces are cooked, transfer them to absorbent paper toweling to drain.

YIELD: 4 SERVINGS

JASON EPSTEIN'S
UPTOWN FRIED CHICKEN

Jason Epstein: "I had learned to imitate the Harlem chefs and could make soul food dinners, to use the culturally correct term, at home. There are endless ways to fry chicken. You can marinate the chicken in garlic powder, cumin, paprika and cayenne or in Lawry's seasoning. Or simply in salt and pepper, with or without paprika or lemon juice, or dipped in milk or buttermilk and coated with flour, egg wash and crumbs or simply in crumbs or panko or crushed cornflakes, with or without honey, and so on and on. But the uptown version is simply to dust the pieces in flour with a little seasoning and fry it in real (not packaged) lard, for which downtown cooks can substitute corn or canola or peanut oil.

> 2 3½- to 4-pound chickens for frying
> 2 tablespoons Lawry's seasoned salt or 2 tablespoons of a mixture of equal
>   parts sea salt, freshly ground pepper, garlic powder, paprika and cumin
> Vegetable oil for frying
> 1 cup all-purpose flour
> 1 cup rice flour

1. Rinse chickens inside and out under running cold water and pat dry with paper towels. Remove extra skin and excess fat. Cut off the first joint of wings and the backs and discard. Keeping skin on, cut legs into thighs and drumsticks. Remove the wings, split the breast and cut each half crosswise into two (or ask your butcher to do this). Place pieces in a single layer in a shallow baking dish; sprinkle with seasoned salt or seasoning mix and rub to coat on all sides. Cover and set aside to marinate 1 hour.

2. Preheat oven to 250 degrees. Heat 1½ inches oil, enough to cover the chicken pieces ⅔ of the way but no more, in one or two wide, deep skillets or kettles to 325 to 350 degrees over medium-high heat. As the oil heats, mix the flours in a plastic food storage bag. Add the thighs and drumsticks; shake to coat. Remove each piece with tongs, shake off excess flour and place skin-side down in the hot oil without crowding. Fry until skin is browned and crisp, about 7 minutes; turn with tongs and fry until browned and crisp and cooked through, about 7 minutes longer, adjusting heat so chicken doesn't brown too quickly.

3. Drain chicken on a wire rack set over a baking pan and keep chicken warm in the oven while coating and frying the remaining pieces: breast pieces next, about

5 minutes on each side, and wing parts last, about 4 minutes on each side. Serve while still warm. The meat will be less moist when served cold the next day, but still very tasty.

NOTE: Jason Epstein serves this chicken with its traditional Harlem accompaniments: black-eyed peas and collard greens. For collard greens, simply wash the greens, discard the stems, cut the leaves into 2-inch strips, simmer a ham hock covered in 3 inches of water for an hour, then add the greens and simmer till tender, 40 minutes to an hour. Drain the greens, flavor them with vinegar and hot sauce, and serve.

YIELD: 4 SERVINGS (WITH LEFTOVERS) *Jason Epstein*

✦ EASY ✦
SPICY FRIED CHICKEN BALTIMORE-STYLE

2 chickens, each cut in 8 pieces
1 quart buttermilk
2 teaspoons garlic powder
2 teaspoons cumin
2 teaspoons salt
2 tablespoons ground black pepper
1 tablespoon cayenne pepper
2 cups flour
1 quart vegetable oil

1. Cover the chicken with the buttermilk. Refrigerate for at least 8 hours and drain. In a separate bowl, mix together the garlic powder, cumin, salt, black pepper and cayenne and sprinkle evenly over the chicken.

2. Place the flour in a plastic bag and add the chicken pieces a few at a time, shaking to coat. Place floured pieces on a dry sheet pan and let them stand for 30 minutes.

3. Heat the oil in a cast-iron skillet over high heat until it is nearly smoking. Cook the pieces until golden brown on each side, about 12 minutes per side. Drain on paper towels. Finish off in a 350-degree oven for about 15 minutes or until cooked through.

YIELD: 4 SERVINGS *Mitchell Owens*

BATTER-FRIED CHICKEN FINGERS

(Adapted from *The Best of Craig Claiborne*)

The success of deep frying depends on the temperature of the oil and on the batter. A good fritter batter is one of the simplest things to make and its uses are countless. This batter-fried chicken is delectable when served with lemon wedges and a simple fresh-tasting tomato sauce of your choice.

> 2 large, whole, skinless, boneless chicken breasts, about 1¼ pounds
> Salt and freshly ground pepper to taste
> ¼ cup peanut, vegetable or corn oil
> ¼ cup lemon juice
> 4 tablespoons finely chopped parsley
> Fritter Batter (see recipe, page 141)
> Oil for deep frying
> Lemon wedges for garnish
> Tomato sauce

1. Place the chicken breasts on a flat surface. Split each whole breast in half. Slice the meat on the bias into about 18 pieces.

2. Put the pieces of chicken in a bowl and add the salt and pepper, ¼ cup oil, lemon juice and parsley. Let stand for 20 minutes.

3. Remove the chicken pieces from the marinade, one piece at a time, and add them to a small bowl that contains the fritter batter. Manipulate the pieces in the batter so that they are well coated.

4. Heat the oil for deep frying and, when it is quite hot, or 365 degrees, add the batter-coated chicken pieces, one at a time. Do not crowd them in the oil. Cook, turning the pieces occasionally, for about 2 minutes, or until each piece starts to float. Remove with a slotted spoon and drain on paper towels.

5. Add the remaining chicken pieces to the oil and cook until done. When drained, sprinkle with salt to taste. Garnish with lemon wedges and serve with tomato sauce.

YIELD: 4 SERVINGS

FRITTER BATTER

1½ cups flour
3 tablespoons peanut, vegetable or corn oil
1 teaspoon salt
2 large eggs
½ cup water

Sift the flour into a mixing bowl. Add the oil and salt. Add the eggs and stir with a wire whisk. Add the water gradually, beating with the whisk.

YIELD: ABOUT 2 CUPS

CLEO JOHNS'S DELECTABLE
BAKE-FRIED CHICKEN

Soaking the pieces in milk flavored with grated onion, dried mustard, sugar and garlic results in an uncommonly tasty fried chicken. The recipe was created by Cleo Johns, a soft-voiced African-American woman whose Cleo's La Cuisine Catering in Maplewood, N.J. was for many years the official caterer for the weddings and bar mitzvahs at nearby Temple Israel.

> 1 fryer, cut in 6 or 8 pieces
> 1 cup milk
> 2 tablespoons grated onion
> 1 tablespoon dry mustard
> 1 tablespoon sugar
> 1 clove garlic, mashed
> Salt and pepper to taste
> Flour for dusting
> Wesson oil or Crisco shortening for frying

1. Mix milk with seasonings and soak chicken pieces in milk for at least half an hour.
2. Drain chicken, press liquid from each piece and dust lightly with flour.
3. Heat in heavy frying pan enough Wesson oil or Crisco to just cover chicken. Brown chicken pieces 10 minutes on each side.
4. Remove chicken with slotted spoon and place in baking pan. Bake in 350-degree oven for 30 minutes.

YIELD: 4 SERVINGS   *B. H. Fussell*

LINDY BOGGS'S
OVEN-FRIED CHICKEN

Lindy Boggs, the former congresswoman who represented the French Quarter of New Orleans, doesn't make fried chicken anymore. She prefers this oven-baked version.

¼ cup butter

⅓ cup flour

2 eggs

Salt to taste

1 tablespoon paprika

2 tablespoons lemon juice

1 cup cracker crumbs

2½ pound chicken, cut in equal-size pieces

1. Place butter in a 13-by-9-by-2-inch baking dish and place in 350-degree oven to melt butter.

2. Flour chicken pieces and set aside.

3. Beat together eggs, salt, paprika and lemon juice. Dip chicken pieces, one at a time, in egg mixture, then in cracker crumbs. Arrange pieces, skin-side down, in melted butter in baking dish and bake for 45 minutes at 350 degrees, turning once.

YIELD: 2 TO 3 SERVINGS *Marian Burros*

JUNIOR'S GOLDEN FRIED CHICKEN, SOUTHERN-STYLE

(Adapted from *Welcome to Junior's*)

FOR THE BATTER

2 cups all-purpose flour

¼ cup yellow cornmeal

2 tablespoons salt

1 tablespoon baking powder

½ teaspoon ground white pepper

5 extra-large eggs

1½ cups milk

FOR THE CHICKEN AND BREADING

3 pounds chicken pieces on the bone
    (drumsticks, breasts, thighs,
    wings)

2 cups all-purpose flour

¼ cup whole wheat flour

¼ cup yellow cornmeal

2 tablespoons cornstarch

3 tablespoons fried chicken
    seasoning

2 tablespoons dried thyme leaves

1 tablespoon paprika

Ground white pepper

Vegetable oil for frying

1. To make the batter, combine the all-purpose flour, cornmeal, salt, baking powder and pepper in a bowl. In another bowl, whisk the eggs and milk together for 2 minutes until thick and light. Add the flour mixture to the egg mixture and whisk until smooth, about 1 minute. Let stand for 15 minutes before using.

2. To make the chicken and breading, pat the chicken dry with paper towels. Combine the flour, whole wheat flour, cornmeal, cornstarch, chicken seasoning, thyme, paprika and pepper in a shallow dish and mix well. Dip the chicken pieces first in the batter, then roll in the breading until evenly coated. Place on a sheet pan and refrigerate for 15 minutes.

3. Heat 1 inch of oil in a large skillet. When very hot, fry the chicken pieces, turning, until golden brown and the juices run clear when pierced with a fork, 20 to 30 minutes. Transfer to a wire rack to drain. Serve piping hot.

YIELD: 4 TO 6 SERVINGS   *Molly O'Neill*

MARK BITTMAN'S
RICE KRISPIES OR CORN FLAKE
OVEN-BAKED "FRIED" CHICKEN

4 garlic cloves, peeled and minced

1 small onion, peeled and sliced

1 teaspoon dried oregano

1 tablespoon ground cumin

¼ cup fresh orange juice

¼ cup fresh lime juice (or use all orange juice)

1 chicken, cut into serving pieces, or use 8 to 10 leg pieces (drumsticks and thighs), trimmed of excess fat

4 tablespoons melted unsalted butter

2 cups Rice Krispies, lightly crushed, or corn flakes crumbs

1. In a large bowl, combine garlic, onion, oregano, cumin and juices. Add chicken and toss; let sit while you heat oven, or marinate it, refrigerated, for up to a day.

2. Heat oven to 425 degrees. Spread half the butter on a 9-by-12 baking dish. Put Rice Krispies or corn flakes on a plate and roll chicken in them, patting to help crumbs adhere. Carefully transfer to baking dish.

3. Drizzle chicken with remaining butter and bake, rotating pan so pieces brown evenly, until they are browned and cooked through, 30 to 40 minutes. Serve hot.

YIELD: 4 SERVINGS   *Mark Bittman*

SHIZUO TSUJI'S DEEP-FRIED MARINATED CHICKEN

(Adapted from *Japanese Cooking: A Simple Art*)

A recipe from Japan's most famous gastronome, Shizuo Tsuji, a cookbook author and an expert on French and Japanese cuisine.

Marinade (see recipe below)
2 pounds boned chicken
Oil for deep frying
1 cup flour

1. Cut unskinned chicken into generous bite-size pieces.
2. Add chicken pieces to marinade and mix thoroughly with your hands. Marinate 30 minutes.
3. Bring a generous amount of oil to medium temperature (340 degrees) in a heavy-bottomed pot or deep fryer.
4. Drain the marinade from the chicken and dust the chicken lightly with flour. Use your hands to toss and coat individual pieces thoroughly. Let coated chicken rest for 2 to 3 minutes.
5. Slide chicken into hot oil, a few pieces at a time. Turn and separate individual pieces as they deep-fry. Skim the oil occasionally. As the chicken is finished, remove and drain on absorbent paper toweling. Keep hot.

YIELD: 4 SERVINGS

MARINADE

1 knob fresh ginger
6 tablespoons sake
3 tablespoons light soy sauce
2 tablespoons very finely chopped green onions

1. Make ginger juice by grating the ginger and squeezing the gratings in a cloth to extract the juice. There should be about 1 tablespoon.

2. Mix ginger juice and all other ingredients in a bowl.

YIELD: APPROXIMATELY ¾ CUP ⟋ *Susan Chira*

DEEP-FRIED CHICKEN WITH LEMONGRASS (GAI TAKRAI)

(Adapted from Lemongrass Restaurant, Bangkok)

CHICKEN

6 stalks lemongrass

8 scallions

6 chicken thighs, boned and skinned

¼ cup fish sauce (nam pla or Vietnamese nuoc mam) (see Note)

1 teaspoon sugar

3 cups vegetable oil

GARNISH

6 stalks lemongrass

6 scallions

1½ tablespoons sugar

¼ cup chopped roasted peanuts

¼ fresh pineapple, peeled, cored and sliced

1. Remove and discard tough outer stalks of lemongrass. With the back of a cleaver or knife, lightly beat the tender inner stalks to release the oils; chop coarsely. Coarsely chop scallions. Place chicken thighs in a bowl with lemongrass and scallions. Add fish sauce and sugar and mix well. Cover and set aside, refrigerated, for at least 3 hours.

2. In a large pot, heat oil until a small cube of bread dropped into the oil turns golden. Prepare garnish. Trim and discard tough outer stalks of lemongrass and slice the tender inner stalks thinly. Deep-fry the lemongrass until it starts to brown. Remove and drain on absorbent paper. Trim and thinly slice the scallions. Deep-fry scallions until brown and crisp. Remove and drain on absorbent paper.

3. Remove chicken thighs from marinade and shake to release the bits of lemon-

grass and scallion. Deep-fry the chicken thighs, turning once, until they are thoroughly cooked, approximately 15 minutes. Remove and drain on absorbent paper.

4. Combine deep-fried lemongrass and scallions, add sugar and toss to combine well. Slice each chicken thigh into 3 or 4 serving pieces. Arrange chicken slices on a serving platter. Sprinkle lemongrass and scallion mixture over chicken pieces. Sprinkle chopped peanuts over top. Arrange thin slices of pineapple around the platter and serve immediately.

NOTE: See "Selected Sources for Ingredients," page 352.

YIELD: 4 SERVINGS ⌢ *Nancy Harmon Jenkins*

✦ EASY ✦

RAYMOND SOKOLOV'S DOMINICAN CRACKLING CHICKEN

This recipe is adapted from a dish that is a specialty of a storefront Dominican restaurant in Brooklyn.

½ cup fresh lime juice
½ cup heavy soy sauce or dark soy sauce
½ teaspoon salt
2 2-pound frying chickens, each cut into 16 pieces
1 quart vegetable oil
2 cups flour
2 teaspoons freshly ground pepper
2 teaspoons cayenne pepper
2 limes, cut into sixths

1. In a large stainless steel or glass bowl, combine lime juice, soy sauce and salt. Add chicken; stir, refrigerate and allow to marinate at least 3 hours.

2. Pour oil into a wok or large pot and heat over medium heat until very hot, but

not smoking. Meanwhile, combine flour, pepper and cayenne in a paper bag and set aside.

3. Drain chicken and pat dry. Drop 3 or 4 chicken pieces into the bag with the seasoned flour and shake until well coated; repeat with remaining chicken.

4. Using a slotted spoon, slowly add the chicken, a few pieces at a time, to the oil and deep-fry until golden brown, about 3 minutes per side. Drain on paper towels and keep warm until served. Serve with lime wedges.

YIELD: 6 SERVINGS *Molly O'Neill*

+ EASY +

CHICKEN NUGGETS WITH SPICY CUCUMBER

(Adapted from *Simple Menus for the Bento Box*)

A bento box is a lacquered wooden box with four small compartments and was derived from a farmer's seed box. Early in the twentieth century, Japanese cooks began using it to make a bento, or boxed meal, with a different dish in each compartment.

1 seedless cucumber

¼ teaspoon Vietnamese chili paste (see Note) or Tabasco sauce, more to taste

3 tablespoons champagne vinegar or white wine vinegar

Salt and freshly ground black pepper

1 quart peanut or canola oil

1 pound skinless, boneless chicken breast or thigh

Flour for dusting

2 large eggs, lightly beaten

1 cup panko or dried bread crumbs, more if needed

1. Cut cucumber lengthwise into quarters. Cut quarters into ⅛-inch slices on an angle. In a medium bowl, combine cucumber, chili paste and vinegar, and toss well. Season with salt, pepper and chili paste. Set aside.

2. In a 2-quart saucepan, heat oil to 350 degrees. Cut chicken into 1-inch cubes, and season with salt and pepper. Dredge chicken cubes in flour, dip them in beaten egg and roll in the bread crumbs to coat evenly. Add half the chicken to the oil, and fry until crust is golden brown, about 3 minutes for breast meat, 5 minutes for thigh. Using a slotted spoon, remove chicken from oil, and drain on paper towels. Repeat with remaining chicken.

3. In each of 6 small bowls, place a small, tight mound of cucumbers. Divide chicken nuggets among bowls, propping them against cucumbers. Serve.

NOTE: See "Selected Sources for Ingredients," page 352.

YIELD: 6 APPETIZER SERVINGS ⟋ *Amanda Hesser*

DAVID K'S HUNAN CHICKEN

At David K's in Manhattan, the Taiwan-born chef Jui-Hsiang Teng prepared chicken with a marinade flavored with hot-sweet hoisin sauce, sugar and vinegar.

THE CHICKEN
**2 chicken legs with thighs, boned,
    fat and membranes removed,
    washed thoroughly and cut into
    bite-size pieces
1 large egg, beaten
Pinch of salt
Pinch of white pepper
2 teaspoons cornstarch
3½ cups peanut oil**

**2 tablespoons scallions, white
    portions cut into ⅛-inch slices
8 to 10 small, dried hot chili peppers**

THE SAUCE
**4 teaspoons dark soy sauce
1 clove garlic, minced
1 slice fresh ginger, in small pieces
2 teaspoons hoisin sauce
1 teaspoon sugar
1 teaspoon white vinegar**

1. Make sauce of soy sauce, garlic, ginger, hoisin, sugar and white vinegar in bowl and reserve.

2. Marinate chicken pieces in beaten egg with salt and pepper and teaspoon of cornstarch for 5 minutes.

3. Heat wok for 1 minute over high heat, add peanut oil. When wisp of white smoke appears, oil is ready. Sprinkle remaining teaspoon of cornstarch over chicken pieces and place in hot oil. Deep-fry for 1½ to 2 minutes until chicken is crisp. Drain.

4. Empty wok of oil. Place back over heat and when remaining residue of oil heats add scallions and chili peppers. Stir about 40 seconds. Add chicken and stir until well mixed.

5. Add sauce and mix all ingredients until chicken pieces are thoroughly coated with sauce, about 3 minutes. There should be no liquid in wok. Remove and serve immediately.

YIELD: 2 PORTIONS IF SERVED ALONE;
4 PORTIONS IF SERVED AS PART OF LARGER MEAL ✌ *Fred Ferretti*

SHUN LEE WEST'S
SICHUAN KUMPAO CHICKEN

(Adapted from Man Sundao, Shun Lee West, New York City)

With a hot and spicy Chinese dish, the hot comes from chili and the spicy comes from ingredients like garlic, ginger and scallions.

> 1 large egg white
> ⅛ teaspoon salt
> 1 tablespoon water
> 2 tablespoons cornstarch
> 8 ounces skinless chicken breast (the breast from one
>   3- to 4-pound chicken), cut into bite-size cubes
> 1 tablespoon sugar
> 1 tablespoon white wine vinegar
> 2 tablespoons rice wine or dry Sherry
> 2 tablespoons dark soy sauce
> 1 tablespoon chili paste
> ¼ cup chicken stock
> 1 tablespoon cornstarch mixed with 1 tablespoon water
> 1 tablespoon sesame oil
> 2½ cups vegetable oil for cooking
> 10 small, dried hot red peppers
> ½ tablespoon diced garlic
> 1 cup diced scallion
> 1 cup peanuts, walnuts or any favorite nuts

1. In a bowl, combine the egg white, salt, water and cornstarch and add chicken. Marinate for at least half an hour.

2. In another bowl make the chili-paste sauce by combining sugar, vinegar, rice wine, soy sauce, chili paste, chicken stock, cornstarch and sesame oil. Mix well and set aside.

3. Heat vegetable oil in a wok or skillet to 350 degrees. Add chicken and marinade and stir-fry quickly to avoid sticking. Cook about 1 minute. Remove and drain chicken well. Remove all but 2 tablespoons of vegetable oil.

4. Cook dry hot peppers in the wok over medium high heat until they begin to darken (about 1 minute). Add garlic and scallions and stir for 5 to 10 seconds. Add partially cooked chicken to the wok and pour the chili paste sauce over it. Stir-fry over high heat until the sauce thickens (about 1 minute). Add nuts, stir-fry briefly and serve with white rice.

YIELD: SERVES 2 AS A MEAL, 4 AS AN APPETIZER (INGREDIENTS MAY BE INCREASED PROPORTIONATELY TO MAKE LARGER SERVINGS) *Bryan Miller*

PEARL'S LEMON CHICKEN

(Adapted from *The Best of Craig Claiborne*)

One of the most popular recipes The Times *has ever printed is the lemon chicken devised by chef Lee Lum of the once-popular but now closed Pearl's restaurant in Manhattan.*

3 skinless, boneless chicken breasts	¼ cup chicken broth
2 tablespoons light soy sauce	1 carrot, trimmed and scraped
1 tablespoon vodka	1 scallion, trimmed
½ teaspoon sesame oil	¼ cup thin julienne strips of green pepper
1 teaspoon salt	
1 large egg white, lightly beaten	¼ cup drained pineapple chunks, cut in half
¾ cup sugar	
1 tablespoon cornstarch	Peanut oil for deep-frying
½ cup white vinegar	¾ cup water chestnut powder
Grated rind of 1 lemon	1 tablespoon lemon extract
Juice of 1 lemon	

1. Trim off any fat and membranous fibers surrounding the chicken pieces.
2. Combine the soy sauce, vodka, sesame oil, salt and egg white in a bowl. Add the chicken breasts and set aside.
3. When ready to cook, combine the sugar, cornstarch, vinegar, lemon rind and

lemon juice in a saucepan. Bring to the boil, stirring. Add the chicken broth and return to the boil, stirring until thickened. Set aside until chicken has been fried.

4. Cut the carrot into 2-inch lengths then cut the lengths into thin slices. Cut the slices into thin slivers. Cut the scallions into thin slivers.

5. Add the carrot, scallion, green pepper and pineapple chunks to the sauce. Bring to the boil and set aside.

6. Heat the oil for deep frying. Dip the chicken pieces into the water chestnut powder and shake off any excess. Cook the chicken pieces in the oil for about 10 minutes, or until the coating is crisp and the chicken is cooked through.

7. Place each piece of chicken on a flat surface. Using a sharp knife, cut it crosswise into 1- or 2-inch lengths. Arrange the pieces on a platter. Heat the sauce, add the lemon extract, if desired, and pour it over the chicken. Serve immediately.

YIELD: 6 SERVINGS ⌒ *Craig Claiborne*

CLASSIC CHICKEN KIEV

(Adapted from *The Best of Craig Claiborne*)

¼ to ½ pound butter
1 to 2 tablespoons chopped chives
Salt to taste
3 whole or 6 halved skinless, boneless chicken breasts
Freshly ground pepper to taste
2 large eggs
¼ cup water
½ cup flour
3 cups fresh bread crumbs
Oil for deep-frying

1. Cream the butter with the chives. If unsalted butter is used, beat in salt to taste. Chill briefly. If the chicken breast pieces are small, use the lesser amounts of butter and chives. If quite large, use the greater amounts.

2. Place the chicken breasts between sheets of plastic wrap and pound lightly with a flat mallet to make them larger. Sprinkle with salt and pepper.

3. Put 1½ to 3 tablespoons of filling in the center of each chicken breast. Fold the edges over to enclose the filling. Place the stuffed chicken breasts briefly in the freezer before breading them.

4. Beat the eggs with water in a flat container. Dip the stuffed chicken breasts first in flour to coat well, then in the egg mixture, coating all over. Finally, roll them in bread crumbs.

5. Cook in deep fat until golden brown and cooked through, 10 minutes, more or less, depending on the size of the stuffed pieces.

YIELD: 6 SERVINGS

JANICE OKUN'S
BUFFALO CHICKEN WINGS

Janice Okun, who was the food editor of the Buffalo Evening News, *created this recipe, which she claimed duplicates what is said to be the original recipe for Buffalo chicken wings that is served at Frank & Theressa's Anchor Bar on Main Street in Buffalo, NY. The "secret" ingredient, she said, is a special brand of hot sauce called Frank's Louisiana Red Hot Sauce, which is available in supermarkets.*

24 chicken wings, about 4 pounds
Salt, if desired
Freshly ground pepper
4 cups peanut, vegetable or corn oil
4 tablespoons unsalted butter
2 to 5 tablespoons (1 2½-ounce bottle) Frank's Louisiana Red Hot Sauce
1 tablespoon white vinegar
Blue cheese dressing (see recipe, page 156)
Celery sticks

1. Cut off and discard the small tip of each wing. Cut the main wing bone and second wing bone at the joint. Sprinkle the wings with salt, if desired, and pepper to taste.

2. Heat the oil in a deep-fat fryer or large casserole. When it is quite hot, add half of the wings and cook about 10 minutes, stirring occasionally. When the chicken wings are golden brown and crisp, remove them and drain well.

3. Add the remaining wings and cook about 10 minutes or until golden brown and crisp. Drain well.

4. Melt the butter in a saucepan and add 2 to 5 tablespoons of the hot sauce and vinegar. Put the chicken wings on a warm serving platter and pour the butter mixture over them. Serve with blue cheese dressing and celery sticks.

YIELD: 4 TO 6 SERVINGS

BLUE CHEESE DRESSING

1 cup homemade mayonnaise (see
    recipe, below)
2 tablespoons finely chopped onion
1 teaspoon finely minced garlic
¼ cup finely chopped parsley
½ cup sour cream

1 tablespoon lemon juice
1 tablespoon white vinegar
¼ cup crumbled blue cheese
Salt to taste, if desired
Freshly ground pepper to taste
Cayenne pepper to taste

1. Combine all of the ingredients in a mixing bowl.
2. Chill for an hour or longer.

YIELD: ABOUT 2½ CUPS

MAYONNAISE

1 large egg yolk
Salt, if desired
Freshly ground pepper

1 teaspoon imported mustard, such as
    Dijon or Düsseldorf
1 teaspoon vinegar or lemon juice
1 cup peanut, vegetable or olive oil

1. Place the yolk in a mixing bowl and add salt, if desired, and pepper to taste, mustard and vinegar or lemon juice. Beat vigorously for a second or two with a wire whisk or electric beater.

2. Start adding the oil gradually, beating continuously with the whisk or electric beater. Continue beating and adding oil until all of it is used.

YIELD: ABOUT 1 CUP   *Craig Claiborne with Pierre Franey*

✦ EASY ✦
ALFRED PORTALE'S BUFFALO CHICKEN WINGS

Alfred Portale, the chef and an owner of Gotham Bar and Grill in New York City, is from Buffalo. That city's famous chicken wings are not on the menu at his restaurant, but for the Super Bowl he makes them for his staff.

16 chicken wings, disjointed	½ tablespoon of minced garlic
Canola oil	3 tablespoons butter
Salt and pepper to taste	Tabasco sauce to taste
Frank's Red Hot Sauce or	Blue Cheese Dip (see recipe
Crystal Hot Sauce	below)
Dash of Worcestershire sauce	Celery, cut in 3-inch sticks

1. Preheat oven to 200 degrees.

2. Disjoint the chicken wings and discard the wingtips.

3. Heat the oil until very hot. Deep-fry the wings until golden brown. Salt and pepper the wings and keep them warm in the oven.

4. Simmer the Frank's Red Hot Sauce or Crystal Hot Sauce with the Worcestershire sauce, minced garlic, butter and Tabasco to taste.

5. Before serving, toss the wings in the sauce. Serve with dip and celery sticks.

BLUE CHEESE DIP

1 cup crumbled blue cheese
⅓ cup sour cream, mayonnaise or crème fraîche, or a mixture of them

Mix the blue cheese with the sour cream, mayonnaise or crème fraîche or a mixture of them.

YIELD: 4 PORTIONS   *Florence Fabricant*

ASIAN CHICKEN WINGS WITH PEANUT SAUCE

In this preparation, Craig Claiborne blended two recipes, serving Indonesian-flavored, deep-fried chicken wings with a Thai-style, somewhat spicy peanut sauce. The result is delicious.

THE WINGS

16 large, meaty chicken wings, about 3½ pounds
Salt to taste, if desired
2 teaspoons soy sauce
1 teaspoon sugar
1 teaspoon freshly squeezed lemon juice
1 tablespoon powdered cumin
1½ teaspoons turmeric
Oil for deep-frying

THE PEANUT SAUCE

1 sweet red pepper, about ½ pound
1 tablespoon corn, peanut or vegetable oil
2 tablespoons finely chopped shallots
2 tablespoons curry powder or curry paste
1 cup canned unsweetened coconut cream
½ cup chunky peanut butter
1 teaspoon sugar

1. Cut the chicken wings into three parts, main wing bone, second joint and wing tip. Discard the tips or use them for soup.

2. Put the chicken pieces into a mixing bowl and add salt, soy sauce, sugar, lemon juice, cumin and turmeric. Blend well. Let stand while preparing the peanut sauce.

3. Preheat the broiler to high and roast the pepper all over until the skin is charred. Place the pepper under cold running water and pull off the charred skin. Split the pepper open and remove the seeds and veins. Chop the pepper coarsely.

4. Heat the oil in a small skillet and add the shallots. Cook briefly, stirring, and add the curry powder or curry paste. Cook briefly and add the chopped pepper and stir. Remove from the heat.

5. Bring the coconut cream to the boil. Pour and scrape the pepper mixture into the cream. Add the peanut butter and sugar and let simmer about 5 minutes.

6. Pour the mixture into the container of a food processor or electric blender. Blend thoroughly. Return the mixture to a saucepan and bring to the simmer. If desired, the sauce may be thinned with up to ¼ cup of water.

7. Heat enough oil to cover the chicken pieces well when they are added. It may be advisable to cook only half of the chicken pieces at a time. Heat the oil to a temperature of 360 degrees. Add the chicken pieces and cook until they are crisp and golden brown. Remove the pieces and drain on absorbent toweling. Repeat if necessary until all the pieces are cooked and drained.

8. Serve the hot sauce on the side as a dip for the deep-fried chicken pieces.

YIELD: 4 TO 6 SERVINGS   *Craig Claiborne with Pierre Franey*

STEAMING AND POACHING YOUR WAY TO THE DINNER TABLE

Play Misty

By Molly O'Neill

Steaming is a brutal but mercifully brief technique that enables the cook to be both generous and firm. Place an inch of liquid in the bottom of a pot and bring it to a vigorous boil. Arrange the ingredients on a rack, suspended above the bubbling vapor and cover—firmly—to let nature take its course. Luxuriating in such a mist is more powerful than total submersion. It is hotter, it moves more rapidly, it has a determined fury. The broth will absorb nearly nothing of what it cooks; rather, it warms the food in its own essence, making it more of what it is.

Steaming has been made simpler recently, with the proliferation of heavy-duty cookware containing steaming baskets. Or the food can be placed on a collapsible steamer basket in a pot or skillet, or on a plate set over simmering liquid.

Also, for the most intense flavor possible, it is crucial that you tightly seal the pot; otherwise, the results of a steamed piece of chicken are indistinguishable from chicken that has been blanched or boiled.

Finally, it should be noted that despite the intense spices used, and the powerful perfume emitted from the liquid, the flavor steam imparts is invariably subtle. Culinarily speaking, it's a hint that life is more complicated than the tender impulses of youth.

CHICKEN BREASTS STEAMED WITH FENNEL AND TARRAGON

A little crème fraîche adds a tangy note to this delicious and nutritious dish.

4 chicken breasts, skinned
Coarse salt and freshly ground pepper to taste
2 tablespoons minced fresh tarragon (or chives if tarragon is not available)
1 cup water
1 cup dry white wine
1 carrot, coarsely chopped
1 onion, quartered
2 heads fennel
⅓ cup crème fraîche
Juice of ½ lemon

1. Trim the chicken breasts and cut them in half. Season with salt and pepper and a tablespoon tarragon or chives. Set aside.

2. Bring the water, wine, carrot and onion to a boil in the bottom of a steamer. Slice the bulb end of the fennel and reserve. Coarsely slice the stalk and leaves and add to the stock.

3. Place the chicken breasts in alternating layers with the fennel in the top of the steamer. Cover and steam for about 12 minutes, or until cooked but still slightly pink in the center. Remove to a heated plate, cover loosely with foil and keep warm.

4. Strain off 2 cups steaming liquid and reduce over high heat to 1 cup. Add the crème fraîche and reduce the liquid to 1 cup. Correct seasoning and add lemon juice. Pour the sauce over the chicken breasts and sprinkle with remaining tarragon or chives. This goes well with rice.

YIELD: 4 SERVINGS ⌒ *Moira Hodgson*

CITRONELLE'S STEAMED CHICKEN WITH FENNEL AND GARLIC

(Adapted from Citronelle, Washington, D.C.)

Michel Richard, the chef/owner of Citronelle in Washington, D.C., loves the steamed version of pot-au-feu, the melange of chicken and vegetables in rich broth: "If you put a chicken in a liquid medium, it dilutes the flavor. When you steam it, there is more concentration of the flavors of the chicken and the vegetables, and the meat is firmer."

40 cloves of garlic, peeled	1 lemon, cut in half
2 sprigs thyme	1 teaspoon aniseed
2 fennel bulbs, thinly sliced crosswise	1 4-pound whole chicken
3 cups chicken stock or canned broth	½ teaspoon coriander seeds, crushed
	Salt and freshly ground black pepper

1. In the lower part of a large steamer, combine garlic, thyme, fennel, chicken stock, lemon and aniseed (see Note).

2. In the upper part of the steamer, place chicken and sprinkle with coriander seeds and salt and pepper to taste.

3. Fit steamer pieces together and cover pot tightly. Place over high heat to bring to a boil, then simmer for 1 hour.

4. Check to see if chicken is thoroughly cooked by slicing into joint where leg meets breast. Meat should be white and juices should run clear. If necessary, steam for an additional 15 minutes.

5. Set top half of steamer aside. Bring vegetable mixture to a boil, and reduce by one third. Remove lemon and thyme sprigs. To serve, cut chicken into four pieces. Place a serving in each of four large soup plates, and top with vegetables and broth.

NOTE: Steaming can be done in pots designed for it that contain a basket to hold the food, or on a collapsible steamer basket in a pot or skillet, or on a plate set over simmering water. A tight-fitting lid is crucial.

YIELD: 4 SERVINGS ⤳ *Marian Burros*

MICHEL RICHARD'S A STEAMED CHICKEN IN EVERY TEAPOT

(Adapted from *Michel Richard's Home Cooking With a French Accent*.)

1 medium rutabaga (about 6 ounces), peeled and cut into 1-inch pieces
1 medium turnip (about 6 ounces), peeled and cut into 1-inch pieces
1 large carrot, peeled and cut into 1-inch lengths
2 medium red boiling potatoes (about 4 ounces each), peeled and cut into
    1-inch pieces
1 large leek (white and light green parts only), halved lengthwise and sliced
    into ⅛-inch pieces
1 small onion, peeled and diced
4 cups low-sodium chicken broth
1 3¾- to 4-pound roasting chicken, at room temperature
Salt and freshly ground black pepper to taste
3 chamomile or other tea bags
1 tablespoon Dijon mustard
2 tablespoons minced fresh chervil or Italian parsley

1. Place vegetables in bottom of a large steamer (see Note). Pour chicken broth over vegetables. Bring to boil over medium-high heat. Place steamer basket above vegetables. Season chicken with salt and pepper, place in basket. Cover pot tightly, reduce heat and steam chicken for 20 minutes. Add tea bags to basket and pour in additional broth if liquid is reduced below about 2 cups. Turn chicken. Cover and steam until chicken is cooked and juices run yellow when thigh is pierced, about 1 hour more.

2. Remove tea bags. Transfer chicken to cutting board, carve into serving pieces. Remove skin if desired. Bring vegetable mixture back to boil. Whisk in mustard. Season with salt and pepper. Ladle vegetables and broth into four soup plates. Place chicken pieces on top of vegetables. Sprinkle with chervil, serve immediately.

NOTE: Steaming can be done in pots designed for it that contain a basket to hold the food, or on a collapsible steamer basket in a pot or skillet, or on a plate set over simmering water. A tight-fitting lid is crucial.

YIELD: 4 SERVINGS ⌁ *Marian Burros*

BETTY SOO HOO'S CANTONESE STEAMED CHICKEN

A simple and savory Cantonese steamed chicken dish with black mushrooms and sausage is the favorite of Betty Soo Hoo, who was born in Canton, where her grandfather was a noodle maker.

1½ pounds of boneless chicken, in small pieces

1 tablespoon light soy sauce

1 tablespoon mushroom soy sauce

1 tablespoon oyster sauce

1 tablespoon cornstarch

½ teaspoon sugar

2 teaspoons rice wine

1 teaspoon ginger juice (see Note)

1 teaspoon Oriental sesame oil

2 teaspoons cooking oil

6 dried black mushrooms

2 Chinese sausages, cut in thin diagonal slices (see Note)

2 scallions, diced

1. Place chicken in a bowl. Add soy sauce, mushroom soy, oyster sauce, cornstarch, sugar, rice wine, ginger juice, sesame oil and cooking oil. Mix ingredients and pour over chicken. Allow to marinate at least 20 minutes.

2. While chicken is marinating, place mushrooms in warm water and soak until soft, about 20 minutes. Then remove stems and cut into thin strips.

3. Lightly oil a heatproof plate or dish that will fit into your steamer (a large Chinese bamboo steamer that fits into a wok is best). Spread the chicken on the plate with the marinade, scatter the mushroom strips over the chicken and then place the sausage slices on top.

4. Heat water in wok or steam pot so rack fits over, not in, it. When the water begins to boil, add the plate to the steamer, cover tightly and steam 20 minutes.

5. Remove dish from steamer, sprinkle with scallions and serve.

NOTES:

1. Ginger juice is made by pressing peeled, fresh ginger in a garlic press.

2. If Chinese sausage is unobtainable, ¼ pound smoked kielbasa or other garlic sausage may be substituted.

YIELD: 4 TO 6 SERVINGS ⤳ *Florence Fabricant*

KEN HOM'S STEAMED CHICKEN (ZHENG JI)

The simple but powerful sauce is an Asian equivalent of salsa or pesto. It radically changes the character of anything it touches, whether it's soup or a bowl of noodles with meat sauce. But also like salsa or pesto, this sauce is actually best reserved for the simplest, mildest dishes like this one, those with little flavor of their own.

1 chicken, about 3½ pounds	2 tablespoons finely chopped
1 tablespoon kosher salt	peeled fresh ginger
	5 tablespoons finely chopped
THE DIPPING SAUCE	scallions
Pinch of sugar	2 tablespoons peanut oil
½ teaspoon salt	1 teaspoon sesame oil
2 teaspoons light soy sauce	

1. Rinse the chicken under cold running water and blot completely dry with paper. Rub the salt inside the cavity and on the skin of the chicken. Place the chicken, breast-side down, on a heatproof platter, and set aside for 15 minutes.

2. Set up a steamer or put a rack into a wok or deep pan. Fill the steamer with about 2 inches of hot water. Bring the water to a simmer. Put the plate with the chicken into the steamer or onto the rack. Cover the steamer tightly and gently steam over medium heat for 1 hour. Replenish the water in the steamer from time to time. Remove the platter with the cooked chicken and pour off all the liquid and reserve to serve over the rice.

3. In a small bowl, combine the sugar, salt, soy sauce, ginger and scallions and mix well. In a small pan, heat the peanut and sesame oils until they are smoking. Pour the hot oils over the ginger mixture. Chop the chicken into serving portions (it can be served with or without the skin) and serve immediately with the sauce.

YIELD: 4 SERVINGS AS PART OF A CHINESE MEAL,
OR 2 AS A SINGLE DISH ⌒ *Ken Hom*

FLORENCE LIN'S STEAMED AND SMOKED CHICKEN

1 4-pound (approximately)
   roasting chicken
4 tablespoons coarse salt
1 tablespoon Sichuan peppercorns

¼ cup hickory chips (see Note)
2 tablespoons black tea leaves
2 teaspoons sesame oil

1. Clean the chicken by rinsing it with water. Drain and dry well. Brown the salt and peppercorns in a dry frying pan over moderate heat until the salt turns slightly brown and the peppercorns smell fragrant. Use a spoon to sprinkle the hot salt and pepper on the inside and outside of the chicken. With your hand rub the mixture in thoroughly and evenly. Place the chicken in a container with a cover, and store in the refrigerator overnight, or for up to two days for a more concentrated flavor.

2. Use a steamer or pot with a cover that is large enough to hold a deep dish that can hold the chicken. Pour water into the large pot until it is at least 1½ inches deep. Place a rack or ovenproof glass above the water. Set the chicken dish on the rack. Cover tightly, bring water to a boil, and steam for 45 minutes. Take the chicken out to cool and dry completely. Save the chicken liquid for other uses, such as soup stock or gravy.

3. Line the inside of a wok and its domed cover with aluminum foil. Sprinkle hickory chips and black tea over the bottom of the wok. Place an oiled rack in the wok. Lay the chicken on it. Cover the wok with the domed cover, and smoke over moderate heat for 15 minutes. Turn off the heat, and let stand for 5 minutes to allow the smoke to dissipate before removing the cover. If the hickory chips and tea leaves are not fully burned and the chicken's skin is not brown in color, continue smoking for 5 to 10 minutes.

4. Remove the chicken, and brush with sesame oil. Cut the chicken into small pieces. Smoked chicken can be made in advance and will keep for days in the refrigerator.

NOTE: If hickory chips are unobtainable, ¼ cup raw rice, ¼ cup black tea leaves, and 1 tablespoon sugar may be used instead. Smoke for 5 minutes only.

YIELD: 6 SERVINGS   *Fred Ferretti*

MOLLY O'NEILL'S STEAMED CHICKEN ROLLS STUFFED WITH RICE, LEMON AND HERBS

1 cup fresh basil leaves

1 cup fresh cilantro leaves

1 cup fresh mint leaves

1½ teaspoons grated lemon zest

3 tablespoons fresh lemon juice

3 large cloves garlic, peeled

1 teaspoon kosher salt, plus more to taste

2 tablespoons water

2 boneless, skinless chicken breasts (about 8 ounces each), split

Freshly ground pepper to taste

2 cups cooked white rice

Roasted-Lemon-and-Garlic Steaming Liquid or Chardonnay, Lemon and Herb
   Steaming Liquid (see recipes, page 171)

1. Place the basil, cilantro, mint, lemon zest, lemon juice, garlic, salt and water in a food processor. Process until the herbs are finely chopped, stopping several times to scrape down the sides of the bowl.

2. Pound the chicken to a scant ¼-inch thickness and season with salt and pepper. Press ½ cup of the rice over the surface of each piece of chicken. Spread the herb mixture over the rice. Starting with one of the long sides of the chicken, roll it up tightly, like a jelly roll. Repeat with the remaining chicken.

3. Place the chicken rolls in a steamer, cover and steam over the liquid for 12 minutes. Trim off the ends and cut across into 1-inch-thick slices. Divide among 4 plates and serve immediately.

YIELD: 4 SERVINGS  *Molly O'Neill*

MOLLY O'NEILL'S STEAMING LIQUIDS

CHARDONNAY, LEMON AND HERB STEAMING LIQUID

3 cups chardonnay
½ cup water
1 bay leaf
1 teaspoon dried rosemary
2 teaspoons dried thyme
½ teaspoon black peppercorns
1 lemon, thinly sliced

Combine the wine, water, bay leaf, rosemary, thyme, peppercorns and lemon in the bottom of the desired steaming equipment. Bring to a boil. Reduce heat and simmer for 1 minute. Begin steaming. Add boiling water if too much of the liquid evaporates before cooking is complete.

YIELD: ABOUT 3½ CUPS

✤ EASY ✤
ROASTED-LEMON-AND-GARLIC STEAMING LIQUID

2 small heads garlic, smashed
2 lemons, cut across into ⅛-inch slices
2 tablespoons olive oil
1 bay leaf
½ teaspoon black peppercorns
3 cups water

1. Preheat the oven to 375 degrees. Place the garlic on a large sheet of aluminum foil and surround with the lemon slices. Drizzle with the olive oil. Wrap the foil into a package and roast until the garlic is soft, about 1 hour.

2. Place the garlic, lemon slices and accumulated juices into the desired steaming equipment with the bay leaf, peppercorns and water. Bring to a boil. Reduce heat and simmer for 1 minute. Begin steaming. Add boiling water if too much of the liquid evaporates before cooking is complete.

YIELD: ABOUT 3½ CUPS

✦ EASY ✦

LEMONGRASS, CHILI AND MINT STEAMING LIQUID

3 stalks fresh lemongrass, coarsely chopped
1 large jalapeño, cut across into thin slices
½ bunch fresh mint, with stems
3 cups water

Combine lemongrass, jalapeño, mint and water in the bottom of the desired steaming equipment. Bring to a boil. Reduce heat and simmer for 1 minute. Place food in top of vessel and begin steaming. Add boiling water if too much of the liquid evaporates before cooking is done.

YIELD: ABOUT 3½ CUPS

+ EASY +
CURRY-MUSTARD STEAMING LIQUID

2 tablespoons Dijon mustard
3 tablespoons curry powder
3½ cups water

Whisk together the mustard, curry powder and water. Place in the desired steaming equipment. Bring to a boil. Reduce heat and simmer for 1 minute. Begin steaming. Add boiling water if too much of the liquid evaporates before cooking is complete.

YIELD: ABOUT 3½ CUPS

+ EASY +
SOY-GINGER STEAMING LIQUID

½ cup soy sauce
3 tablespoons sherry
3 tablespoons minced fresh ginger (unpeeled)
4 large cloves garlic, coarsely chopped
2½ cups water

Combine the soy sauce, sherry, ginger, garlic and water in the bottom of the steaming equipment. Bring to a boil. Reduce heat and simmer for 1 minute. Begin steaming. Add boiling water if too much of the liquid evaporates before cooking is complete.

YIELD: ABOUT 3½ CUPS *Molly O'Neill*

better ✓✓
day after

FLORENCE FABRICANT'S
BASIC POACHED CHICKEN
WITH CHICKEN SOUP

1 4-pound chicken, whole or split	2 stalks celery
Juice of ½ lemon	2 cloves garlic, peeled
Water	2 sprigs parsley
2 medium onions	2 sprigs fresh dill
2 leeks, well rinsed	10 whole black peppercorns
2 carrots, peeled	Salt

1. Remove the gizzards, heart, neck and liver from the chicken. Pull off any excess fat from the edges of cavity. Rinse the chicken in cold water, pat dry on paper towels and rub with the lemon juice. Place in a large, deep pot and cover with cold water to a depth of 2 inches. If necessary to fit the chicken comfortably in the pot, it can be split in half. Rinse the gizzards, heart and neck and add them as well. Reserve the liver for another use. It should not be added to poached chicken, because it will make the stock bitter. It can be frozen. The excess fat can be sautéed slowly in a small skillet to use for frying or it can also be frozen for future use.

2. Bring the water with the chicken to a boil.

3. While the water is coming to a boil, cut the root and top ends off the onions but do not peel them. The skin will enhance the color of the soup. Trim the roots and most of the green off the leeks and trim the root ends off the carrots. Cut or break the celery if necessary to fit it into the pot. Add the garlic. Tie the parsley and dill together in a piece of cheesecloth.

4. When the chicken has come to a boil, reduce the heat to a steady simmer and skim the surface of the water, removing the scum as it accumulates. Do this for at least 5 minutes, until relatively little scum reappears.

5. Add the vegetables, herbs and peppercorns. Continue simmering the chicken and vegetables slowly, skimming the surface from time to time, for one hour, until the juices of the chicken run clear when the thigh is pricked with a sharp fork. If necessary, additional water can be added to the pot during the cooking.

6. Remove the chicken from the pot, allowing it to drain well. Set it aside, covered, in a shallow bowl.

7. Pour the contents of the pot through a colander set into another large pot or a deep bowl that holds at least 6 quarts. Clean the original cooking pot. Pour the soup

through a large, very fine strainer into the cooking pot. If you do not have a large, very fine strainer, use a large strainer with a coarser mesh and line it with a clean linen napkin.

8. Bring the soup to a gentle simmer and allow it to cook for 20 to 30 minutes, until it has reduced and concentrated somewhat. Do not allow it to come to a boil or it will turn cloudy. When the soup tastes rich enough, season it with salt.

9. While the soup is simmering, retrieve vegetables you wish to serve with it and cut them into 1-inch pieces. Remove the skin from the chicken and cut it into serving pieces.

10. Serve the chicken and vegetables in bowls, with the hot soup spooned over them. If desired, noodles or rice can be cooked separately and added to the soup as well.

YIELD: 4 SERVINGS ⟿ *Florence Fabricant*

POACHED CHICKEN WITH GREEN SAUCE

3 quarts well-seasoned chicken stock

1 3½-pound chicken

6 cloves garlic

1 teaspoon whole white peppercorns

1 teaspoon whole coriander seeds

1 large onion, peeled and halved

Salt

1 cup, loosely packed, flat-leaf
    parsley leaves

1 teaspoon drained capers

2 tablespoons white wine vinegar

⅓ cup extra-virgin olive oil

Juice of ½ lemon

1 tablespoon Dijon mustard

Freshly ground black pepper to taste

Parsley sprigs and lemon wedges
    for garnish

1. Bring stock to a simmer in a saucepan or pot large enough to hold chicken. Lightly crush four cloves of garlic, peppercorns and coriander seeds. Add along with onion and salt to taste. Add chicken. Bring to a fast simmer, just under a boil, and cook

5 minutes, skimming constantly. Lower heat to very slow simmer and poach chicken about an hour, skimming from time to time, until leg juices run clear. Remove from heat and allow to cool in stock 30 minutes.

2. Turn on food processor. Drop remaining garlic in through feed tube and process until chopped. Shut off processor, scrape down sides of container and add parsley, capers and vinegar. Process until blended. Drizzle in olive oil and lemon juice. Remove to small bowl and stir in mustard. Season to taste with salt and pepper.

3. Remove chicken from poaching liquid. Reserve poaching liquid for another use, as stock or soup.

4. Remove skin from chicken. Cut up chicken in serving pieces and put on a platter. Decorate with parsley sprigs and lemon wedges and serve with green sauce.

YIELD: 4 SERVINGS   *Florence Fabricant*

POACHED CHICKEN WITH WATERCRESS SAUCE

1 lemon
1 chicken, 3 to 3½ pounds
1 onion, cut in half
2 cloves garlic, cut in half
2 stalks celery, with leaves
1 small bunch parsley
A few sprigs of thyme
Coarse sea salt and freshly
    ground pepper to taste

FOR THE SAUCE

1 bunch watercress, leaves only
¾ cup heavy cream
1 medium potato, boiled and
    mashed
3 to 4 tablespoons walnut oil
Coarse sea salt and freshly
    ground pepper to taste
Freshly grated nutmeg to taste

1. Cut the lemon in half, squeeze half over the chicken inside and out. Put the remaining half inside the chicken and truss the bird.

2. Put chicken in heavy casserole or kettle and add onion, garlic, celery, parsley, thyme, salt and pepper. Pour in 2 cups water and bring to boil. Reduce heat and cover. Simmer gently for 45 minutes to 1 hour, or until chicken is cooked: breast should be

firm, and legs should move at the joint but still be fairly firm. It is important not to overcook the chicken. When it is done, put it on a serving platter and keep warm in a low oven. Strain and skim chicken broth and reserve it for future use.

3. Meanwhile, wash the watercress leaves and blanch them in boiling, salted water. Drain and refresh under cold running water. Squeeze out as much water as possible.

4. Bring cream to a boil. Boil for 30 seconds, then put in blender with potato and walnut oil. Add watercress and blend till smooth. (If it needs liquid, add a little chicken poaching broth.) Season to taste with salt, pepper and nutmeg. Keep warm in a low oven. Serve the chicken with the sauce on the side.

YIELD: 4 SERVINGS   *Moira Hodgson*

+ EASY +

WHITE-CUT CHICKEN WITH TWO SAUCES

(Adapted from *The New York Times International Cook Book*)

In many Chinese restaurants "white cut" is a term for a delicate dish of poached chicken that is dipped in tangy sauces.

> 6 to 8 cups chicken stock
> 4 thin slices fresh ginger
> 1 scallion, trimmed and cut into 2-inch lengths
> 1 3- to 4-pound chicken

1. Heat the stock in a kettle and add the ginger and scallion. There should be enough stock to completely cover the chicken when it is added.

2. Place a metal teaspoon inside the chicken to help retain the heat, then add the chicken to the stock. If the stock does not completely cover the chicken, add boiling water to make up the difference.

3. When the stock starts to boil, reduce the heat to a simmer. Cover and simmer

20 minutes. Turn off the heat and leave the chicken in the stock for 2 hours, then remove from the stock and cut into 2½-inch cubes. Serve with Sesame-Flavored Dipping Sauce or Ginger-Pepper Dipping Sauce.

SESAME-FLAVORED DIPPING SAUCE

1 tablespoon sesame oil
½ cup soy sauce

1. Combine the oil and soy sauce and blend.

GINGER-PEPPER DIPPING SAUCE

1 tablespoon finely shredded peeled ginger
4 scallions, white part only, trimmed and shredded
½ teaspoon sugar
¼ cup vegetable oil
1 teaspoon salt
½ teaspoon hot pepper flakes or chopped hot green or red pepper

1. Place the ginger, scallions and sugar in a small heatproof dish.
2. Heat the oil and salt until hot but not smoking. Add the hot pepper and pour the mixture over the ginger mixture. Let cool. Serve as a dip or pour over the chicken as a sauce.

YIELD: 4 TO 6 SERVINGS

DAVID WALTUCK'S CHILLED WHITE-COOKED CHICKEN WITH GREEN SAUCE

(Adapted from *Staff Meals at Chanterelle*)

1 pound fresh ginger, unpeeled, plus 1 tablespoon peeled and finely grated

3 bunches scallions, trimmed

1 cup dry sherry

1 3- to 3½-pound chicken

¼ cup, packed, cilantro, minced, plus sprigs for garnish

1 large jalapeño, seeded and minced

1 tablespoon Asian sesame oil

½ teaspoon coarse salt, or to taste

⅓ cup canola or extra virgin olive oil, or ½ cup plain yogurt or mayonnaise

1. Rinse pound of ginger and, without peeling, cut it into ¼-inch dice. Place in large stockpot. Cut scallions, white and green parts, into 1-inch pieces. Place in stockpot. Add sherry and 8 cups water. Bring to a boil and boil 10 minutes.

2. Rinse chicken inside and out under cold running water. Pull off excess fat. Carefully place chicken in stockpot. When liquid returns to boil, reduce heat to very low, cover the pot and cook until chicken juices run clear, 45 minutes to 1 hour.

3. While chicken is cooking, combine minced cilantro, grated ginger, jalapeño, sesame oil and salt in small bowl. Warm canola or olive oil, if using, until hot. Pour over cilantro mixture, stir, check salt and set aside to cool to room temperature to use as dipping sauce. If not using oil, cilantro mixture can be folded into plain yogurt or mayonnaise for topping.

4. A few minutes before chicken is done, place a large bowl in kitchen sink and fill with cold water and 2 to 3 pounds ice. Remove cooked chicken from stockpot, draining well as you lift it out, and transfer chicken to ice bath. Chicken should be submerged. Allow to chill about 20 minutes, until cool to the touch inside and out.

5. Skin chicken, cut up at the joints, then cut breast and thighs in half or in thirds. Arrange on platter garnished with cilantro sprigs and serve with dipping sauce.

YIELD: 8 AS FIRST COURSE, 3 OR 4 AS MAIN COURSE   *Florence Fabricant*

CHICKEN TONNATO

(Adapted from *The New York Times Menu Cook Book*)

4 large chicken breasts, halved and skinned
1¼ cups dry white wine
1 onion, finely chopped
1 clove garlic, finely minced
1 can (7 ounces) tuna fish
6 anchovy fillets, chopped
½ teaspoon salt
¼ teaspoon freshly ground black pepper
1 teaspoon grated lemon rind
3 tablespoons lemon juice
4 cups cooked rice, cold
3 tablespoons chopped parsley
Capers

1. Combine the chicken with the wine, onion, garlic, tuna, anchovies, salt, pepper and lemon rind in a heavy saucepan. Cover, bring to a boil and simmer gently for 25 minutes, or until chicken is tender.

2. Transfer the chicken to a bowl. Put the sauce in which the chicken was cooked into the container of an electric blender or a food processor and puree it. Add the oil and lemon juice, blend and pour over the chicken. Cover and let stand overnight.

3. Spread the cold rice on a serving platter. Slice the chicken into large oval pieces, discarding the bones. Place the chicken over the rice. Add parsley to the sauce, pour over the chicken and rice, and sprinkle with capers.

YIELD: 6 SERVINGS

CIRCASSIAN CHICKEN IN WALNUT SAUCE

(Adapted from *Classical Turkish Cooking*)

The most interesting part of any Turkish meal is the meze (pronounced MEZZ-eh), or Turkish tapas, and the piece de resistance of the most elaborate meze table is Circassian chicken, poached chicken in a spicy ground walnut sauce. Although it is traditionally an appetizer, it may also be served as a main course, either hot or at room temperature.

1 large onion plus ½ cup minced
1 cup coarsely chopped carrots
8 peppercorns
Salt
2 bay leaves
6 sprigs parsley
3 pounds chicken, cut up
1 tablespoon walnut oil (see Note)
1 teaspoon plus 1 tablespoon paprika
4 slices day-old white bread, crusts removed
3½ cups walnuts
2 medium cloves garlic, crushed
⅛ to ¼ teaspoon cayenne pepper

1. Simmer the large onion, carrots, peppercorns, salt, bay leaves and parsley in 1½ quarts of water for 20 minutes. Add the chicken and continue simmering for 20 minutes longer, just until the chicken is done. Cool the chicken in the broth.

2. Meanwhile, heat the walnut oil over very low heat, stirring in 1 teaspoon of the paprika. Set aside in a warm place.

3. Soak the bread in a little water and squeeze it dry.

4. Grind the walnuts in a food processor or blender until fine. Spoon into a large bowl, and set aside.

5. When chicken is cool enough to handle, remove from broth; discard skin and bones, and tear meat into bite-size pieces and set aside. Strain the chicken stock and reserve.

6. Crumble the bread into the walnuts. Stir in garlic, ½ cup minced onion, 1 tablespoon paprika, cayenne and 2 cups of reserved stock. Mix and process in batches to make smooth paste, using more stock as needed to make a thick sauce of pouring consistency. Season with salt.

7. Mix half the sauce with the chicken pieces. Arrange the mixture on a serving platter, and pour the remaining sauce over it. Drizzle with hot walnut-paprika oil. Serve cold or at room temperature.

NOTE: Olive oil may be substituted for the walnut oil, or the teaspoon of paprika may be sprinkled over the sauce, although this will somewhat diminish the nutty flavor.

YIELD: 8 APPETIZER SERVINGS OR 4 MAIN SERVINGS *Marian Burros*

CHARLIE TROTTER'S STUFFED CHICKEN BREASTS POACHED IN TOMATO CONSOMMÉ

2 tablespoons fresh lemon juice
1 teaspoon apple cider vinegar
½ teaspoon salt, plus more to taste
1 teaspoon freshly ground pepper, plus more to taste
1 cup cooked wild rice
¼ cup minced celery leaves
¼ cup ground hazelnuts, lightly toasted
4 5-ounce chicken breasts
4 very thin slices prosciutto
1 quart tomato broth (see recipe below, which needs to be doubled)
1 tablespoon port wine

1. Combine lemon juice, vinegar, salt and pepper in a glass or ceramic bowl. Add the rice, 2 tablespoons of the celery leaves and 2 tablespoons of the hazelnuts. Toss and set aside.

2. Put each chicken breast in a large plastic bag or between two sheets of plastic wrap and gently pound with a rolling pin until each piece is ¼ inch thick. Lay the breast skin-side down, season with salt and pepper and spread with 3 tablespoons of the rice mixture. Cover with a thin sheet of prosciutto. Carefully roll the breast like a jelly roll. Tuck in the ends and tie with string in 4 or 5 places so that the breast will stay intact during poaching.

3. Heat the tomato broth to a boil and skim. Slide the chicken rolls into the broth. Lower heat and cook gently for 10 minutes, turning frequently. Make sure that the chicken remains covered with liquid. Remove the chicken and set aside. Add the port and continue cooking the tomato broth until it is thick and measures about 2 cups, about 5 minutes.

4. Use a knife to remove the ties from the chicken. Carefully slice each breast into pieces 1½ inches thick. Fan each in a circle on a plate. Ladle ½ cup of reduced tomato broth over each, sprinkle with the remaining celery leaves and hazelnuts and serve.

YIELD: 4 SERVINGS

TOMATO BROTH

Very ripe late-summer farm stand tomatoes are the key ingredient in this broth. You will need to double the recipe for the Stuffed Chicken Breasts.

> 2 pounds ripe tomatoes, pureed to equal 5 cups
> 1 tablespoon chopped basil
> 1 tablespoon chopped parsley
> 1 tablespoon chopped celery leaves
> ½ teaspoon salt
> ¼ teaspoon freshly ground pepper

Combine all the ingredients in a saucepan over medium heat. Bring to a boil and remove immediately. Pass through a fine mesh strainer, whisking occasionally to help the liquid pass through. The broth will keep for up to 1 week in the refrigerator. It will separate and need only be stirred. It can be frozen for up to 2 months.

YIELD: 3 CUPS 〜 *Molly O'Neill*

MIMI SHERATON'S
SUBGUM CHICKEN CHOW MEIN

(Adapted from *My Mother's Kitchen*)

This dish was a favorite of Mimi Sheraton's mother. It can be made with any cooked leftover meat (other than lamb), in place of the chicken. Although somewhat overcooked for today's tastes, Ms. Sheraton says that these dishes, with their meltingly tender vegetables and soothing garlic overtones, are for her what Federico Fellini once described as "the soft and gentle flavors of the past."

⅔ cup whole almonds, blanched
3 large half breasts chicken, poached, boned and skinned
2 teaspoons cornstarch
Pinch sugar
2 tablespoons dry sherry
3 tablespoons corn oil
Pinch salt
1 medium-size clove garlic, minced
4 stalks celery, diced
2 medium-size onions, peeled and thinly sliced vertically
10 small mushroom caps, sliced
¾ cup fresh bean sprouts, trimmed (optional)
8 small canned water chestnuts, cut in half and sliced
½ cup diced cooked ham
½ cup fresh green peas
⅔ to 1 cup hot chicken broth
2 medium-size tomatoes, chopped coarsely
White pepper to taste
3 cups Chinese fried noodles

1. Preheat the oven to 425 degrees.

2. Place the almonds in a single layer in a pie tin and roast for about 15 to 20 minutes. Check them every 7 or 8 minutes to see that they are toasting but not burning. When they are golden brown on one side, shake the pan to turn them and toast the other side. Remove and set aside.

3. Trim the bone, fat and gristle from the chicken breasts and cut the meat into cubes (⅓ to ½ inch each). You should have about 2 cups of meat. In a small bowl, combine the cornstarch with the sugar, dry sherry and 2 tablespoons of water. Set aside.

4. Heat the oil in a 12-inch iron skillet. Add the salt and garlic and sauté for 1 minute, or until the garlic loses its raw look. Do not let it brown. Add the celery and onion and sauté over moderate heat, stirring, for about 5 minutes, or until the vegetables are bright and begin to soften. Add the mushrooms and sauté, stirring, until their liquid evaporates.

5. Add the bean sprouts, if desired, and the water chestnuts, ham, peas and chicken. Ladle in about ⅔ cup of the chicken broth, bring to a simmer, then cover the pan and cook for 2 minutes. Add a little more broth if the mixture is too dry.

6. Over moderate heat, stir in the tomatoes and season with salt and white pepper. Reduce the heat and add the cornstarch mixture. Simmer for 1 or 2 minutes, or until the sauce is clear and the subgum is glossy. (If it is too gelatinous, ladle in more broth and stir until smooth.)

7. Serve at once on heated plates atop fried noodles and with rice on the side. Top each portion with a few roasted almonds.

YIELD: 4 SERVINGS *Mimi Sheraton*

THE CRISPY, THE CRUNCHY AND THE QUICKLY PREPARED

Three Steps to Crispiness

By Mark Bittman

Sautéed chicken should have the same attributes as fried chicken: meat that is moist and flavorful inside and crisp outside. Getting it that way is easy, but it took me nearly thirty years of experimentation to discover that the best method is also the simplest one. Only three rules apply.

First, you need a good chicken. This is not the time for a cotton-textured, mass-produced bird. I prefer kosher chicken, but that may be because for me the paradigm of pan-cooked chicken is my maternal grandmother's, and she kept a kosher kitchen.

Second, you need a large nonstick skillet, or two smaller ones, because there is no oil used to sauté and because crowding the chicken pieces prevents them from browning. The skillet should be large enough so that the pieces barely touch each other; they should certainly not overlap.

Finally, you have to pay attention. If the heat is too high, the chicken pieces will scorch and dry out; if it is too low, they will get soggy and never brown. The best heat level is medium, but some adjustments may be needed to guarantee even browning.

To finish, all you need is a squeeze of lemon.

MARK BITTMAN'S
SAUTÉED CHICKEN

Mark Bittman:"This recipe has only two or three crucial ingredients, but it is easy to vary. I like to add garlic and paprika, but a mild chili powder, like ancho, would work as well with the garlic. Other seasonings, in small amounts, are also good, like curry powder, five-spice powder or a mixture of cinnamon and allspice with a pinch of ground cloves."

> 1 chicken, 2 to 3 pounds, cut into serving pieces
> Salt and ground black pepper
> ½ teaspoon paprika or mild chili powder
> 1 teaspoon minced garlic
> Lemon wedges, optional

1. Season the chicken with salt and pepper, and arrange skin-side down in a nonstick skillet large enough to accommodate all the pieces without crowding; use two skillets if necessary. Turn heat to medium.

2. About 5 minutes after pieces begin to make cooking noises, peek at their undersides. If they are browning evenly leave them alone; otherwise, shift them as needed so they will brown evenly. Let every piece cook until evenly golden brown and crisp-looking before turning over and seasoning with paprika or chili powder. Adjust heat as needed. If pieces are scorching or spattering, turn heat down; if the chicken is cooking too slowly, raise it a bit.

3. When chicken is nearly done, add garlic to skillet. As pieces finish browning, turn them skin-side down once again. To test for doneness, cut into a piece or two; there should be no traces of blood, but some pinkness is okay. Breast pieces will finish first; you can keep them warm in an oven that's on low. Serve with lemon.

YIELD: 4 SERVINGS 〰 *Mark Bittman*

✦ EASY ✦
MARK BITTMAN'S
CHICKEN UNDER A BRICK

(Adapted from *The Minimalist Cooks at Home*)

Mark Bittman: "It isn't easy to cook chicken so that its skin is crisp and its interior juicy. Grilling, roasting and sautéing all have their problems. But there is an effective and easy method for getting it right, using two ovenproof skillets. A split chicken is placed in one of them, skin-side down. The other skillet goes on top as a weight, which helps retain moisture and insures thorough browning. The chicken is seasoned and marinated for a few minutes, or longer if there's time. Then it's seared in one skillet and weighted with the other before being transferred to a hot oven. Moving the hot, heavy pan from range to oven takes two hands, but the effort is well worth it. As a bonus at the end, much of the chicken's natural juices remain at the bottom of the pan; they make a perfect sauce, especially for rice. The dish is well known in Italy, where it is called chicken al mattone (a mattone is a heavy tile), but as a knowledgeable friend points out, it has roots in Russia as well. There it's called chicken tapaka (a tapa is a heavy skillet)."

1 whole 3- to 4-pound chicken, trimmed of excess fat, rinsed, dried and split,
    backbone removed
1 tablespoon fresh minced rosemary or 1 teaspoon dried rosemary
Salt and freshly ground black pepper to taste
1 tablespoon peeled and coarsely chopped garlic
2 tablespoons extra virgin olive oil
2 sprigs fresh rosemary, optional
1 lemon, cut into quarters

1. Place the chicken on a cutting board, skin-side down, and using your hands, press down hard to make it as flat as possible. Mix together the rosemary leaves, salt, pepper, garlic and 1 tablespoon of the olive oil, and rub this all over the chicken. Tuck some of the mixture under the skin as well. If time permits, cover and marinate in the refrigerator for up to a day (even 20 minutes of marinating boosts the flavor).

2. When you are ready to cook, preheat the oven to 500 degrees. Preheat an ovenproof 12-inch skillet (preferably nonstick) over medium-high heat for about

3 minutes. Press rosemary sprigs, if using, into the skin side of the chicken. Put remaining olive oil in the pan and wait about 30 seconds for it to heat up.

3. Place the chicken in the skillet, skin-side down, along with any remaining pieces of rosemary and garlic; weight it with another skillet or with one or two bricks or rocks wrapped in aluminum foil. The idea is to flatten the chicken by applying weight evenly over its surface.

4. Cook over medium-high to high heat for 5 minutes, then transfer to the oven. Roast for 15 minutes more. Remove from the oven and remove the weights; turn the chicken over (it will now be skin-side up) and roast 10 minutes more, or until done (large chickens may take an additional 5 minutes or so). Serve hot or at room temperature, with lemon wedges.

Until recently, I had always seasoned this dish as described above—with olive oil, garlic, rosemary and lemon, a standard quartet often found in Italian chicken dishes. But I have found several successful variations.

- Use different herbs; sage, savory and tarragon are all great. Russians use paprika.
- Try a light dusting of cinnamon, ginger and/or other "sweet" spice.
- Use minced shallots instead of garlic.
- Vary the acidic ingredient: balsamic or sherry vinegar, or lime can all pinch-hit for the lemon, depending upon the other flavors.
- Use clarified butter or a neutral oil, like canola or corn, in place of the olive oil.
- Leave European flavors behind entirely and make the dish Asian, using peanut oil and a mixture of minced garlic, ginger and scallions. Finish the dish with lime and cilantro, or soy sauce and sesame oil.

NOTE: A couple of clean rocks or bricks can be used instead of the second skillet. (If the weight of choice doesn't seem terribly pristine, it can be wrapped in foil.)

YIELD: 4 SERVINGS   *Mark Bittman*

PIERRE FRANEY'S SAUTÉED CHICKEN WITH RED WINE VINEGAR GLAZE

Glazes are sauces that are so thoroughly reduced that they can be used to coat meat, poultry or seafood. They are full flavored because of the heavy reduction. To save time and work in this recipe, everything is cooked in one pan, and the chicken rests in its own glaze. Since this sauce has little natural gelatin, a few tablespoons of butter are added at the last minute to bind it together.

1 whole chicken, about 3½ pounds	3 tablespoons red wine vinegar
6 ripe plum tomatoes, about 1 pound	2 sprigs fresh thyme or 1 teaspoon dried
Salt and freshly ground pepper to taste	1 bay leaf
2 tablespoons vegetable oil	2 tablespoons unsalted butter
4 tablespoons finely chopped shallots	4 tablespoons finely chopped fresh basil or parsley
2 teaspoons finely chopped garlic	

1. Cut the chicken into 10 serving pieces.

2. Drop the tomatoes into a pot of boiling salted water. Immediately remove from heat and let stand for about 10 seconds. Drain tomatoes and peel. Cut away and discard the core. Cut the tomatoes into ¾-inch cubes. There should be about 2 cups.

3. Sprinkle the chicken with salt and pepper to taste.

4. Heat the oil on medium heat in a large, heavy skillet. Brown chicken about 10 minutes on the skin side. Turn and brown 8 minutes on the other side. Drain off all the fat.

5. Sprinkle the shallots and garlic between the pieces of chicken and cook briefly, stirring, but do not brown. Add the vinegar and cook over medium heat until most of the vinegar has evaporated. Add the tomatoes, thyme and bay leaf. Cover tightly and simmer for 10 minutes.

6. Uncover and remove the sprig of thyme and bay leaf. Reduce the liquid by half. Swirl in the butter. Sprinkle with the basil and serve.

YIELD: 4 SERVINGS   *Pierre Franey*

LE PETIT TRUC'S CHICKEN WITH WHITE WINE VINEGAR AND TARRAGON

3 tablespoons extra-virgin olive oil

3 tablespoons unsalted butter

1 chicken, 3 to 4 pounds, cut into serving pieces, at room temperature

Salt and freshly ground black pepper to taste

4 shallots, minced

2 medium tomatoes, cored, peeled, seeded and chopped

½ cup dry white wine, such as Riesling

½ cup white wine tarragon vinegar

1 bunch fresh tarragon leaves, minced

1. In a large and deep-sided 12-inch skillet, melt the oil and 1 tablespoon of the butter over high heat. Season the chicken liberally with salt and pepper, and when the fats are hot but not smoking, add the chicken and brown on both sides until the skin turns an even, golden brown, cooking to desired doneness, about 12 minutes on each side. Carefully regulate the heat to avoid scorching the skin. (If you do not have a pan large enough to hold all of the chicken pieces in a single layer, do this in several batches.)

2. Transfer the chicken to a serving platter, cover loosely with aluminum foil and keep warm.

3. Discard the fat in the skillet. Return the skillet to the heat and, over medium-high heat, deglaze the pan with the wine. Add the shallots and tomatoes and cook for several minutes. Slowly add the vinegar and cook for an additional 2 or 3 minutes, stir in remaining 2 tablespoons of butter then return the chicken to the skillet. Coat well with the sauce, cover and continue cooking over medium heat until the chicken absorbs some of the sauce, just 2 or 3 minutes. Sprinkle with the tarragon and toss the chicken to coat. Serve immediately.

YIELD: 4 TO 6 SERVINGS   *Patricia Wells*

CHICKEN WITH SAUSAGE, ITALIAN-STYLE

4 sweet or hot Italian sausages
2 tablespoons olive oil
6 leg-thigh pieces of chicken, skinned and cut apart
1 onion, chopped
12 ounces fresh mushrooms, sliced
1 cup dry white wine
½ cup chicken stock
¼ teaspoon crushed red pepper, or to taste
Salt to taste

1. Prick sausages and brown them in the olive oil in a large skillet.

2. Add the chicken pieces and sauté them until lightly browned. Add the onion and mushrooms and sauté 10 minutes, stirring often.

3. Drain off surplus fat. Add all remaining ingredients, cover and simmer 15 minutes. Uncover and cook 5 to 10 minutes, or until the sauce is reduced by half. Serve with pasta.

YIELD: 6 SERVINGS   *Robert Farrar Capon*

⚝ CHICKEN SAUTÉ WITH PROSCIUTTO AND MUSHROOMS

(Adapted from *The New York Times Cook Book*)

2 3½-pound chickens, cut into serving pieces
Salt and freshly ground pepper
Flour for dredging
Oil for shallow frying
¾ cup dried porcini mushrooms
12 tablespoons unsalted butter
2 cloves garlic, finely minced
⅓ cup finely chopped onion
¼ pound prosciutto, cut into fine julienne strips
1 tablespoon chopped fresh sage
3 tablespoons lemon juice
¾ cup dry white wine

1. Sprinkle the chicken pieces with salt and pepper and dredge lightly in flour.

2. Heat the oil to a depth of about ⅓ inch in 1 or 2 large, heavy skillets. Cook the chicken pieces, turning often, until golden brown all over. Drain.

3. Place the mushrooms in a saucepan and add water to barely cover. Bring to a boil. Simmer for 1 minute and set aside.

4. Heat 8 tablespoons of butter in a skillet and add the garlic, onion and shallots. Cook, stirring, until wilted and add the prosciutto. Cook briefly and sprinkle with sage. Cook for about 3 minutes and add the browned chicken pieces.

5. Drain the mushrooms but reserve the cooking liquid. Add the mushrooms, lemon juice and white wine to the chicken. Add a little of the reserved mushroom cooking liquid and stir. Boil gently for about 5 minutes and add the remaining butter. When it melts, stir to blend and serve.

YIELD: 8 SERVINGS

IMAM BAYELDI
(CHICKEN BREASTS ON EGGPLANT)

Pierre Franey: "Imam bayeldi, *in Turkish, means 'the priest fainted' and indicates dishes that contain a combination of eggplant, onions, garlic and tomatoes, plus olive oil. Every time I have attempted to explain the origin of the term, I receive letters from readers offering their particular interpretations. The basic version is that the priest's wife was an outrageously good cook; she presented him with a dish that contained eggplant plus oil and the other ingredients, and he found it so excessively to his liking that he swooned. Other versions have it that he fainted because of the outlandish quantity of oil she used. I recently prepared chicken breasts sautéed and served on the* imam bayeldi *base and found it uncommonly good. It consists of fairly thick slices of eggplant, quickly sautéed and topped with the chicken plus a quickly made sauce of tomatoes, onions and garlic. It is easy to prepare in less than an hour.*"

  4 boneless chicken breast halves, about 1 pound
  Salt to taste, if desired
  Freshly ground pepper to taste
  4 eggplant slices, peeled, each about ¾-inch thick
  ¼ cup flour
  ¼ cup olive oil
  2 tablespoons corn, peanut or vegetable oil
  1 teaspoon finely minced garlic
  1½ cups crushed canned tomatoes, preferably imported
  ¼ teaspoon dried, crushed hot red pepper flakes
  1 teaspoon crumbled dried oregano
  ½ cup crumbled feta cheese

1. Preheat oven to 425 degrees.
2. Sprinkle chicken pieces with salt and pepper to taste and set aside.
3. Sprinkle eggplant slices with salt and pepper and coat lightly with flour. Shake off excess.
4. Heat olive oil in a skillet and when it is quite hot add eggplant slices. Cook about 2 minutes on each side until golden brown. Drain on paper towels. Arrange slices in one layer in baking dish.
5. Heat corn oil in clean skillet and add chicken pieces skin-side down. Cook

until golden brown, about 2 or 3 minutes. Turn pieces and cook until golden brown on second side, 2 or 3 minutes.

6. Top each slice of eggplant with one chicken breast half, skin-side up.

7. Add garlic to oil remaining in skillet and cook briefly. Add tomatoes, pepper flakes and oregano and cook down, stirring often, about 5 minutes.

8. Spoon equal portions of sauce over chicken pieces. Sprinkle evenly with cheese. Place in oven and bake 10 minutes.

YIELD: 4 SERVINGS   Pierre Franey

✢ EASY ✢

MARK BITTMAN'S CHICKEN WITH APRICOTS

(Adapted from The Minimalist Cooks Dinner)

Mark Bittmann: "I brown the chicken in a nonstick skillet with no fat, and that works well. A tablespoon or two of butter, stirred in at the end, will make the sauce richer. Or you can render some bacon, remove it, and brown the chicken in the bacon fat, then crumble the bacon and stir it in at the end of cooking

1 cup dried apricots	**1 chicken, cut into serving pieces**
¼ cup red wine vinegar	**1 medium onion, chopped**
½ cup red wine	**Salt and freshly ground black pepper**

1. Combine apricots in a bowl with vinegar, wine and ¼ cup water. Let soak while you brown the chicken.

2. Turn the heat to medium-high under a 12-inch nonstick skillet, and add chicken pieces, skin-side down. Cook, rotating but not turning pieces so they brown evenly. When they are nicely browned—take your time—turn them so they are skin-side up. Make a little space to add the onion, and cook, stirring the onion occasionally until it has softened a bit, a minute or two.

3. Add apricot mixture and bring to a boil; cook for a minute, then turn heat to low and cover. Cook until chicken is done, 15 to 20 minutes. Uncover, raise heat and season chicken well with salt and pepper. Boil away any excess liquid; sauce should not be too watery. Serve with white rice or any other cooked grain, or bread.

NOTE: Any dried fruit can be used, or a combination; with the short cooking time, even prunes will remain intact. But be aware that fruit dried with sulfur (the common method) becomes tender much faster than fruit dried organically, which needs a couple of hours of soaking before cooking.

YIELD: 4 SERVINGS ⤳ *Mark Bittman*

CHICKEN CHASSEUR

(Adapted from *The Best of Craig Claiborne*)

Craig Claiborne: "Chicken chasseur *is the French way of saying 'chicken hunter's-style.' The term actually means that mushrooms are included, and the original recipe, of course, was for wild mushrooms picked up on the way to the chase."*

     1 2½-pound chicken, cut into serving pieces
     Salt and freshly ground pepper to taste
     2 tablespoons peanut, vegetable or corn oil
     ¾ pound mushrooms, cut into thin slices, about 4 cups
     2 tablespoons finely minced shallots
     1 teaspoon finely minced garlic
     1 teaspoon dried tarragon
     1 bay leaf
     ½ cup plus 1 tablespoon dry white wine
     1 cup chopped tomatoes
     ¼ cup water
     ½ teaspoon arrowroot or cornstarch
     2 teaspoons finely chopped fresh tarragon or parsley

1. Sprinkle the chicken with salt and a generous grinding of pepper.

2. Heat the oil in a heavy skillet large enough to hold the chicken pieces in one layer. Add the chicken pieces skin-side down and cook for about 5 minutes, or until golden brown on one side.

3. Turn the pieces and cook until browned on the other side, about 5 minutes. Carefully pour off the fat from the skillet. Add the mushrooms and stir. Add the shallots and garlic and stir. Cook for about 5 minutes and add the dried tarragon and bay leaf. Cook the liquid in the skillet until it has evaporated.

4. Add the ½ cup wine and cook until the wine has almost evaporated. Add the tomatoes and water. Cover and cook for about 10 minutes.

5. Blend the arrowroot and the remaining 1 tablespoon of wine and stir it into the sauce. Cover and continue to cook for about 5 minutes. Serve sprinkled with chopped tarragon.

YIELD: 4 SERVINGS

✢ EASY ✢

CHICKEN IN APPLE-FLAVORED CREAM (VALLE D'AUGE)

(Adapted from *The New York Times Cook Book*)

This dish originated in Normandy, the French province famous for its apples and calvados, its apple brandy. The calvados gives the dish its unique, subtle flavor. Like all brandies, it can be old and smooth or quite rough, and it is worthwhile to spend the money to get a good quality. If no calvados is available, Apple Jack may be substituted.

6 tablespoons unsalted butter
2 broiling chickens, quartered
¼ cup warmed calvados (or other apple brandy)
2 small white onions, minced
1 tablespoon minced parsley

1 sprig fresh thyme or ⅛ teaspoon of dried thyme
Salt and freshly ground black pepper to taste
6 tablespoons cider
6 tablespoons heavy cream

1. In a large skillet heat the butter, add the chicken pieces and brown on all sides. Continue cooking, uncovered, 20 minutes. Add the calvados and ignite. When the flame has burned out, add the onions, parsley, thyme, salt, pepper and cider. Cover tightly and cook over low heat until the chicken is tender, about 20 minutes.

2. Remove the chicken to a warm platter and keep hot. Slowly stir the cream into the pan and heat thoroughly. Do not boil again. Correct the seasonings. Pour some of the sauce over the chicken and serve the remainder separately.

NOTE: You also may add one or two tart apples, peeled, cored and chopped, to the skillet after the brandy flame has burned out.

YIELD: 4 SERVINGS

SPICY GINGER AND
CITRUS CHICKEN

This easy dish of skinned chicken legs, with a sweet and spicy flavor from a mixture of chili and cumin powders, cayenne pepper, lemon and orange peels, ginger, garlic and apple cider, can be made ahead and reheated just before serving.

2 tablespoons olive oil

6 chicken legs (about 4 pounds), with skin and tips of drumsticks removed

1 teaspoon salt

1 teaspoon chili powder

1 teaspoon cumin powder

½ teaspoon dried thyme leaves

¼ teaspoon cayenne pepper

1 tablespoon flour

6 strips of lemon zest, cut off with a vegetable peeler

6 strips of orange zest, cut off with a vegetable peeler

¼ cup ginger pieces (washed, but not peeled)

4 cloves garlic, peeled

1 cup sweet apple cider

1. Heat the oil in a large saucepan until hot but not smoking. Add the chicken legs in one layer, and brown them over medium to high heat, turning occasionally, for 15 minutes.

2. Add the rest of the ingredients, bring the mixture to a boil, reduce the heat to low, cover, and cook gently for 15 minutes. Serve, 1 leg per person, with some of the cooking juices.

YIELD: 6 SERVINGS ⟶ *Jaques Pepin*

TEQUILA CHICKEN

2 tablespoons extra-virgin olive oil
1 frying chicken, cut up and patted dry
1 medium-size red onion, chopped
1 small sweet red pepper, seeded and chopped
1 jalapeño pepper, seeded and chopped
1 tablespoon pine nuts
1 teaspoon chili powder, or to taste
1 cup finely chopped fresh or canned tomatoes
½ cup silver tequila
Juice of 1 lime
Salt and freshly ground black pepper
1 cup cooked or canned and rinsed black beans
2 tablespoons chopped cilantro

1. Heat the oil in a large, heavy ovenproof skillet. Add the chicken pieces and cook over high heat until nicely browned. Do not crowd the chicken pieces in the pan and remove them as they brown.

2. Lower heat, add the onion and red pepper and sauté until tender.

3. Add the jalapeño and pine nuts and sauté for a minute or so, then stir in the chili powder. Add the tomatoes, tequila and lime juice.

4. Return the chicken to the pan along with any juices that may have been released by the chicken as it cooled. Baste with the pan juices and season with salt and pepper.

5. Cover and cook 40 minutes. Fold in the black beans and heat thoroughly. Sprinkle with cilantro and serve.

YIELD: 4 SERVINGS 〜 *Florence Fabricant*

CHICKEN IN FLAT BREAD

3 tablespoons olive oil

2 cups boneless chicken dark meat (about 4 large boneless thighs), cut into
  ½-inch cubes

1 teaspoon ground cumin

Salt and freshly ground black pepper to taste

1 medium onion, chopped

3 cloves garlic, chopped

1 tablespoon minced fresh ginger

⅛ teaspoon saffron threads crushed into
  ½ cup chicken stock

½ cup small pitted green olives, halved

½ teaspoon grated lemon rind

⅓ cup toasted sliced almonds

4 pieces pocketless pita bread or similar flat bread, each about 5 to 7 inches in
  diameter

½ cup cilantro leaves

1. Put 2 tablespoons of the oil in a large skillet over medium-high heat. Season the chicken with cumin and salt and pepper. Cook the chicken for 5 minutes, stirring so that it browns evenly.

2. Add the onion, garlic and ginger, and cook for 3 to 4 minutes, until the onion softens and turns light brown. Add the saffron stock, olives and lemon rind, and bring to a simmer. Cook for 10 minutes.

3. Preheat the broiler.

4. Adjust the salt and pepper for the tagine if needed, stir in the almonds, and reduce further so only a few tablespoons of liquid remain. Remove from the heat.

5. Brush one side of the bread with the remaining olive oil. Broil for a few minutes until it is lightly browned and slightly crisp.

6. Put the bread, crisp-side down, on a 12-by-12-inch sheet of foil. Divide the chicken among the four pieces of bread, and sprinkle with cilantro leaves. Roll into a cone, and secure the bottom by twisting the foil. Fold the top back to expose the top of the roll.

YIELD: 4 SERVINGS  *Sam Gugino*

All the Flavor, Outside-In

By Mark Bittman

Boneless chicken breasts have been a basic ingredient in France for a long time, but they did not become popular in the United States until at least the mid-1960's, when it was discovered that they made a good substitute for thin-sliced veal (scaloppine), which was considered prohibitively expensive. Now the boneless breast is emblematic of contemporary meat: virtually fat-free, reasonably priced, fast-cooking and, all-too-often, tasteless.

One basic technique, done intelligently, makes the most out of boneless chicken: sautéing. What I mean by intelligently is this: When you pan-fry a piece of chicken, you want to brown it because much of the flavor is coming from the exterior. But to brown a thin slice of chicken breast you must cook it at least three minutes per side over fairly high heat, by which time it is guaranteed to be as dry as sawdust.

But take a thicker piece of chicken breast, a half-breast that has not been sliced or pounded, or a boneless chicken thigh, and you have a piece of meat that takes almost 10 minutes to cook through, long enough to brown both sides gloriously while leaving the interior moist. The thickness gives you the flexibility to adjust the heat, raising it a bit if the exterior is not browning well, lowering it if it's burning, even extending the cooking if necessary.

The standard coating for sautéed chicken is flour. If you're after crunch and flavor, bread crumbs, which adhere to the meat with just a little egg, do the job nicely. Two things markedly improve the crumb coating: making your own, by coarsely grinding dried bread in a food processor, or using panko (Japanese bread crumbs). And you can increase the coating's flavor by adding freshly grated Parmesan. Best with Parmigiano-Reggiano, this is also good with Grana Padano (a Parmesan-like cheese from northern Italy) or dried sheep's milk cheese like pecorino Romano (which is stronger).

Great as this simple preparation is, it is even better when served on a bed of freshly cooked spinach. There is something about the combination that is superb.

MARK BITTMAN'S SAUTÉED CHICKEN BREAST WITH PARMESAN CRUST

¾ cup grated Parmesan

¾ cup coarse bread crumbs or panko

2 large eggs

2 tablespoons extra-virgin olive oil

2 tablespoons unsalted butter (or a little more oil)

1½ to 2 pounds boneless chicken breasts or thighs

Salt and pepper to taste

Chopped parsley leaves for garnish

Lemon wedges

1. Combine Parmesan and bread crumbs on a plate. Beat eggs in a bowl. Put a large nonstick skillet over medium-high heat and add oil and butter. Dip a piece of chicken in egg, then turn it over in bread crumbs once or twice: the more of this coating that adheres, the better. When butter melts, put chicken piece in pan; repeat until all chicken is used.

2. Sprinkle chicken with salt and pepper. Adjust heat so chicken cooks rapidly but coating does not burn. Turn pieces as each side becomes deep golden brown, about 4 minutes a side. As pieces are done—cut into them to make sure there are no traces of blood—remove them to a plate. Garnish with parsley and serve hot, with lemon.

YIELD: 4 SERVINGS *Mark Bittman*

CHICKEN BREASTS
WITH MUSTARD SAUCE

4 whole, skinless, boneless chicken breasts, about 2½ pounds total
Salt to taste
Freshly ground pepper to taste
3 tablespoons unsalted butter
2 tablespoons finely chopped shallots
½ cup dry white wine
1 cup heavy cream
3 tablespoons imported mustard, preferably whole-grain mustard such as
    Pommery Moutarde de Meaux
3 tablespoons finely chopped chives, optional

1. Split the chicken breasts in half lengthwise. Cut away and discard any carti-lage and connecting tissues. Sprinkle the breasts with salt and pepper.

2. Heat the butter in a large, heavy skillet and add the breasts in one layer. Cook over moderately low heat 3 to 4 minutes or until lightly browned. Turn the pieces and continue cooking 7 to 8 minutes.

3. Transfer the pieces to a warm platter. Add the shallots to the skillet and cook, stirring, about 30 seconds. Add the wine and cook, stirring, about 1 minute. Add the cream and cook down until reduced to about ¾ cup. Stir in the mustard; return the breast halves to the skillet and turn them in the sauce. Bring to a boil.

4. Sprinkle with chives and serve. Rice goes well with this dish.

YIELD: 4 SERVINGS ∽ *Craig Claiborne*

CHEF PAUL'S BRONZED
CHICKEN BREASTS

Paul Prudhomme:"Most of us eat a lot of chicken. It is not expensive and we know it is low in fat, especially the breast. Here is an easy way of cooking chicken that changes the taste into something totally delicious . . . my bronzing method causes the seasonings to caramelize on the outside of the chicken. You can serve it alone with vegetables or dice it into small cubes or strips and use it in all your favorite pasta and rice dishes."

SEASONING MIX

1 tablespoon plus 1 teaspoon Chef Paul Prudhomme's Poultry Magic® *or*
    Meat Magic®, Magic Barbecue Seasoning®, *or* Fajita Magic® (see Note)
or
1 tablespoon plus 1 teaspoon home-made seasoning blend of the following,
    mixed together:
    1 teaspoon salt
    1 teaspoon garlic powder
    ½ teaspoon red pepper, preferably cayenne
    ½ teaspoon onion powder
    ½ teaspoon black pepper
2 tablespoons melted unsalted butter, olive oil or vegetable oil
4 boneless, skinless, chicken breast halves (about 3 ounces each), about ¾-inch
    thick at thickest part, at near room temperature

1. Place a heavy nonstick skillet over medium-high heat until hot, about 7 minutes (375 to 400 degrees).

2. In order to have even-sized chicken breasts, you may wish to pound the thick end of the breasts slightly before cooking.

3. As soon as the skillet is hot, lightly drizzle or brush each side of each chicken breast-half with butter, then sprinkle one side of each breast-half evenly with ½ teaspoon of the Magic seasoning blend of your choice or the home-made seasoning blend (a total of 2 teaspoons). Place the chicken in the skillet, seasoned sides down, and sprinkle the topsides of the chicken breasts evenly with the remaining 2 teaspoons of seasoning blend.

Deviled Chicken Thighs (page 75).

PHOTOGRAPH AND STYLING BY ANDREW SCRIVANI

PRECEDING PAGE: *A Classic Roasted Chicken.*

FOODPIX/GETTY IMAGES

Steven Raichlen's Beer Can Chicken (page 106).

GREG SCHNEIDER

Alfred Portale's Buffalo Chicken Wings (page 157).

FACING PAGE:

Mark Bittman's Corn Flake Oven-Baked "Fried" Chicken (page 145).

Nigella Lawson's Chicken Tikka (page 216).

Georgian Chicken in Pomegranate and Tamarind Sauce (page 266).

PHOTOGRAPH AND STYLING BY ANDREW SCRIVANI

Nigella Lawson's Chicken and Apricot Masala (page 276).

4. Cook chicken until underside is bronze in color, 2 to 3 minutes. (Do not over-cook. Watch and you'll see a white line coming up the sides as the chicken cooks; when line is about one-half the thickness, chicken is ready to be turned.) Turn and cook until done, 2 to 3 minutes more, or to an internal temperature of 160 degrees. You can turn the chicken more than once or continuously until cooked to desired doneness. All cooking times are approximate.

5. Serve immediately.

NOTE: See "Selected Sources for Ingredients," page 352.

YIELD: 4 SERVINGS ✒ *Richard Flaste*

✦ EASY ✦
SAUTÉ OF CHICKEN BREASTS WITH LEMON

½ cup flour for dredging
Salt and freshly ground pepper to
taste
4 skinless boneless chicken breasts,
about 6 ounces each
2 tablespoons olive oil
4 sprigs fresh thyme or 1 teaspoon
dried

2 tablespoons finely chopped shallots
2 teaspoons finely chopped garlic
2 teaspoons grated lemon rind
3 tablespoons lemon juice
½ cup chicken broth, fresh or
canned
2 tablespoons unsalted butter

1. Season flour with salt and pepper, and dredge the chicken all over. Remove the excess flour.

2. Heat the oil in a heavy skillet large enough to hold the chicken pieces in one layer. Add chicken and cook, uncovered, over medium heat for 5 minutes or until lightly browned.

3. Flip the chicken and cook for 5 minutes more, or until cooked through. Carefully remove the oil from the skillet, leaving the chicken. Discard the oil.

4. Add the thyme, shallots and garlic, and cook for about a minute. Do not burn the garlic. Add the lemon rind, the lemon juice and the broth.

5. Scrape the skillet to dissolve the brown particles that cling to the bottom. Add the butter, and cook for 3 minutes longer. Serve immediately.

YIELD: 4 SERVINGS ∽ *Pierre Franey*

✦ EASY ✦
CHICKEN BREASTS
WITH MUSHROOMS AND CAPERS

4 boneless, skinless chicken breasts, about 1¼ pounds
Salt and freshly ground pepper to taste
2 tablespoons olive oil
¼ cup finely chopped onion
1 teaspoon finely chopped garlic
1 tablespoon chopped fresh rosemary or 1 teaspoon dried

½ pound small mushrooms; if large, cut in quarters
2 tablespoons red wine vinegar
4 tablespoons drained capers
½ cup fresh or canned chicken broth
1 tablespoon tomato paste
4 tablespoons chopped parsley

1. Sprinkle the chicken with salt and pepper.

2. Heat the oil in a heavy-bottomed skillet. Add the chicken breasts. Sauté them over medium-high heat, turning often, until lightly browned, about 5 minutes.

3. Add the onion, garlic, rosemary and mushrooms. Cook, stirring, about 5 minutes.

4. Pour off the fat and add the vinegar, stirring to dissolve the brown particles clinging to the skillet. Add the capers, broth and tomato paste and blend well. Bring to a boil, cover and simmer 5 minutes. Add the parsley and stir to coat the chicken well. Serve.

YIELD: 4 SERVINGS ∽ *Pierre Franey*

CHICKEN BREASTS
WITH MARSALA AND FRESH FIGS

1½ pounds skinless and boneless
    chicken breasts

3 tablespoons flour

1½ tablespoons extra-virgin olive oil

½ cup dry marsala wine

6 fresh green calmyrna figs, sliced

Juice of ½ lemon

Salt and freshly ground black pepper

½ tablespoon finely shredded
    basil leaves

1. Cut the chicken into about 12 pieces of uniform size. Dry them and toss them in the flour.

2. Heat the oil in a large skillet and cook the chicken over medium heat until it is lightly browned and cooked through, about 12 minutes. Remove the chicken from the pan.

3. Stir in the marsala, bring it to a simmer and add the figs. Heat the figs briefly, then stir in the lemon juice and season the sauce with salt and pepper. Return the chicken to the pan, stir gently to mix the ingredients then serve. Sprinkle each serving with some basil.

YIELD: 4 SERVINGS   *Florence Fabricant*

PIERRE FRANEY'S CHICKEN BREASTS WITH FENNEL SAUCE

4 skinless, boneless chicken breast halves, about 1¼ pounds
Salt and freshly ground white pepper to taste
1 head fennel, about ¾ pound
2 tablespoons olive oil
4 tablespoons finely chopped shallots
¼ cup dry white wine
¼ cup fresh or canned chicken broth
1 bay leaf
2 sprigs fresh thyme or ½ teaspoon dried
Dash Tabasco sauce
2 tablespoons unsalted butter
4 fennel leaves, finely chopped

1. If the chicken breast halves are connected, separate and trim membrane or fat. Salt and pepper to taste.

2. Trim the fennel and save 4 green leaves for chopping, leaving only the white bulb at the bottom. Cut the bulb into ¼-inch cubes. There should be about 1½ cups.

3. Heat the oil in a nonstick skillet over medium-high heat. Add the chicken breasts and cook until lightly browned, about 3 minutes. Add the shallots.

4. Turn the chicken breasts and scatter the fennel around them. Continue cooking, shaking the skillet and redistributing the fennel, until it is cooked evenly. Cook about 3 minutes. Add the wine, broth, bay leaf, thyme and Tabasco sauce. Cover tightly and cook over medium heat for 10 minutes. Turn the pieces occasionally.

5. Transfer the chicken to a warm platter, cover with foil and keep warm.

6. With a slotted spoon, remove about ½ cup of the fennel cubes. Remove the bay leaf and thyme sprig. Pour the remaining fennel mixture into a blender or food processor. Add the butter and blend to a very fine puree. Pour the mixture into a saucepan, season with salt and pepper as needed. Add any liquid that may have accumulated around the chicken. Add the reserved fennel cubes and the chopped fennel leaves. Bring to a simmer and spoon the sauce over the chicken breasts. Serve immediately.

YIELD: 4 SERVINGS ⟋ *Pierre Franey*

CHICKEN BREASTS
WITH SWEET PEPPER STRIPS

(Adapted from *The Best of Craig Claiborne*)

4 skinless, boneless chicken breast halves, about 2 pounds
Salt and freshly ground pepper
3 tablespoons unsalted butter
½ teaspoon finely minced garlic
½ pound sweet red or green peppers, cored, seeded and cut into thin strips,
 about 2 cups
½ cup dry white wine
1 tablespoon finely chopped parsley

1. Sprinkle the chicken with salt and a generous grinding of pepper.

2. Heat 2 tablespoons of butter in a skillet and add the chicken pieces, skin-side down. Cook for about 4 minutes, or until golden brown on one side. Turn and continue cooking for about 4 minutes.

3. Add the garlic and pepper strips. Cook for about 4 minutes. Add the wine. Cover and cook about 4 minutes longer.

4. Remove the chicken pieces to a warm serving dish.

5. Add the remaining tablespoon of butter to the peppers and stir. Pour the peppers and sauce over the chicken. Sprinkle with parsley.

YIELD: 4 SERVINGS

CHICKEN BREASTS CREOLE-STYLE

Many of the building blocks of Creole cooking are incorporated into this dish: onion, olive oil, tomato, hot-pepper sauce and green pepper. The quick sauce is made in a pan, and then the pounded chicken breasts are sautéed until golden. The result is richly flavored and distinctively Creole dish.

4 skinless, boneless chicken breasts, halved, about 1¼ pounds
1 tablespoon olive oil
¾ cup onion strips
¾ cup cored, seeded and julienned green pepper
¾ cup sliced celery
1 tablespoon finely chopped garlic
1 bay leaf
1 tablespoon paprika
1 cup peeled, diced tomatoes, or 1 cup canned crushed tomatoes
Salt and freshly ground pepper to taste
1 teaspoon Worcestershire sauce
1 teaspoon hot-pepper sauce (like Tabasco)
1 tablespoon unsalted butter
1 tablespoon wine vinegar
4 tablespoons water or chicken broth
4 tablespoons finely chopped parsley

1. Place half a chicken breast between sheets of plastic wrap. Pound lightly to a thickness of ¼ inch with a flat mallet or meat pounder. Repeat with the remaining halves.

2. Heat the olive oil in a large skillet. Add the onions, green peppers, celery, garlic and bay leaf. Cook, stirring, until the onions become transparent. Add the paprika, the tomatoes, and salt and pepper to taste. Stir well. Continue cooking for 3 to 4 minutes.

3. Add the Worcestershire sauce and the hot-pepper sauce. Simmer until the sauce is reduced, about 5 minutes. Set aside.

4. Meanwhile, sprinkle the chicken with salt and pepper to taste. Heat the butter in a heavy skillet over medium heat, and cook the chicken breasts until golden on one side, about 4 minutes. Turn the pieces and cook for 4 minutes more or until done. Be careful not to overcook.

5. Add the vinegar, water or chicken broth, cover, bring to a boil, and simmer for 2 minutes. Remove the bay leaf. Keep warm.

6. To serve, divide the Creole sauce among 4 serving plates. Place the chicken breasts over the sauce and pour the gravy from the skillet over them. Sprinkle with parsley.

YIELD: 4 SERVINGS

CHICKEN BREASTS BASQUAISE

2 tablespoons olive oil

2 boneless chicken breasts

Coarse salt and freshly ground
    pepper to taste

3 ounces prosciutto, chopped

1 medium onion, thinly sliced

1 clove garlic, minced (green part
    removed)

1 teaspoon thyme leaves

1 cup dry white wine

1 cup canned or fresh, peeled Italian
    plum tomatoes, chopped, with
    their juice

2 pimentos or red peppers

¼ cup black oil-cured olives, pitted

2 tablespoons flat-leaf parsley

1. Heat the oil in a large skillet. Cut the chicken into inch-and-a-half pieces, and season with salt and pepper. Brown the chicken pieces; remove and set aside.

2. Add the prosciutto, onion and garlic. Sauté for 2 to 3 minutes over low heat, stirring from time to time. Add the thyme, wine and tomatoes. Stir well to scrape up the cooking juices. Cover and cook for 15 minutes.

3. Add the pimentos and olives, and cook for 10 more minutes or until the sauce is quite thick.

4. Return the chicken pieces to the pan, and cook for 3 to 5 minutes, or until they are done. Sprinkle with parsley and serve.

YIELD: 4 SERVINGS ~ *Moira Hodgson*

NIGELLA LAWSON'S
CHICKEN TIKKA

Nigella Lawson: "Tikka refers to the marinade—hot spices in cool yogurt—which tenderizes the chicken and infuses it with aromatic, mellow fire. It also happens to be just about the most beautiful way of cooking a chicken breast: the meat is tinted a deep gold as the marinade that clings to the surface is cooked (forgo the butter and use a nonstick pan if you prefer, but be careful the yogurt doesn't burn). The heat and sharpness of the tikka is emphatically echoed in the red onion relish. I always make sure I have enough chicken to eat cold for another meal. I eat it as is, or pile lettuce on a plate, and add some sliced chicken with some onion relish on top. I find this a particularly addictive meal, and I often leave some breast fillets in their marinade in the fridge so that they are ready for me to cook up in a day or two."

2 garlic cloves, peeled

1 2-inch piece of ginger, peeled and coarsely chopped

2 small red chilies

1 teaspoon ground cumin

1 teaspoon ground coriander

½ teaspoon turmeric

½ teaspoon garam masala (available in many supermarkets and specialty stores)

Juice of 1 lime

1 cup plain yogurt

3 tablespoons plus 1 teaspoon peanut oil

4 6- to 8-ounce boneless, skinless chicken breast halves

2 tablespoons unsalted butter

1 or 2 limes cut into thin wedges

Spicy Red Onion Relish, optional (see recipe below)

1. In a food processor or blender, combine garlic, ginger and chilies. Process until finely chopped. Add cumin, coriander, turmeric, garam masala, lime juice, yogurt and 3 tablespoons peanut oil. Process again to make a smooth paste.

2. Place yogurt mixture in a wide, shallow bowl. Add chicken pieces, turning them to coat them well. Cover bowl with plastic wrap and refrigerate a minimum of 4 hours.

3. Allow chicken to come to room temperature before cooking. Remove chicken from marinade, scraping off excess. Place a large skillet over medium-low heat, and add butter and remaining teaspoon peanut oil. When butter has melted, add chicken. Sauté, turning once or twice, until chicken is golden brown on surface and white in center, 15 to 20 minutes. (Adjust heat as necessary so that yogurt does not burn.) Arrange chicken on a platter, and garnish with lime wedge and Spicy Red Onion Relish, if desired.

YIELD: 4 SERVINGS ⌒ *Nigella Lawson*

SPICY RED ONION RELISH

2 small or 1 large red onion, peeled
1 tomato
3 tablespoons chopped cilantro leaves
½ teaspoon hot red pepper flakes, more to taste
Salt and freshly ground black pepper
Juice of 1 lemon

1. Cut onions in half, and slice into thin half moons. Place in a bowl.
2. Halve tomato and discard seeds and pulp. Dice tomato and add to onion.
3. Add cilantro and pepper flakes, and season with salt and black pepper to taste. Add lemon juice, and stir well. Allow to macerate at room temperature for 30 minutes before serving.

YIELD: 4 SERVINGS ⌒ *Nigella Lawson*

BREAST OF CHICKEN
INDONESIAN-STYLE

4 skinless boneless chicken breast halves, about 1¼ pounds
Salt and freshly ground pepper to taste
1 tablespoon soy sauce
1 teaspoon honey or brown sugar
2 tablespoons fresh lemon juice
1 tablespoon ground cumin
⅛ teaspoon cayenne pepper
½ teaspoon turmeric
1 tablespoon ground coriander
2 teaspoons finely chopped garlic
2 tablespoons vegetable oil

1. Place the chicken in a mixing bowl. Add salt, pepper, soy sauce, honey, lemon juice, cumin, cayenne, turmeric, coriander and garlic. Blend well so that the pieces are well coated. Cover with plastic wrap and refrigerate for at least 30 minutes or overnight.

2. Heat the oil in a skillet large enough to hold the pieces in one layer without crowding. Over medium heat, add the pieces of chicken and cook until browned on one side. Turn the pieces and reduce the heat to medium high. Cook until done. Total cooking time is about 10 minutes. After the pieces are cooked, transfer them to paper towels and keep them in a warm place. Serve hot.

YIELD: 4 SERVINGS   *Pierre Franey*

CHICKEN WIENER SCHNITZEL

4 whole chicken breasts, boned
Coarse sea salt and freshly ground pepper to taste
Flour for dredging
2 large eggs
¼ cup milk
2½ cups bread crumbs
5 tablespoons unsalted butter, approximately
6 tablespoons olive oil, approximately
2 lemons, cut into wedges

1. Cut the chicken breasts in half, and pound them flat with a rolling pin.

2. Season the breasts with salt and pepper, and dredge them lightly with flour. Beat the eggs with the milk, and dip the breasts first in the milk, then in the bread crumbs.

3. Meanwhile, heat 1½ tablespoons butter and 2 tablespoons olive oil in a large, heavy frying pan. Working in three batches, sauté the chicken breasts over high heat without crowding them, until they are golden on both sides. Drain on paper towels. After each batch, wipe the pan clean with a paper towel. Heat more butter and oil, and sauté the remaining pieces of chicken a few at a time.

4. Arrange the wiener schnitzel on a platter and serve at room temperature, garnished with lemon wedges.

YIELD: 4 TO 6 SERVINGS ✏ *Moira Hodgson*

ORIGINAL CHICKEN CORDON BLEU

(Adapted from *American Gourmet*)

4 large, boned and skinned chicken breast halves (about 1½ pounds)
4 thin slices smoked ham
2 ounces Swiss cheese, cut into 4 equal "fingers"
¼ cup flour
½ teaspoon salt
¼ teaspoon pepper
1 large egg, beaten
¾ cup fresh bread crumbs
¼ cup unsalted butter
½ cup plus 2 tablespoons chicken stock
½ cup white wine, heavy cream or additional chicken stock

1. Lay the chicken breasts between pieces of wax paper and use a mallet to pound them to between ¼ inch and ⅛ inch thick. Take care not to pound holes in the chicken. Layer each breast with the ham, then place a finger of cheese in the center. Roll up to completely enclose the ham and cheese and secure with toothpicks.

2. In a medium bowl, combine the flour, salt and pepper. Lightly dredge the chicken in the seasoned flour, then dip in the egg and coat with bread crumbs. Place on a baking sheet and chill at least 15 minutes and up to 4 hours.

3. In a large skillet over medium heat, heat the butter. Add the chicken and cook, turning carefully with tongs, until browned, about 8 to 10 minutes. Add ½ cup of the stock to the skillet, reduce the heat to medium-low, cover and simmer until the chicken is cooked through, 10 to 15 minutes. Move the chicken to a warm platter.

4. Add the remaining 2 tablespoons of stock to the skillet, raise the heat to high, and cook, stirring up browned bits clinging to the bottom, for 1 minute. Add the wine (or heavy cream or additional stock), lower the heat and simmer uncovered until the consistency of gravy, about 45 seconds. Pour over the chicken breasts and serve.

YIELD: 4 SERVINGS   *Molly O'Neill*

Meuniere and Its Many Variations

By Mark Bittman

Traditionally, the term "meuniere" has a specific meaning, usually referring to fillets of sole that are floured and sautéed quickly, then finished with lemon juice, parsley and browned butter.

But there's no reason to be parochial about it. This is a fast, surprisingly elegant approach to boneless, skinless chicken breasts, or cutlets of pork, turkey, veal or a variety of other foods, like shrimp, scallops and calf's liver. As long as the slice won't fall apart in the pan and will cook through in the time it takes to form a crust—just six to eight minutes—it's a suitable candidate.

Once you have the technique perfected (it won't take much practice, I promise), you'll be able to apply it to so many foods that months will pass before you repeat yourself.

Other than the chicken breasts, the remaining ingredients are insignificant. You might dip the meat in a quick milk bath to help the flour adhere, but it is usually moist enough to make this treatment superfluous. Although the traditional cooking medium is clarified butter, it is also perfectly acceptable to use a neutral oil like grape seed or canola. Varying the oil is one way of varying the dish; extra-virgin olive oil or peanut oil will modify the flavor.

Beyond that, there are several points to keep in mind:

- Use a large, flat-bottomed skillet, preferably one with deep, sloping sides, which makes turning easier and minimizes spattering.
- Preheat the skillet before adding the oil, and make sure the oil is hot before adding the meat (a pinch of flour will sizzle when tossed into the oil). This will prevent sticking and insure proper browning.
- Use enough oil or clarified butter to cover the bottom of the skillet; meat that does not come in contact with the oil will steam rather than sauté, and become soggy instead of crisp.
- Do not crowd the meat; if necessary, work in batches (finished pieces keep well in a 200-degree oven). Add when cooking the first side, keep the heat high (or medium-high, depending on your stove). Lower it a bit after you turn the cutlets if the coating starts to scorch.

The little bit of browned butter added at the end is a luxury, but hearing and see-ing the lemon juice and parsley sizzle when the butter hits it—preferably at the table, so everyone can enjoy it—is a thrill.

MARK BITTMAN'S CHICKEN CUTLETS MEUNIERE (AND VARIATIONS)

(Adapted from *The Minimalist Cooks at Home*)

4 boneless, skinless chicken cutlets (2 breasts), 1 to 1½ pounds
Salt and freshly ground black pepper
1 cup (approximately) flour or cornmeal for dredging
Oil or clarified butter to a depth of ⅛ inch in a 12-inch skillet (about 1 cup)
1 to 2 tablespoons unsalted butter, optional
1 tablespoon fresh lemon juice
2 tablespoons minced parsley

1. Heat a 12-inch skillet, preferably nonstick, over medium-high heat for about 2 minutes. While it is heating, sprinkle the chicken breasts with salt and pepper, and place the flour or cornmeal on a plate.

2. Place the oil or clarified butter in the skillet, and turn the heat to high. When the oil is hot, dredge the cutlets in the coating, turning them a few times and pressing them down so they are well covered. After you dredge each, add it to the pan.

3. Cook until the chicken is nicely brown, 3 to 5 minutes, then turn. Cook 2 to 4 minutes until the chicken is firm to the touch (lower the heat if the coating begins to scorch).

4. Meanwhile, if using the optional butter, melt over medium heat until it is nut brown.

5. When the chicken is done, drain it briefly on a paper towel, then transfer to a warm platter. Drizzle with lemon juice, and top with half the parsley. At the last minute, pour the browned butter over the chicken, add the remaining parsley and serve.

Chicken meuniere is a dish made for variations. Here are a few to try:

1. Instead of flour or cornmeal, substitute bread crumbs (seasoned with finely minced garlic and parsley if you like), ground nuts or sesame seeds.
2. Stir a tablespoon or more of a spice mixture like chili powder or curry powder into the coating.
3. Add a garlic clove or some chopped herbs (or both) to the butter as it browns.
4. Add a teaspoon of balsamic vinegar or a tablespoon of capers (or both) to the browned butter, and omit the lemon juice.

YIELD: 4 SERVINGS   *Mark Bittman*

These Patties Need No Filler Or Buns

By Mark Bittman

Calling something a chicken burger makes it sound like either fast food or a 1950's throwback. But if you make this dish with up-to-the-minute ingredients, the result is far better than any burger alternative I know.

Using chicken is not new. Even before fat was an issue, cooks were making flat patties from scraps of poultry and calling them cutlets, because they were designed to replace veal or pork. They were kept moist by mixing the chicken with cream or a thickened but not flavorful white sauce—little more than flour and milk. (Of course, there was also the barely mentionable addition: canned cream of mushroom soup.)

The same concept can be improved (minus fatty sauces or soups) with some potent ingredients most people have on hand—garlic, dried mushrooms and grated Parmesan. These burgers have no filler and need no buns. Nearly pure protein, they couldn't be more contemporary.

This is a simple winning combination, but you still have to be careful preparing the burgers. The chicken must be chopped, not pureed; too fine a texture will create an almost impenetrable patty. The chopping can be done in a food processor as long as you pay attention. And although the meat must be cooked through, it should not overcook or, again, it will become tough. When the burger feels just firm to the touch, it's done. Grill these burgers if you like or sauté in olive oil or, better still, butter.

As for serving, they're too good for buns and ketchup. I like them with mustard or lemon juice, with a salad on the side. Vary the taste by adding a little chopped ginger, by substituting a fistful of cooked spinach (nearly squeezed dry) for the mushrooms, or by adding a quarter of a cup of chopped parsley or other herb. Of course, you could substitute turkey for the chicken; pork, beef, veal or a combination will also work.

MARK BITTMAN'S CHICKEN-MUSHROOM BURGERS

(Adapted from *The Minimalist Cooks Dinner*)

1 ounce dried porcini or shiitake mushrooms
4 ounces Parmesan (about 1 cup grated)
2 cloves garlic, peeled
1 teaspoon freshly ground black pepper
Pinch salt
1½ pounds boneless, skinless chicken or turkey breasts
2 tablespoons olive oil or unsalted butter

1. Put the dried mushrooms in a bowl and cover with hot water.

2. Cut Parmesan into chunks; put it in container of food processor with garlic; process until grated (if Parmesan is already grated, just pulse a couple of times).

3. Add the pepper, salt and chicken or turkey and pulse the machine on and off until the mixture is chopped but not pureed.

4. Squeeze excess water from mushrooms, but do not wring them completely dry, and add to the machine. Pulse 2 or 3 more times, until mixture is more or less combined but, again, not pureed.

5. Put olive oil in a 12-inch nonstick skillet, and turn heat to medium. Wait a couple of minutes, then shape chicken mixture into 8 small burgerlike cakes. Cook 3 minutes a side, or until nicely browned. Do not overcook; when burgers are firm, they are done. Serve hot or at room temperature.

YIELD: 4 SERVINGS   *Mark Bittman*

✦ EASY ✦
CRAIG CLAIBORNE'S
CLASSIC CHICKEN BURGERS

(Adapted from *The Best of Craig Claiborne*)

Craig Claiborne: "Do not be put off by the pedestrian name of this dish. It is a variation of chicken cutlet pojarski without the sour cream."

2 pounds skinless, boneless chicken breasts
Salt and freshly ground pepper to taste
½ cup finely chopped parsley
1 cup fine fresh bread crumbs
1 teaspoon ground cumin
¼ cup chicken broth or water
4 tablespoons unsalted butter, approximately

1. Trim the breasts to remove all nerve fibers, cartilage, and so on. Cut the chicken into cubes.

2. Put the prepared breast meat into the container of a food processor and process until chopped fairly, but not totally, smooth.

3. Scrape the chicken into a mixing bowl. Add the salt, pepper, parsley, bread crumbs, cumin and broth or water. Blend well with the hands.

4. Divide the mixture equally into 12 portions. Using dampened hands, pat the portions into flat, round patties. Chill until ready to cook.

5. These patties are excellent when cooked on a preheated charcoal grill, about 4 minutes to a side. Or cook them in a little butter in a heavy skillet, 4 to 5 minutes to a side. Do not overcook. Serve with a little melted butter poured over.

YIELD: 6 SERVINGS

CHICKEN PATTIES
WITH TARRAGON

(Adapted from *The Best of Craig Claiborne*)

3 whole skinless, boneless chicken breasts, about 1½ pounds
½ cup bread crumbs
⅛ teaspoon grated nutmeg
Pinch of cayenne
Salt and freshly ground pepper to taste
2 teaspoons plus 1 tablespoon chopped fresh tarragon
½ cup heavy cream
4 tablespoons peanut, vegetable or corn oil
2 cups tomato sauce of your choice

1. Trim off all fat, cartilage, and membranes from the chicken. Cut the chicken into 1-inch cubes. Put the cubes into the container of a food processor and process until the meat is coarse-fine. Do not overprocess or it will be like pulp.

2. Put the ground chicken into mixing bowl and add the bread crumbs, nutmeg, cayenne, salt and pepper, 2 teaspoons of the tarragon and the cream. Blend well by beating with a wooden spoon. Chill the mixture.

3. Shape the mixture into 12 patties.

4. Heat the oil in a skillet and add the patties. Cook until golden brown on one side, about 3 minutes. Turn and cook on the other side for about 3 minutes.

5. Serve the patties with the tomato sauce of your choice and the remaining chopped tarragon sprinkled over.

YIELD: 6 SERVINGS

CHICKEN BREASTS
WITH SWEET RED PEPPERS
AND SNOW PEAS

The addition of red onions, water chestnuts, sesame seeds, ginger and cilantro make this dish exceptionally colorful.

4 chicken breast halves, skinless and boneless, about 1¼ pounds
1 tablespoon cornstarch
2 tablespoons light soy sauce
2 tablespoons dry white wine or water
3 tablespoons olive oil
½ teaspoon red pepper flakes (optional)
Salt and freshly ground pepper
2 large sweet red peppers, cored, seeded and cut into ½-inch cubes

¼ pound snow peas, trimmed and washed
½ cup sliced water chestnuts or bamboo shoots
¼ cup coarsely chopped red onion
1 tablespoon sesame seeds
1 tablespoon finely chopped garlic
1 tablespoon grated fresh ginger
¾ cup fresh or canned chicken broth
4 tablespoons coarsely chopped cilantro

1. Using a sharp knife, cut chicken breasts in half lengthwise then crosswise into slices ½ inch thick.

2. In a small mixing bowl, combine the cornstarch, soy sauce and white wine or water, blend well and set aside.

3. In a wok or a large nonstick skillet, add oil over high heat. Add chicken, pepper flakes and salt and pepper. Cook and stir about 1 minute. Scoop out the chicken pieces, leaving the oil. Set aside.

4. Add red peppers, snow peas, water chestnuts or bamboo shoots, onions and sesame seeds and cook over high heat, stirring, about 1 minute or until crisp and tender. Add garlic and ginger. Cook briefly over high heat. Add chicken and chicken broth. Cook stirring and tossing for 1 more minute.

5. Add cornstarch mixture, cook and stir for 15 seconds. Sprinkle with cilantro and serve immediately.

YIELD: 4 SERVINGS   *Pierre Franey*

✢ EASY ✢
VATCH'S STIR-FRY CHICKEN
WITH GINGER

(Adapted from *Vatch's Southeast Asian Cookbook*)

2 tablespoons canola oil
½ pound boneless chicken breast, sliced in thin strips across the grain
2 tablespoons Chinese oyster sauce
1 2-inch piece of fresh ginger, peeled and cut in matchsticks
1 teaspoon sugar
3 scallions, cut in 1-inch lengths
Freshly ground black pepper to taste
2 to 3 tablespoons chicken stock or water
Steamed long-grain white rice, preferably jasmine

1. Heat the oil in a wok or deep skillet. Add the chicken, stir-fry briefly, then add the oyster sauce, stirring.

2. Stir in the ginger, sugar, scallions and pepper. Continue cooking about 5 minutes longer, just until the chicken is cooked through. Moisten the mixture with a little stock or water to make a sauce that coats the chicken.

3. Remove from heat, and serve with rice.

YIELD: 2 SERVINGS   *Florence Fabricant*

KATHY OSIP'S CHICKEN WITH CASHEWS AND SNOW PEAS

2 large egg whites

½ teaspoon salt

2 teaspoons cornstarch

1 pound skinless and boneless chicken breasts, cut into ½-inch cubes

¾ cup plus 2 tablespoons peanut oil

4 scallions, cut on the diagonal into 1-inch pieces

½ cup unsalted cashews

2 tablespoons soy sauce

½ pound fresh snow peas

1. Whip the egg whites, salt and cornstarch with wire whisk until frothy. Add the chicken, and coat the cubes with the egg white mixture. Cover and refrigerate for 30 minutes.

2. Heat the ¾ cup oil in a wok or sauté pan. Add the chicken and, stirring to make sure the cubes do not stick, cook about 3 minutes. Remove the chicken with slotted spoon, and set aside. Discard the oil and clean the wok.

3. Heat the remaining 2 tablespoons oil in the wok over high heat. Add the scallions and cashews and stir-fry 1 minute. Add the soy sauce and chicken and stir-fry for 1 minute more. Add the snow peas, and stir-fry for 1 minute more. Transfer immediately to a heated platter and serve.

YIELD: 4 SERVINGS *Dena Kleiman*

✤ EASY ✤
CHICKEN AND WATERCRESS
STIR-FRY

1 tablespoon vegetable oil

2 teaspoons finely minced fresh ginger

1 teaspoon minced garlic

1 whole skinless and boneless chicken breast (about ½ pound), cut in slivers

½ cup chicken stock

2 teaspoons light soy sauce

1 teaspoon rice vinegar

½ bunch watercress

⅓ cup minced scallions

½ teaspoon sesame oil

1. Heat the oil in a wok or skillet. Add the ginger and garlic and stir-fry a minute or two. Add the chicken and stir-fry over medium heat until it loses its pinkness, 6 to 8 minutes. Stir in the chicken stock, increase the heat to high and cook until most of the stock has evaporated and the mixture is just moist.

2. Stir in the soy sauce, vinegar and watercress, stirring just until the watercress begins to wilt.

3. Stir in the scallions and sesame oil and serve.

YIELD: 2 TO 4 SERVINGS ⌒ *Florence Fabricant*

✤ EASY ✤
CHICKEN WITH PEANUTS

¾ pound boneless chicken

5 dried black Chinese mushrooms

2 scallions

1 clove garlic

1 piece of fresh ginger the size of an acorn

1 tablespoon brown bean sauce

2 tablespoons water

1 teaspoon cornstarch mixed with a little water

½ teaspoon Chinese thick soy (Chinese bead molasses)

¼ teaspoon cayenne pepper, or to taste

2 tablespoons peanut oil

1 tablespoon sake or dry sherry

⅓ cup shelled roasted peanuts

1. Cut chicken into ⅜-inch-square pieces. Soak mushrooms 15 minutes in warm water, discard the stems, and dice.

2. Mince scallions, garlic and ginger.

3. Mix brown bean sauce and water. Mix cornstarch solution with the thick soy and cayenne pepper

4. Over high heat, heat a wok, and add oil, ginger and garlic. Stir-fry 10 seconds. Add the chicken and wine, and stir-fry 1 minute. Add the mushrooms, and stir-fry 30 seconds. Add the brown bean sauce solution, scallions and peanuts and stir well.

5. Add the cornstarch mixture. Stir to coat all ingredients evenly and serve.

YIELD: SERVES 2 AS A MAIN COURSE OR 4 TO 6 IF PART OF A MEAL OF SEVERAL COURSES ⌒ *Robert Farrar Capon*

SPICY STIR-FRY CHICKEN AND ASPARAGUS

1 pound boneless chicken breast

1 large egg white

1 tablespoon cornstarch

Coarse salt to taste

1 tablespoon rice wine or dry sherry

1 tablespoon soy sauce

½ cup chicken stock (preferably homemade)

6 tablespoons peanut or vegetable oil

1 clove garlic, minced

1 tablespoon fresh ginger, minced

3 scallions, sliced

¾ pound asparagus, sliced on the bias in 1½-inch pieces

1 tablespoon chili paste

1 teaspoon sesame oil

2 tablespoons fresh cilantro

1. Cut the chicken in 1-inch cubes. Beat the egg white lightly and mix it with half the cornstarch and salt to form a smooth paste. Set aside.

2. In another bowl, mix the rice wine, soy sauce, stock and remaining cornstarch to form a smooth paste.

3. Toss the chicken into the egg white–cornstarch mixture. Heat the oil in a wok or large skillet. Fry the chicken cubes until golden and remove with a slotted spoon. Drain on paper towels. Pour off the oil, leaving about one tablespoon in the wok.

4. Add the garlic, ginger and scallions and stir-fry for 1 minute. Add the asparagus and stir-fry for 2 minutes, or until bright green. Add the chicken and chili paste and mix thoroughly. Add the rice wine mixture and stir well. Just before removing from heat, stir in the sesame oil. Sprinkle with cilantro and serve.

YIELD: 4 SERVINGS   *Moira Hodgson*

HOT AND NUMBING
SICHUAN CHICKEN

(Adapted from *Land of Plenty*)

Fuchsia Dunlop, an Englishwoman who had a grant to live and study in Sichuan, was the first foreigner allowed to attend chef training classes in the provincial cooking school in Chengdu.

1 pound boneless, skinless chicken breasts
1 1½-inch-piece fresh ginger, peeled and lightly crushed
8 scallions, white parts only, trimmed
1 teaspoon Sichuan peppercorns
4 teaspoons sugar
3 tablespoons light (or thin) soy sauce
3 to 6 tablespoons Chinese chili oil
2 teaspoons Asian sesame oil
Salt

1. Place chicken in a medium saucepan and add cold water to cover. Remove chicken and bring water to a boil. Return chicken and when water returns to a boil, skim surface. Add ginger and two scallions and reduce heat to low; cover and simmer for 10 minutes. Remove from heat and allow chicken to cool in pan.

2. Place a dry wok or a skillet over low heat, add Sichuan pepper and stir-fry for 5 minutes, until pepper is fragrant. Remove from wok, allow to cool, then grind in a mortar. Set aside.

3. Thinly slice remaining scallions on a sharp angle and set aside. In a small bowl, mix sugar and soy sauce until sugar dissolves, then stir in oils.

4. Drain chicken, pat it dry and slice it about ¼-inch thick. Arrange slices on a platter. Season lightly with salt. Scatter scallions around. Dust chicken with ground Sichuan pepper. Mix sauce and drizzle on top, then serve.

YIELD: 4 SERVINGS *Florence Fabricant*

BACH GNU'S VIETNAMESE CHICKEN WITH LEMONGRASS AND CHILI PEPPERS

(Adapted from *The Classic Cuisine of Vietnam*)

Bach Gnu prepares this dish from her native city, Hue, in central Vietnam. It calls for marinating slices of poultry, meat or fish in strips of lemongrass, chopped fresh chili peppers, sesame seeds, fish sauce (called nuoc mam), sugar, garlic, shallots and black pepper for a minimum of a half hour (or overnight). There is a vital balance here between sweetness and hotness.

½ pound skinless chicken breast, cut into 1-inch cubes (roughly the breast meat from 1 3- to 4-pound chicken)

2 to 3 fresh hot chili peppers, diced (or 2 teaspoons dried, crushed chili peppers)

½ teaspoon freshly ground black pepper

1 stalk fresh lemongrass (see Note)

1 tablespoon vegetable oil

4 cloves garlic, chopped

4 teaspoons fish sauce (nuoc mam)

1½ teaspoons sugar

2 tablespoons vegetable oil for cooking

¼ large onion, quartered

1 cup chicken stock

1 scallion, chopped into 1-inch pieces

1. In a bowl, mix the chicken cubes with the chili peppers, black pepper, lemongrass, 1 tablespoon vegetable oil, 2 cloves garlic, fish sauce and sugar. Let stand for a half hour minimum, or overnight.

2. Heat 2 tablespoons of vegetable oil in a wok over medium-high flame. Add the onion and stir-fry for a minute, then add the remaining 2 cloves of garlic. Sauté until the garlic is golden but not brown.

3. Add the marinated chicken to the wok with the marinade. Stir quickly and constantly for 5 minutes over high heat.

4. Add the chicken stock, reduce heat to simmer and cook for 5 minutes. Add scallions, simmer another minute and serve with steamed rice.

NOTE: Fresh lemongrass looks somewhat like giant scallion stalks. Cut off the top third and remove any hard, dry outer strips. Slice the lemongrass lengthwise as finely as possible, then dice it extremely well. If you buy dried lemongrass, which is sold in packages, soak it in warm water a minimum of 30 minutes before chopping and using.

YIELD: SERVES 2 AS A MAIN COURSE OR
4 AS PART OF A MULTICOURSE MEAL ✍ *Bryan Miller*

THAI SPICY GROUND CHICKEN IN LETTUCE LEAVES (LAAB)

(Adapted from *The Taste of Thailand*)

3 tablespoons rice
4 tablespoons fresh lemon juice
¼ cup chicken stock
2 tablespoons fish sauce (nam pla or Vietnamese nuoc mam) (see Note)
½ to 1 teaspoon, or to taste chili powder
½ pound chicken breast, minced very fine or ground
3 shallots, peeled and chopped
1 stalk lemongrass, trimmed and sliced thin
2 scallions or spring onions, chopped
Romaine lettuce leaves
Cilantro sprigs for garnish

1. Place rice in a dry pan and toast over medium-high heat, 4 to 5 minutes, until rice is pale brown. Watch carefully and stir so that rice does not burn. Remove from heat, let cool slightly, then grind rice in a coffee or spice grinder to make a powder. This should yield about 2 tablespoons ground rice. Set aside.

2. Combine lemon juice, stock, fish sauce and chili powder in a small pan and heat quickly. Add minced chicken and continue cooking, stirring briskly, until meat is

opaque and cooked through. Add shallots, lemongrass, scallions and browned rice and cook a few seconds more, stirring continuously.

3. Serve chicken on a bed of lettuce leaves and garnish with sprigs of cilantro. Use the lettuce leaves as a boat to hold the chicken.

NOTE: See "Selected Sources for Ingredients," page 352.

YIELD: 4 SERVINGS, IF SERVED AS ONE OF SEVERAL DISHES; OTHERWISE, 2 SERVINGS ⌁ *Craig Claiborne*

THE GOLDEN FLOWER HOTEL'S CHICKEN WITH BAMBOO SHOOTS AND CHILI

A recipe created by Li Cheng Heng, the Sichuan chef at the Golden Flower Hotel, a joint venture operated by the Chinese government and a Scandinavian company in Xi'an.

6 ounces julienned white chicken meat

½ large egg white

1 teaspoon cornstarch

½ cup finely chopped bamboo shoots

1 teaspoon black vinegar

1 teaspoon soy sauce

½ teaspoon sugar

⅛ teaspoon white pepper

3 tablespoons peanut oil

2 tablespoons finely chopped celery

1 thinly sliced spring onion

2 tablespoons finely chopped red bell pepper

1½ teaspoons chili paste

2 tablespoons chicken stock

1. Cut chicken into strips about ⅛ inch wide and 2 inches long. Mix with egg white and cornstarch. Set aside.

2. Rinse and drain bamboo shoots and slice with a thick slicing blade in food processor. Cut slices into small dice.

3. Combine vinegar, soy sauce, sugar and white pepper and set aside.

4. Heat 1 tablespoon peanut oil in wok until it shimmers. Stir-fry bamboo shoots, celery, spring onion and red pepper about 2 minutes; remove and set aside. Wipe out wok.

5. Heat remaining 2 tablespoons peanut oil in wok until it shimmers. Stir-fry chicken until it turns white.

6. Add chili paste; stir-fry. Add vinegar mixture and stir-fry.

7. Return the vegetables to wok and stir in chicken stock; stir-fry to mix well.

YIELD: 2 SERVINGS AS PART OF A CHINESE MEAL ⟋ *Marian Burros*

✦ EASY ✦

CHINESE BROCCOLI WITH CHICKEN AND TOFU

After the tofu and broccoli are steamed together, the chicken and the rest of the broccoli are quickly stir-fried in the same sauce—and there's only one pan to wash.

3 tablespoons peanut oil	¼ pound tofu, cut into slices ½ inch
1 clove garlic, minced	by 2 inches
1 teaspoon chopped fresh ginger root	1 tablespoon bean sprouts
1 scallion, chopped	2 tablespoons soy sauce
½ cup dry sherry	½ boneless chicken breast, cut into
2 medium stalks broccoli (about 12	slices ½ inch by 2 inches
ounces), cut into large chunks	1 tablespoon almonds

1. Heat the oil in a wok. Add the garlic, ginger and scallion, and sauté for about 3 minutes.

2. Add the sherry and half of the broccoli, and arrange the tofu on top of the broccoli. Cover and turn the heat down to low. Let the broccoli and tofu steam for about 10 minutes.

3. Stir in the bean sprouts and 1 tablespoon of the soy sauce.

4. Use a slotted spoon to remove the broccoli, tofu and bean sprouts from the

wok, and place them on a warm platter. Pour half the pan liquid over them and cover. Set aside while you cook the chicken briefly.

5. Place the rest of the broccoli and the chicken in the same wok with the remaining pan liquid. Stir-fry about 5 minutes, until the chicken is cooked through. Add the remaining soy sauce, and stir in the almonds until they are just glazed. Serve with white or brown rice.

YIELD: 2 SERVINGS *Jean Grasso Fitzpatrick*

✦ EASY ✦
HOMER C. LEE'S SPECIAL CHICKEN

For the Chinese New Year, chef Homer C. Lee, owner of Homer's Szechuan Star in Woodbury, New York, and Homer's Szechuan South in Massapequa Park, N.Y., prepared this stir-fried dish with pheasant, a bird that is also called "chicken of the mountains."

½ cup dried black mushrooms

2 teaspoons peanut oil

¾ pound boneless dark meat of chicken, in 1-inch squares (see Note)

1 tablespoon finely shredded fresh ginger

6 to 8 canned baby corn

1½ cups fresh broccoli florets

½ carrot, scraped and sliced thin

1 teaspoon salt

1 teaspoon sugar

½ teaspoon rice vinegar

1 teaspoon rice wine or dry sherry

2 to 3 tablespoons water or chicken stock (optional)

1 teaspoon cornstarch mixed with 1 tablespoon cold water

1 teaspoon light soy sauce

½ teaspoon Oriental sesame oil

1. Place mushrooms in warm water and allow to soak until softened, about 20 minutes. Drain, remove stems and set aside.

2. Heat wok. Add oil, then chicken. Stir-fry a few minutes, until meat changes color but is only half cooked. Add ginger and stir once; then add mushrooms, corn, broccoli and carrot and stir-fry 2 minutes.

3. Add salt, sugar, vinegar and wine. Cover and allow to cook 3 minutes. If there is not much liquid in the wok, add additional water or stock. Add cornstarch, stir until thickened; then add soy sauce and sesame oil. Stir once, then serve.

YIELD: 4 SERVINGS *Florence Fabricant*

+ EASY +
# CHIN CHIN'S
# THREE-GLASS CHICKEN

(Adapted from Chin Chin's, New York City)

Jimmy Chin's stove-top interpretation of the traditional dish, in which chicken pieces are smothered with a glass of rice wine, a glass of soy sauce and a glass of water and then braised in the wok over high heat after stir-frying.

4 pounds chicken thighs, skinned and boned

THE MARINADE
2 tablespoons rice wine
2 teaspoons salt
2 teaspoons sesame oil
½ teaspoon freshly ground black pepper
2 teaspoons cornstarch
1 cup Chinese dried black mushrooms
2 tablespoons peanut oil
3 tablespoons finely chopped fresh ginger
2 tablespoons finely chopped scallions

2 tablespoons finely chopped garlic
1½ tablespoons finely chopped fresh coriander

THE SAUCE
1 tablespoon light soy sauce
2 tablespoons oyster sauce
2 teaspoons sugar
¾ cup chicken stock
2 tablespoons rice wine
½ teaspoon cornstarch mixed with 1 teaspoon water
2 teaspoons sesame oil

1. Cut the chicken thighs into bite-sized pieces and combine them with the marinade ingredients. Let them stand for 40 minutes.

2. Soak the mushrooms in a bowl of warm water for about 20 minutes or until they are soft and pliable. Squeeze out the excess water and cut off and discard the woody stems.

3. Heat a wok or large skillet until it is hot. Add the peanut oil, then add the chicken and stir-fry for about five minutes or until the chicken is lightly browned. Remove the chicken to a clay pot or casserole with a slotted spoon.

4. Drain off all but one tablespoon of oil. Reheat the wok, add the ginger, scallions, garlic and coriander and stir-fry for 30 seconds. Then add the sauce ingredients. Bring the mixture to a boil and pour this into the pot together with the mushrooms. Cover and braise over high heat for about 15 minutes. Serve at once.

YIELD: 4 TO 6 SERVINGS   *Ken Hom*

KEN HOM'S CHICKEN
COOKED WITH RICE

(Adapted from *The Taste of China*)

On a trip to China, the foods that most impressed Ken Hom, the noted cookbook author, were the simple dishes like this one.

> 1½ cups long-grain white rice
> ½ pound skinless and boneless chicken thigh meat, coarsely chopped
> 1 tablespoon light soy sauce
> 2 teaspoons plus 1 tablespoon dark soy sauce
> 2 teaspoons rice wine or dry sherry
> 1 teaspoon salt
> 2 teaspoons Oriental sesame oil
> 1 teaspoon cornstarch
> 1½ tablespoons peanut oil
> 2 teaspoons finely chopped peeled fresh ginger
> 2 tablespoons finely chopped scallions

1. Put the rice in a Chinese clay pot or a heavy medium-size saucepan. Pour in enough water to cover the rice by 1 inch. Bring to a boil and cook until most of the water has evaporated, about 15 minutes. Reduce heat to very low and cover tightly.

2. Combine the chicken with the light soy sauce, 2 teaspoons of the dark soy sauce, the rice wine, salt, sesame oil and cornstarch.

3. Heat a wok or skillet until it is hot. Add the peanut oil and the ginger and stir-fry for 10 seconds. Add the chicken and stir-fry for 2 minutes. Pour the mixture on top of the rice, cover and continue to cook over very low heat for 10 minutes.

4. Drizzle the remaining tablespoon of dark soy sauce over the chicken, sprinkle with scallions and serve.

YIELD: 4 TO 6 SERVINGS AS PART OF A CHINESE MEAL,
2 TO 3 SERVINGS AS A SINGLE DISH ✦ *Florence Fabricant*

THE SLOW ROAD TO TENDERNESS

CRAIG CLAIBORNE'S CHICKEN FRICASSEE

½ cup all-purpose flour

1 tablespoon salt

½ teaspoon freshly ground black pepper

½ teaspoon paprika

1 chicken (3½ to 4 pounds), well rinsed, patted dry, and cut into 8 pieces

¼ cup vegetable oil

1 small onion, thinly sliced

1 stalk celery, thinly sliced

1 cup dry white wine

1. Combine the flour, salt, pepper and paprika in a bag. Add the chicken and shake well to coat. Remove chicken pieces to a plate and reserve the remaining flour.

2. Warm the oil over medium-high heat in a nonreactive 12-inch skillet. Add chicken pieces and brown on all sides. Add the onion, celery and wine and bring to a boil. Reduce the heat to low, cover, and simmer until fork-tender, about 2½ hours.

3. Transfer chicken pieces to a warm platter. In a small cup, mix together 1 tablespoon of the reserved flour mixture with ¼ cup water and stir until smooth. Stir into the skillet and cook over medium heat, stirring constantly, until the mixture thickens. Pour sauce over the chicken, season to taste if necessary, and serve.

YIELD: 4 SERVINGS ✍ *Craig Claiborne*

SLOW-COOKED COQ AU VIN

(Adapted from *The New York Times Cook Book*)

The classic wine for coq au vin is Chambertin, but any good dry red wine will do.

> 1 5-pound roasting chicken, cut into serving pieces
> Flour for dredging
> ½ cup unsalted butter
> 1 slice raw ham, chopped
> 10 small white onions, peeled and left whole
> 1 clove garlic, finely chopped
> ¼ teaspoon dried thyme, or ½ teaspoon fresh thyme
> 1 sprig parsley
> 1 bay leaf
> 8 whole mushrooms
> Salt and freshly ground black pepper to taste
> ¼ cup warmed cognac (see Note)
> 1 cup dry red wine

1. Preheat oven to 300 degrees.
2. Dredge the chicken with flour. In a skillet heat the butter, add the chicken and brown on all sides. Transfer the chicken to an earthenware casserole and add the ham, onions, garlic, thyme, parsley, bay leaf, mushrooms, salt, and pepper.
3. Pour the cognac over the chicken and ignite. When the flame dies, add the wine.
4. Cover and bake until the chicken is tender, about 2½ hours.

NOTE: Flaming cognac is a traditional step that intensifies the flavor of the dish. But you may omit it and simply add the wine after step 2 and proceed to step 4.

YIELD: 6 SERVINGS

BRAISED CHICKEN WITH GINGER, AND SNOW PEAS

1 tablespoon peanut oil
1 frying chicken, cut up and patted dry
1 tablespoon minced shallots
2 tablespoons finely slivered fresh ginger
3 cloves garlic, minced
½ teaspoon five-spice powder
2 tablespoons dark soy sauce
½ cup rice wine or dry sherry
Salt and freshly ground black pepper
4 ounces snow peas, trimmed
2 tablespoons finely chopped scallions
1 tablespoon chopped cilantro

1. Heat the oil in a large, heavy ovenproof skillet. Add the chicken pieces and cook over high heat until nicely browned. Do not crowd them and remove them to a bowl as they brown.

2. Lower the heat and add the shallots, ginger and garlic. Sauté for a minute or so, then stir in the five-spice powder, soy sauce and rice wine or sherry.

3. Return the chicken to the pan along with any juices that may have been released by the chicken as it cooled. Baste with the pan juices and season with salt and pepper.

4. Cover and cook over low heat, about 40 minutes, basting once or twice.

5. When the chicken is done, remove it from the pan. Increase the heat, add the snow peas and sauté for about a minute, until they turn bright green. Stir in the scallions and cilantro. Return the chicken to the pan, reheat briefly, check the sauce for seasoning and serve at once.

YIELD: 4 SERVINGS   *Florence Fabricant*

CHICKEN WITH GINGER, MUSHROOMS AND SCALLIONS

Because there is such a small amount of liquid, enhanced by the juices from the chicken and vegetables, there is no need to add thickeners to this dish. It can be prepared in advance and reheated.

1 tablespoon peanut oil
1 frying chicken, cut up and patted
   dry
1 tablespoon minced shallots
1 tablespoon minced fresh ginger
3 cloves garlic, minced
¼ pound shiitake mushrooms, sliced

½ teaspoon five-spice powder
2 tablespoons dark soy sauce
½ cup rice wine or dry sherry
Salt and freshly ground black pepper
2 tablespoons finely chopped
   scallions
1 tablespoon chopped fresh cilantro

1. Heat the oil in a large, heavy ovenproof skillet. Add the chicken pieces and cook over high heat until they are nicely browned. Do not crowd them in the pan and remove them to a bowl as they brown. You may have to brown the chicken in several shifts.

2. Preheat oven to 350 degrees.

3. Lower the heat and add the shallots, ginger and garlic to the pan. Sauté for a minute or so, then add the mushrooms. Increase the heat to medium-high and sauté until the mushrooms begin to brown. Stir in the five-spice powder, soy sauce and rice wine or sherry.

4. Return the chicken to the pan along with any juices that may have been released by the chicken as it cooled. Baste with the pan juices and season with salt and pepper.

5. Cover and place in the oven. Bake 40 minutes, basting once or twice during baking.

6. To serve, remove the chicken pieces from the pan and place them on a warm serving platter. Stir scallions and cilantro into the sauce, check sauce for seasoning and pour it over the chicken. Serve at once.

YIELD: 4 SERVINGS   *Florence Fabricant*

CHICKEN WITH MIXED MUSHROOMS AND RIESLING CREAM

The acidity in Riesling is bright and generous, and it leavens the heft in an old-fashioned dish like braised chicken with mushrooms and cream.

2 tablespoons olive oil

4 tablespoons unsalted butter

3 cups mushrooms (any mix, such as cremini, chanterelle, blue foot and shiitake), sliced ¼-inch thick

3 sprigs thyme

Sea salt and freshly ground black pepper

4 chicken thighs, preferably organic

4 chicken drumsticks, preferably organic

½ cup chicken broth

¼ cup finely diced onion

⅓ cup Riesling

¼ cup heavy cream

1. Heat oven to 325 degrees. Heat 1 tablespoon oil and 1 tablespoon butter in a medium skillet over medium heat. When melted and bubbling, add mushrooms and thyme. Cook, stirring occasionally, until softened and browned on edges, 10 to 15 minutes. Discard thyme, and season with salt and pepper to taste; set aside.

2. Heat remaining oil and 1 tablespoon butter in a large sauté pan over medium-high heat. Season chicken with salt and pepper and add it skin-side down to the hot pan. Brown well on all sides, about 10 minutes. Pour in broth and bring to a boil. Cover and place in oven until very tender, about 30 minutes.

3. Transfer chicken to a plate, and pour pan juices into a bowl. Return pan to medium heat, and add remaining 2 tablespoons butter. When it foams, add onion and sauté until translucent. Add Riesling and bring to a boil, reducing by half. Add ½ cup of cooking juices, and reduce by half.

4. Add cream and simmer for 3 minutes. Return chicken to pan, and add mushrooms. Simmer, basting, about 2 minutes. Serve hot.

YIELD: 4 SERVINGS ~ *Amanda Hesser*

BRAISED CHICKEN LEGS
IN MUSTARD SAUCE

3 tablespoons extra-virgin olive oil
12 chicken legs
½ cup finely chopped onion
½ cup finely chopped celery
½ teaspoon rosemary, fresh or dried
¼ cup dark beer
½ cup chicken stock or brown stock
¼ cup wholegrain prepared mustard
Salt and freshly ground black pepper
2 tablespoons chopped fresh Italian parsley

1. Heat the oil in a heavy casserole large enough to hold the chicken tightly in a single layer. Add half the chicken legs, brown over high heat, remove from the pan and repeat with the remaining chicken. Lower heat, add the onion and celery and sauté until the vegetables are tender, about 8 minutes. Stir in the rosemary, beer and stock.

2. Return all the browned chicken to the pot, cover and cook over low heat until it is cooked through, about 45 minutes. Turn the chicken once during cooking.

3. Remove the chicken from the casserole and increase the heat to high. Stir in the mustard, season to taste with salt and pepper and return the chicken to the pan, basting it with the sauce. Transfer the chicken to a serving platter or individual plates and spoon the sauce over each portion. Sprinkle with parsley and serve.

YIELD: 4 SERVINGS ⏤ *Florence Fabricant*

CHICKEN PAPRIKASH

(Adapted from *The Best of Craig Claiborne*)

The innocuous powder that stores often pass off as paprika has little more character than chalk. In its finer forms, paprika is a distinctive and much-prized spice. There are three types—sweet, mild and hot—each with a pronounced flavor. The best is imported from Hungary and, logically enough is called Hungarian or rose paprika. It is available in the gourmet or spice sections of most high-quality supermarkets and in fine specialty food shops.

> 1 3-pound chicken, cut into serving pieces
> Salt and freshly ground pepper to taste
> 2 tablespoons unsalted butter
> 1 cup thinly sliced onions
> 1 tablespoon finely minced garlic
> 1 tablespoon sweet paprika
> ½ cup fresh or canned chicken broth
> 1 cup sour cream
> 1 tablespoon flour

1. Sprinkle the chicken with salt and pepper.
2. Melt the butter in a heavy skillet and add the chicken pieces, skin-side down. Cook over moderately high heat for about 5 minutes and turn the pieces. Continue cooking for about 5 minutes until brown on second side.
3. Sprinkle the onions and garlic around the chicken pieces. Sprinkle with paprika and stir. Add the chicken broth and cover. Simmer for 10 minutes or longer, until the chicken is cooked.
4. Remove the chicken to a warm serving dish.
5. Blend the sour cream and flour and stir it into the sauce. Cook, stirring, for about 1 minute. Pour the sauce over the chicken.

YIELD: 4 SERVINGS

JAMIE OLIVER'S
BRAISED LIGURIAN CHICKEN

(Adapted from Jamie Oliver)

"When you eat this dish, it's quite delicately flavored," says Jamie Oliver, one of London's acclaimed chefs, about the braised chicken reminiscent of one he ate in Liguria. *"It's perfumed with the wine and the rosemary . . . When you cook olives whole like this, it's almost like an anchovy. The salt comes out of the olives, and the olive becomes more like a vegetable. And the salt from the olive flavors the chicken really wonderfully."*

> 2 heaping tablespoons flour
> Sea salt and freshly ground black pepper
> 1 4-pound chicken, cut into 8 pieces
> ¼ cup extra-virgin olive oil
> 4 to 5 fresh rosemary sprigs
> 6 cloves garlic, peeled and thinly sliced
> 1½ cups white wine
> 4 anchovy fillets (optional)
> ½ cup kalamata olives (with pits)
> 3 ripe plum tomatoes, halved, seeded and coarsely chopped

1. In a large bowl, combine flour with salt and pepper to taste. Add chicken pieces and toss until evenly coated.

2. Place a large flameproof casserole dish over medium-high heat, and heat olive oil. Add chicken pieces, and fry until golden underneath, about 5 minutes. Turn chicken, and add rosemary and garlic. Continue to fry until garlic is softened but not colored, about 3 minutes. Add wine. When it comes to a boil, add anchovies, olives and tomatoes.

3. Partly cover pan, and reduce heat to medium low. Simmer until chicken is cooked and tender, and broth is reduced to a rich sauce, 15 to 20 minutes. To serve, discard rosemary sprigs, and season well with salt and pepper to taste. Place a piece or two of chicken on each plate, and top with a spoonful of sauce.

YIELD: 4 SERVINGS   *Amanda Hesser*

BRAISED CHICKEN WITH
ESCAROLE AND SICILIAN OLIVES

love!!!

*Bitter greens, like escarole, work well in braised dishes. They are, in fact, lettuce, but a trail of bit-
terness jogs through their veins. Escarole hearts are mild enough for a salad. In Italian cuisine, the
outer leaves of escarole are chopped up and thrown in soups. Lightly stewed, whole escarole leaves
are also a wonder: the stem remains succulent, but the leaf wilts into a tidy, compact sauce rag.*

8 chicken thighs with bone
Fine sea salt
Freshly ground black pepper
2 tablespoons extra-virgin olive oil
8 large garlic cloves, sliced (¼ cup)
2 large shallots, sliced (½ cup)
1½ tablespoons fresh minced thyme
1½ tablespoons fresh minced rosemary
3 tablespoons white wine
½ cup chicken broth
½ cup jumbo pitted Sicilian olives, quartered
1 large or 2 small heads escarole, separated into individual leaves
Juice of ½ lemon
4 tablespoons cold, unsalted butter, cut into pieces

1. Trim chicken thighs of excess fat, and dry well on paper towels. Heat a 10-
inch nonstick skillet over medium heat for 5 minutes. Place chicken in skillet, skin-
side down, and sear until skin is well browned, about 5 minutes. Turn thighs with
tongs, sprinkle with salt and pepper, and sear until second side is golden, about 3 minutes more.

2. Pour off fat. Reduce heat to low, add olive oil, and half of the sliced garlic,
shallots and the herbs, and sauté until soft and fragrant, about 40 seconds. Add wine
and chicken broth, cover, and simmer 7 minutes. Turn chicken, and simmer until meat
pulls easily from bone, about 7 minutes more.

3. Transfer chicken from skillet to plate. Add remaining garlic, shallots and
herbs, olives, escarole and lemon juice to skillet. Sprinkle with salt and pepper, increase heat to medium-high, and cover. Steam escarole until it wilts, about 5 minutes.

4. Return chicken to skillet on top of escarole. Add butter, increase heat to high,

and simmer until butter melts and sauce has emulsified slightly. (If sauce appears thin, transfer escarole and chicken to warm platter, then boil sauce until it has reached a pleasing consistency.) Taste to correct seasoning. Serve immediately.

YIELD: 4 TO 6 SERVINGS   *Kay Rentschler*

EASY
CHICKEN WITH SAGE AND WINE

(Adapted from *The New York Times International Cook Book*)

1 2½- to 3-pound chicken, cut into serving pieces
Salt and freshly ground black pepper
5 tablespoons unsalted butter
3 tablespoons peanut oil
4 ounces sliced prosciutto, cut into bite-size pieces
1 tablespoon chopped fresh sage, preferably with stems, or dried whole-leaf
    sage
¾ cup dry white wine

1. Sprinkle the chicken pieces with salt and pepper.

2. Heat 3 tablespoons of the butter and the oil in a large skillet and cook the chicken until golden brown all over. Pour off most of the fat from the skillet and add the prosciutto, sage and wine. Cover and cook until tender, about 20 minutes. Remove the chicken to a hot platter.

3. Bring the pan juices to a boil, then remove the skillet from the heat. Swirl in the remaining butter by rotating the pan gently and serve the sauce separately.

YIELD: 4 SERVINGS

254 • *THE NEW YORK TIMES CHICKEN COOKBOOK*

FLORENCE FABRICANT'S CHICKEN CACCIATORE

1 3½-pound chicken, quartered

2 tablespoons extra-virgin olive oil

1 cup onion, sliced very thin

2 cloves garlic, sliced very thin

Salt and freshly ground black pepper to taste

¼ cup dry white wine

1½ cups fresh ripe tomatoes, skinned with a peeler and chopped, or canned
   Italian plum tomatoes, cut up, with their juice

1. Rinse chicken in cold water and pat dry.

2. Put olive oil and onion in a sauté pan large enough to hold the chicken without crowding. Place over medium heat and cook, stirring occasionally, until onion is translucent. Add garlic. Add chicken, skin-side down, and sauté until skin turns golden. Turn and cook chicken on the other side.

3. Add salt and pepper and turn the chicken a few times. Add the wine, and simmer until it is reduced by half.

4. Add the tomatoes, reduce the heat to a very slow simmer, partly cover the pan, and cook the chicken about 40 minutes, until it is very tender and comes away from the bone easily. Turn and baste it from time to time during cooking. If necessary add a little water.

5. Transfer the chicken to a warm dish and serve. If desired, it can be prepared in advance and reheated.

YIELD: 4 SERVINGS ⌁ *Florence Fabricant*

MEDITERRANEAN CHICKEN WITH SWEET PEPPERS

1 small frying chicken, preferably free range or naturally raised, cut in
    6 serving pieces (or use 2 pounds of chicken parts)
¼ cup extra-virgin olive oil
2 tablespoons fresh lemon juice (juice from half a lemon)
1 tablespoon finely chopped fresh rosemary
½ medium yellow onion, thinly sliced
2 cloves garlic, thinly sliced
¼ to ½ cup dry white wine
2 red or yellow (or both) sweet peppers, sliced in strips
1 tablespoon capers
2 tablespoons chopped black olives, Greek or niçoise
2 tablespoons finely chopped flat-leaf parsley

1. Put the chicken in a deep bowl and add the oil, lemon juice and rosemary. Turn to coat well. Cover and set aside to marinate for 1 hour, or refrigerate 10 hours or overnight.

2. To cook, remove about 2 tablespoons of the flavored oil from the marinade. Place the oil in a heavy saucepan large enough to hold the chicken pieces and set over medium-low heat. Add the onion and garlic and cook, stirring occasionally, until the vegetables are soft. Push the vegetables to the edges of the pan and put the chicken in the middle. Raise the heat to medium and brown the chicken lightly on all sides. Add the wine and peppers. Lower the heat again, cover and continue cooking, stirring occasionally and turning the chicken parts over, for about 30 minutes, or until the chicken is thoroughly cooked and the juices run clear yellow when the meat is pricked with a fork. If necessary, add more marinade.

3. When the chicken is done, stir in the capers, olives and parsley. Let the sauce come to a boil, remove from the heat and serve immediately.

VARIATION: Chicken skin adds a lot of flavor to any dish, but if you want, you may remove the skin or prepare this dish with skinless, boneless breasts.

YIELD: 4 TO 6 SERVINGS ✒ *Nancy Harmon Jenkins*

✤ EASY ✤
CHICKEN WITH LEEKS
AND TOMATOES

1 3- to 4-pound chicken, cut into 8 pieces
Coarse sea salt and freshly ground pepper to taste
¼ cup olive oil
1 clove garlic, minced
3 large leeks, well washed and sliced
1 tablespoon fresh thyme leaves
2 tablespoons chopped parsley leaves
1 cup dry white wine
2 cups canned plum tomatoes, peeled and chopped

1. Pat the chicken pieces dry with paper towels. Season them to taste with salt and pepper.

2. Heat the oil in a large skillet. Brown the pieces a few at a time. Remove them and add the garlic, leeks, thyme and parsley. Cook, stirring frequently, until leeks are soft.

3. Add the wine, scraping up the cooking juices. Add the tomatoes and chicken pieces. Cover and cook over low heat, turning occasionally, or until the chicken is tender, about 30 to 45 minutes. Correct seasoning and serve.

YIELD: 4 SERVINGS   *Moira Hodgson*

CHICKEN WITH EGGPLANT

This recipe for chicken browned in olive and then combined with diced eggplant, onions, garlic and tomatoes adds a South-of-France flavor to your table.

1 chicken, 3 pounds, cut into quarters
Salt to taste
Freshly ground pepper to taste
2 small eggplants, about 1¼ pounds total
1 large onion, about ½ pound, peeled
2 small tomatoes, about ½ pound total
2 tablespoons olive oil

1 tablespoon finely minced garlic
¼ cup red wine vinegar
½ cup dry white wine
½ cup fresh or canned chicken broth
1 bay leaf
¼ teaspoon dried thyme
¼ teaspoon dried hot red pepper flakes
Finely chopped parsley for garnish

1. Sprinkle chicken pieces with salt and pepper. Make slight gashes at thigh and wing joints to facilitate cooking. Set aside.

2. Trim off ends of eggplants. Cut lengthwise in half and cut each half lengthwise into 3 long slices. Cut slices crosswise into 1-inch pieces. There should be about 5 cups.

3. Cut onion in half vertically. Cut each half crosswise into very thin slices. There should be about a cup.

4. Cut cores from tomatoes. Cut tomatoes into inch cubes or slightly smaller. There should be about 1½ cups.

5. Heat oil in large skillet and add chicken pieces skin-side down. Cook about 5 minutes on one side and turn, cooking 5 minutes more. Transfer chicken to platter.

6. Add onions, garlic and eggplant to skillet. Cook, stirring, about a minute and add tomatoes. Stir.

7. Add vinegar, wine and broth and bring to boil. Stir. Add bay leaf, thyme, salt, pepper and pepper flakes. Stir and return chicken to the skillet. Turn pieces in sauce.

8. Cover closely and let cook, basting occasionally, about 20 minutes or until chicken is done. Remove bay leaf. Serve with sauce poured over and sprinkled with parsley.

YIELD: 4 SERVINGS　　*Pierre Franey*

CHRISTIAN CHEVILLON'S BRAISED CHICKEN WITH GREEN OLIVES

In Nuits-Saint-Georges, where the Chevillon family makes some of France's most worthy Burgundian reds, Christian Chevillon prepares some of the region's most traditional fare, such as this favorite dish, which also can be made with rabbit.

1 fresh chicken, 2½ to 3 pounds, cut into serving pieces

Sea salt and freshly ground pepper to taste

3 tablespoons extra-virgin olive oil

2 medium onions, coarsely chopped

1 tablespoon flour

2½ cups dry white wine, such as Aligote, Riesling, Pouilly-Fumé or a
     white Cotes du Rhone

4 tomatoes, cored, peeled, seeded and chopped

4 whole bay leaves

1 tablespoon each of fresh herbs, minced, preferably a blend of rosemary,
     thyme and parsley

1 generous cup green olives (preferably the French picholine), pitted

1. Season the chicken pieces liberally with salt and pepper. Heat the oil in a large, deep-sided skillet over medium-high heat. When the oil is hot but not smoking, brown the chicken. Do not crowd the pan, browning each piece on both sides until the meat turns an even golden brown, about 5 minutes on each side. You will probably need to do this in several batches.

2. Remove the chicken from the skillet, brown the onions in the remaining fat for 3 to 4 minutes, then quickly stir in the flour to thicken the sauce. Very slowly add the wine, stirring all the time, then add the chicken, tomatoes, bay leaves, herbs and olives. Stir to mix all the ingredients. Cover, reduce the heat to medium and cook, stirring from time to time, until the chicken is cooked through and the sauce has had time to absorb all the varied flavors, from 30 to 40 minutes. (The dish can easily be prepared ahead and reheated.)

3. Remove the bay leaves and serve with rice or fresh pasta.

YIELD: 4 TO 6 SERVINGS   *Patricia Wells*

CHICKEN WITH MORELS
AND ASPARAGUS

4 teaspoons unsalted butter

2 chicken breasts, split in half and skinned

¼ cup minced shallots

1 cup chicken broth, homemade or low-sodium canned

1 cup white wine

4 sprigs fresh thyme

20 asparagus spears, ends snapped off, cut into 2-inch pieces

1 cup morels, stemmed and cleaned

1½ teaspoons salt, plus more to taste

Freshly ground pepper to taste

2 tablespoons heavy cream

1 tablespoon chopped Italian parsley

1. Heat 2 teaspoons of butter in a large, wide pot over medium-high heat. Add the chicken breasts and sear until browned, about 4 minutes per side. Remove the chicken from the pan. Lower the heat to medium, place 1 teaspoon of butter and the shallots in the pan and cook, stirring constantly, for 30 seconds.

2. Add the broth, wine and thyme and bring to a simmer. Add the chicken and bring back to a simmer. Cover and cook until the chicken is cooked through, about 20 minutes. Remove the chicken and tent with foil to keep warm. Increase the heat and simmer the liquid until it has reduced to 1 cup, about 10 minutes. Remove the thyme.

3. Meanwhile, bring a large pot of water to the boil. Add the asparagus and blanch until crisp-tender, about 3 minutes. Drain and rinse under cold water. Heat the remaining butter in a large nonstick skillet over medium heat. Add the asparagus and the morels and sauté until tender, about 4 minutes. Season with ½ teaspoon of salt and pepper to taste.

4. Stir the cream, 1 teaspoon of salt and pepper to taste into the sauce. Adjust seasoning if necessary. Divide the chicken among 4 plates and spoon the sauce over it. Place the asparagus and morels around the chicken, sprinkle with parsley and serve immediately.

YIELD: 4 SERVINGS *Molly O'Neill*

CHICKEN WITH CHERVIL
AND PERNOD

Chervil is a delicate herb that is best used fresh because its flavor quickly fades in the dried state. If you cannot find fresh chervil, substitute parsley, dill or chives rather than using the dried version.

1 broiling chicken, cut up
1 tablespoon unsalted butter
3 tablespoons finely minced shallots
1 teaspoon minced garlic
2 tablespoons Pernod
½ cup well-flavored chicken stock
Salt and freshly ground white pepper
1 cup heavy cream
2 tablespoons finely minced fresh chervil
Several drops of fresh lemon juice
Sprigs of fresh chervil for garnish

1. Dry the chicken pieces. Heat butter in a large skillet and sauté the chicken until it is golden. Remove the chicken and set aside.

2. Add the shallots and garlic to the pan and sauté until tender but not brown. Stir in the Pernod and deglaze the pan by scraping up any little particles clinging to the bottom. Stir in the chicken stock and return the chicken to the pan. Season to taste with salt and pepper.

3. Cook the chicken, covered, until done, about 25 minutes. Remove chicken from the pan and raise heat to high.

4. Add the cream and cook over high heat until the sauce has thickened and reduced to about 1 cup. Stir in the chervil and lemon juice and return the chicken to the pan. Reheat the chicken, then serve it garnished with sprigs of chervil.

YIELD: 3 TO 4 SERVINGS   *Florence Fabricant*

ED BEHR'S DAUBE OF CHICKEN LEGS
IN TOMATO AND RED WINE SAUCE

(Adapted from *The Art of Eating*)

8 whole chicken legs, drumstick and thigh
¼ cup olive oil or chicken fat
1 medium onion, diced
2 cups medium-bodied red wine
3 carrots, scraped and diced
1 tender rib celery, diced
4 cloves garlic, peeled and crushed with the blade of a knife
2 small bay leaves
¼ teaspoon dried thyme or about 1 teaspoon minced fresh
¼ teaspoon dried oregano or about 1 teaspoon minced fresh
1 teaspoon minced fresh savory (optional)
1 tablespoon minced fresh parsley
1 cup canned imported Italian tomatoes, broken up
3 cups well-flavored chicken stock, preferably homemade

1. Over medium-low heat brown chicken legs in fat or oil; remove and set aside, leaving fat in pan.

2. Brown diced onion in fat, stirring frequently. Remove and set aside.

3. Remove all but 3 tablespoons of fat from the pan. Pour the red wine into the pan and cook over medium-high heat, stirring continuously to deglaze the pan.

4. Preheat oven to 350 degrees.

5. Place chicken, onion and glazing juices in a casserole. Add carrots, celery, garlic, bay leaves, thyme, oregano, savory if desired, parsley, tomatoes and chicken stock. Bring to a boil, cover and place in the oven. Immediately reduce oven temperature to 200 degrees and cook for 1 hour. Serve broth as a first course; chicken legs may be served as a main course with salad or vegetables.

YIELD: 8 SERVINGS   *Nancy Harmon Jenkins*

SMOTHERED CHICKEN
CREOLE-STYLE

Smothered chicken in its most basic form consists of cooking a chicken that has been split down the back and opened up as for broiling, the breast unsplit and left intact. You cook it breast-side down in a black iron skillet (this is essential) with a plate on top. The plate is weighted down and it is this that contributes the name "smothered." The chicken is turned over and continues to cook in a flour-thickened gravy until it is exceptionally tender, the meat almost "falling from the bones."

1 chicken, 3½ pounds, butterflied (split down the backbone,
    breast left intact and unsplit)
Salt to taste, if desired
Freshly ground pepper to taste
2 tablespoons unsalted butter
1 cup finely chopped onion
1 cup finely chopped celery
1 cup cored, seeded and finely chopped green pepper
1½ teaspoons finely minced garlic
2 tablespoons flour
1¾ cups canned imported tomatoes, crushed or chopped
1 bay leaf
2 tablespoons finely chopped parsley

1. A black iron skillet is essential for the authentic preparation of this dish. Sprinkle the chicken on both sides with salt and pepper. Select a skillet large enough to hold the chicken comfortably when it is opened up as for broiling. Fold the chicken wings under to hold them secure.

2. Melt the butter in the skillet and add the chicken skin-side down. Cover the chicken firmly with a plate that will fit comfortably inside the skillet. Add several weights, approximately 5 pounds, to the top of the plate. Cook over low heat, checking the skin side of the chicken, until it is nicely browned, about 25 minutes.

3. Remove the chicken to a warm platter. To the skillet add the onion, celery, green pepper and garlic and cook, stirring, until onions are wilted.

4. Sprinkle with flour and stir to blend. Add the tomatoes, bay leaf, salt and pepper, stirring rapidly with the whisk. Bring to a boil.

5. Return the chicken to the sauce skin-side up. Cover with the plate and weights and continue cooking over low heat 45 minutes longer. Remove the chicken to a warm platter and cook down the sauce briefly, stirring. Pour the sauce over the chicken and sprinkle with parsley.

YIELD: 4 SERVINGS 〜 *Craig Claiborne and Pierre Franey*

DOMINICAN CHICKEN
(POLLO CRIOLLO)

A dish prepared by Bill Eichner, a surgeon in Vermont, based on a family recipe of his wife, the novelist Julia Alvarez.

1 3½- to 4½-pound chicken, cut up

FOR THE MARINADE

3 cloves garlic, minced
¼ teaspoon nutmeg
½ teaspoon salt
½ teaspoon freshly ground black pepper
1 tablespoon cider vinegar
½ cup dry white wine
3 tablespoons olive oil

TO FINISH THE DISH

1 cup flour seasoned lightly with salt and freshly ground black pepper
½ cup olive oil
1 large onion, minced
2 shallots, minced
3 cloves garlic, minced
1 cup tomato puree, or crushed stewed tomatoes
½ cup green olives, chopped
1 tablespoon sun-dried tomatoes, chopped
1 tablespoon capers, rinsed
Salt and freshly ground black pepper to taste

1. Mix the garlic, nutmeg, salt and pepper together with the vinegar and white wine. Whisk in the olive oil. Add the chicken pieces, turning to coat well. Marinate in the refrigerator for 3 hours.

2. Remove the chicken, wipe off excess marinade and pat dry. Lightly dust each piece with the seasoned flour. Over medium-high heat, warm half of the olive oil in a nonstick skillet. Add the chicken and cook for 10 minutes. Turn and cook for 10 more minutes.

3. Remove the chicken and drain on a paper towel, pouring off as much oil as possible. Return the pan to high heat, add 1 cup of water, scrape well and simmer until the liquid is reduced by half. Set aside.

4. In a heavy casserole over medium heat, warm the remaining ¼ cup of olive oil. Add the onion and cook until soft, about 5 minutes, stirring to avoid burning. Add the shallots and garlic and continue cooking, stirring occasionally, for 5 minutes. Add the broth resulting from the deglazing, as well as the tomato puree, and simmer for 5 minutes. Add the olives, sun-dried tomatoes and capers and stir. Simmer for a minute or two, taste and adjust seasoning with salt and pepper.

5. Add the chicken, turning each piece so that it is covered as much as possible. Cover and simmer over low heat for 40 to 50 minutes, until a fork inserted into the thigh yields clear juice. Serve with beans and rice.

YIELD: 4 SERVINGS ⤙ *Molly O'Neill*

✤ EASY ✤

NEW MEXICAN CHICKEN WITH PUMPKIN SEED SAUCE

(Adapted from *The New York Times Heritage Cook Book*)

1 2½- to 3-pound chicken, cut in
    serving pieces
Salt and freshly ground black pepper
2 tablespoons vegetable oil
½ cup pumpkin seeds (pipians or
    pepitas)
¼ cup blanched almonds

¼ cup cumin seeds
1 clove garlic, finely chopped
3 canned green chilies, seeded and
    chopped
¼ cup chopped flat-leaf parsley
1 cup chicken broth

1. Season the chicken pieces with salt and pepper and brown on all sides in the oil. Pour off extra oil.

2. Toast the pumpkin seeds, almonds and cumin in a hot, dry skillet over low heat, shaking often, until almonds are golden.

3. Grind the toasted mixture in a food processor, blender or with a mortar and pestle. Add the garlic, chilies and parsley and mix well. Gradually stir in the broth. Pour into a saucepan. Bring to a boil and pour over the chicken. Cover and simmer 40 minutes, or until chicken is done.

YIELD: 4 SERVINGS

✦ EASY ✦

GEORGIAN CHICKEN IN POMEGRANATE AND TAMARIND SAUCE

(Adapted from *The Essential Book of Jewish Festival Cooking*)

Tamarind, pomegranate and similar formerly exotic ingredients are now readily available and even fashionable, so recipes requiring them do not seem so daunting anymore.

4 medium yellow onions, diced

4 medium red onions, diced

2 cups chopped fresh cilantro

10 garlic cloves, minced

1 teaspoon sweet paprika

1 teaspoon hot paprika or cayenne pepper

1 teaspoon black pepper

3 tablespoons tamarind paste (see Note), diluted in 3 tablespoons water

½ cup pomegranate paste (see Note), diluted in ½ cup water, or 1 cup pomegranate juice

2 tablespoons ketchup

1 teaspoon salt

10 skinless chicken thighs

10 skinless chicken legs

Seeds from pomegranate, for garnish

1. In a large Dutch oven or in a pot with a tight-fitting lid, mix the onions, 1½ cups cilantro, the garlic and the spices. Blend in the diluted tamarind paste, the diluted pomegranate paste, the ketchup and the salt.

2. Add chicken thighs and legs to pot, and submerge in sauce. Cover, and cook on medium-high heat for 10 minutes, then lower heat, and cook for 1 hour. Uncover, adjust seasonings to taste, and continue cooking for 20 minutes.

3. Transfer chicken and sauce to a serving platter, and garnish with remaining cilantro. Sprinkle pomegranate seeds over platter, and serve hot.

NOTE: Sold in Middle Eastern and Indian markets and some supermarkets. Or, see "Selected Sources for Ingredients," page 352.

YIELD: 4 TO 6 SERVINGS ⚮ *Joan Nathan*

✦ EASY ✦

WEST AFRICAN MARINATED CHICKEN (YASSA AU POULET)

(Adapted from *The African-American Kitchen*)

This tangy chicken with lemon and onions is from a compilation of intriguing heirloom and contemporary recipes that Ms. Medearis started recording at the suggestion of family members.

2 cups sliced onion

3 cloves garlic, minced

½ teaspoon minced fresh hot green chili

½ teaspoon ground ginger

1 teaspoon white pepper

1 tablespoon salt, or to taste

1 cup fresh lemon juice

1¼ cups water

5 tablespoons peanut oil

1 2½- to 3-pound chicken, cut in serving pieces

1. In a large baking dish combine the onion, garlic, chili, ginger, pepper and salt. Stir in the lemon juice, 1 cup of the water and 1 tablespoon of the oil. Place the chicken pieces in the dish, coat with this mixture, cover and refrigerate at least 4 hours, turning the chicken every half hour.

2. Remove the chicken from the marinade and pat dry with paper towels. Press the marinade through a fine sieve set over a bowl. Reserve the solids and liquid separately.

3. Heat remaining oil in a heavy skillet. Brown chicken in oil over medium heat, turning to brown pieces evenly. When chicken has browned, remove it from skillet and discard all but 1 tablespoon of oil.

4. Reheat remaining tablespoon of oil in skillet. Add the solids from the marinade to skillet, and cook, stirring constantly, until onion is transparent, about 5 minutes. Return chicken to skillet, add ½ cup of marinade liquid and ¼ cup of water. Bring to a boil, partly cover pan, lower heat to a simmer and cook about 25 minutes, until chicken is done.

YIELD: 4 SERVINGS ⤙ *Florence Fabricant*

✤ EASY ✤
MOIRA HODGSON'S CHICKEN TAGINE WITH ALMONDS AND RAISINS

This tagine (Moroccan for "stew") is low-calorie and very good with plain white rice. Or you could serve it with instant couscous made with rich, preferably homemade, chicken stock.

1 3-pound chicken, cut up	½ teaspoon turmeric
Coarse salt and freshly ground pepper to taste	2 teaspoons ground ginger
1 large onion, sliced	1 teaspoon ground cinnamon
2 carrots, sliced	1 cup water
1 clove garlic, crushed	½ cup whole peeled almonds
Pinch saffron	½ cup raisins

1. Pat the chicken pieces dry with paper towels. Put them in a large heavy pan. Season with salt and pepper. Add the onion, carrots and garlic.

2. Sprinkle on the saffron, turmeric, ginger and cinnamon. Pour in the water, cover and cook for 30 minutes.

3. Add the almonds and the raisins. Cover and cook for another 30 minutes or until the chicken is tender.

YIELD: 4 SERVINGS   *Moira Hodgson*

SHALLOTS'S
CHICKEN TAGINE WITH OLIVES
AND PRESERVED LEMONS

(Adapted from Shallots, New York City)

Tagine (TAH-jean) refers to a Moroccan stew and to the traditional earthenware vessel—a shallow dish with a tall, conical lid—in which the dish is cooked and served.

5 cloves garlic, finely chopped

¼ teaspoon saffron threads,
    pulverized

½ teaspoon ground ginger

1 teaspoon sweet paprika

½ teaspoon ground cumin

½ teaspoon turmeric

Salt and freshly ground black pepper

1 chicken, cut in 8 pieces

2 tablespoons extra-virgin olive oil

3 medium onions, sliced thin

1 cinnamon stick

8 kalamata olives, pitted and halved

8 cracked green olives, pitted and
    halved

1 large or 3 small preserved lemons
    (sold in specialty food shops)

1 cup chicken stock

Juice of ½ lemon

1 tablespoon chopped flat-leaf
    parsley

1. Mix garlic, saffron, ginger, paprika, cumin and turmeric together. If not using kosher chicken, add ½ teaspoon salt. Add pepper to taste. Rub chicken with mixture, cover and refrigerate and marinate 3 to 4 hours.

2. Heat oil in heavy skillet. Add chicken and brown on all sides. Remove to platter. Add onions to skillet, and cook over medium-low heat about 15 minutes, until lightly browned. Transfer to tagine, if you are using one, or leave in skillet. Add cinnamon stick.

3. Put chicken on onions. Scatter with olives. Quarter the lemons, remove pulp and cut skin in strips. Scatter strips over chicken. Mix stock and lemon juice. Pour over chicken.

4. Cover tagine or skillet. Place over low heat, and cook about 30 minutes, until chicken is done. Scatter parsley on top, and serve.

YIELD: 4 SERVINGS ⤚ *Florence Fabricant*

✦ EASY ✦

NICOLE ROUTHIER'S BRAISED VIETNAMESE CHICKEN WINGS WITH GINGER

(Adapted from *The Foods of Vietnam*)

A Vietnamese dish that is quick and simple, with a touch of the exotic. It can be served with rice as a main course or an appetizer.

> 2 pounds chicken wings
> 1 cup sugar
> ¼ cup nuoc mam (fish sauce) (see Note)
> 4 shallots sliced as thinly as possible
> 1 tablespoon finely shredded fresh ginger
> Salt to taste if desired
> Freshly ground pepper to taste

1. Cut each chicken wing into 3 pieces, the main wing joint, second joint and wing tip. Discard the wing tip.

2. Put the sugar in a large, heavy saucepan. Do not add liquid. Cook, stirring and watching carefully to prevent burning and scorching. Shake and swirl the pan over the heat until the sugar becomes liquid and caramel colored. It will smoke slightly. Add the nuoc mam and swirl the pan off heat until blended. Quickly add the shallots and stir. Add the fresh ginger root, salt and ground pepper.

3. Add the wing pieces to the saucepan and cover. Return to moderate heat and cook, stirring occasionally, for 30 to 40 minutes until the pieces are tender. Skim off excess fat. Serve with hot rice, if desired.

NOTE: See "Selected Sources for Ingredients," page 352.

YIELD: 4 SERVINGS 〜 *Craig Claiborne*

✦ EASY ✦
MADHUR JAFFREY'S
LEMONY CHICKEN WITH CILANTRO

(Adapted from Madhur Jaffrey)

Jonathan Reynolds: "Madhur Jaffrey not only changed the way this country views Indian food but also affected the way restaurants do, too, perhaps more than anyone. One of her early books, Indian Cooking, *has sold more than a million copies worldwide, and an updated reissue has just appeared. Altogether, she has written 20 and found time to appear in more than 20 movies."*

2 1-inch cubes fresh ginger, peeled and coarsely chopped

6 tablespoons vegetable oil

3 pounds skinless chicken legs, drumstick and thigh separated

5 cloves garlic, very finely chopped

3 cups finely chopped cilantro leaves

1 bird's-eye chili (tiny, very hot chili), very finely chopped

¼ teaspoon cayenne pepper

2 teaspoons ground cumin

1 teaspoon ground coriander seeds

½ teaspoon ground turmeric

1 teaspoon salt, or to taste

2 tablespoons lemon juice

1. Put the ginger and ¼ cup water into a blender and blend into a paste. Set aside.

2. Place the oil in a wide, heavy, preferably nonstick pot over medium-high heat. When hot, add as many chicken pieces as fit in a single layer and brown on both sides. Remove them and continue until all the chicken is browned.

3. Add the garlic to the hot oil. As soon as it turns medium brown, turn down the heat to medium and pour in the ginger paste. Stir and fry for a minute. Add the cilantro, chili, cayenne, cumin, coriander seeds, turmeric and salt. Cook, stirring, for a minute. Add the chicken pieces as well as any juices that have accumulated. Add ⅔ cup water to the pot and the lemon juice. Stir and bring to a boil. Cover tightly, turn heat to low and cook for 15 minutes. Turn the chicken pieces over. Cover and cook for 10 to 15 minutes more, until chicken is cooked through.

4. Remove the chicken. If the sauce is too thin, boil some of the liquid away over a higher heat. Serve with basmati rice.

YIELD: 6 SERVINGS ⌁ *Jonathan Reynolds*

CORIANDER CHICKEN

(Adapted from *Savoring the Spice Coast of India: Fresh Flavors from Kerala*)

¼ cup vegetable oil

2 cups thinly sliced onion

2 teaspoons minced garlic

2 teaspoons minced ginger

1 teaspoon minced serrano or
   Thai chili

10 to 12 fresh curry leaves (see Note)

2 tablespoons ground coriander

1 teaspoon ground black pepper

½ teaspoon cayenne

¼ teaspoon turmeric

⅛ teaspoon cinnamon

⅛ teaspoon ground cloves

⅛ teaspoon ground cardamom

1½ teaspoons salt

2 pounds boneless, skinless chicken
   breasts, cut into 1-inch cubes

½ cup coconut milk

¼ cup chopped cilantro, plus additional
   leaves for garnish

1. In a large deep pan, heat-oil over medium-high heat. Sauté onions until edges are nicely browned. Add garlic, ginger, chili and curry leaves and fry for 1 minute.

2. Stir in coriander, pepper, cayenne, turmeric, cinnamon, clove, cardamom, salt and a few teaspoons of water to prevent spices from sticking. Fry for 2 minutes, stirring constantly.

3. Add chicken pieces and continue stirring over medium-high heat until the pink color disappears. Add ¼ cup coconut milk and ½ cup water and bring to a boil. Reduce heat and simmer, covered, for 20 minutes.

4. Add remaining coconut milk and chopped cilantro, bring just to a boil and re-move from heat. Check salt. Garnish with cilantro leaves and serve immediately.

NOTE: Fresh curry leaves may be found in almost any Indian grocery store and also in many Southeast Asian grocery stores.

YIELD: 4 SERVINGS   *Amanda Hesser*

CHICKEN COOKED IN COCONUT MILK

(Adapted from Craig Claiborne's Gourmet Diet)

1 2½-pound chicken, cut into serving pieces
Freshly ground black pepper to taste
2 tablespoons peanut, vegetable or corn oil
¾ cup finely chopped onion
2 teaspoons finely minced garlic
1 bay leaf
1 teaspoon turmeric
1 tablespoon chopped fresh ginger, or 1 teaspoon ground
½ teaspoon ground cumin
½ teaspoon ground coriander
¼ teaspoon hot red pepper flakes
1½ cups canned coconut milk

1. Sprinkle the chicken with a generous grinding of pepper.

2. Heat the oil in a heavy skillet large enough to hold the chicken pieces in one layer. Add the chicken pieces skin-side down and cook for about 5 minutes, or until golden brown on one side. Turn the pieces and cook until browned on the other side, about 5 minutes. Carefully pour off the fat from the skillet.

3. Add the onion, garlic, bay leaf, turmeric, ginger, cumin, coriander and hot pepper. Add the coconut milk.

4. Turn the pieces of chicken in the milk. Partly cover and cook for 8 minutes. Uncover and cook 7 minutes longer, turning the pieces of chicken in the sauce as they cook.

YIELD: 4 SERVINGS

✦ EASY ✦
GREEN-CURRY CHICKEN

(Adapted from *Real Thai*)

Thai eggplants—one varietal is called Kermit—are small and round, the size of a tangerine, and retain their shape and texture, despite having a very thin skin. As they roast, they soften slightly but still come out more like a pickled green tomato, with a wet, almost crunchy texture, and with lots of seeds that pop in your mouth.

2 14-ounce cans coconut milk
¼ cup green curry paste (see Note)
1 skinless, boneless chicken breast, cut into bite-size pieces
2 skinless, boneless chicken thighs, cut into bite-size pieces
1½ cups quartered Thai eggplant or purple eggplant, cut into 1-inch cubes
2 tablespoons Thai fish sauce
1 tablespoon palm sugar or brown sugar
½ teaspoon salt
12 kaffir lime leaves, optional (see Note)
½ cup fresh basil leaves
9 long thin strips red bell pepper

1. Remove thick top layer of cream from each can of coconut milk, reserving the thinner liquid. Place cream in a medium-size heavy saucepan and bring to a gentle boil. Cook until oil begins to glisten on the surface, 6 to 8 minutes. Add curry paste, and stir to mix well. Continue cooking over medium heat until curry paste releases a pleasing aroma, 1 to 2 minutes.

2. Add chicken; stir to coat evenly with coconut cream mixture. Cook until mixture thickens slightly, about 2 minutes. Increase heat to high, and add coconut milk left in the cans, eggplant, fish sauce, sugar and salt. Stir well. Add 6 of the lime leaves, if using. Adjust heat to maintain a gentle, active boil. Cook, stirring occasionally, until eggplant is just tender, 8 to 10 minutes.

3. Remove chicken curry from heat, and adjust seasonings with more fish sauce, sugar or curry paste as desired. Transfer to a serving bowl, and garnish with basil leaves, red pepper and remaining 6 lime leaves. Serve hot or warm with rice.

NOTE: Green curry paste and kaffir lime leaves are available in Asian markets. Or, see "Selected Sources for Ingredients," page 352.

YIELD: 4 SERVINGS ∼ *Amanda Hesser*

‡ EASY ‡

NIGELLA LAWSON'S CHICKEN AND APRICOT MASALA

Nigella Lawson: *"This chicken masala is my version of a curry: it demands little effort and delivers a huge amount of flavor. I know a recipe requiring a spice paste is off-putting, but mine involves no more than a few spices and some minced ginger and garlic. After the paste, all you need are some onions, some chicken thighs (better flavor and texture than breasts, in my opinion, but if you feel happier with the latter, be my guest), tomatoes and a cup of dried apricots. Fruit with meat is not to everyone's taste, but there is nothing invasive about the apricots here. Rather, their fragrant sweetness is the perfect complement to the mellow heat of the light sauce. The masala has all the impact you need, so you could freely consider serving no more than a bowlful of rice alongside it."*

1 cup dried apricots	2 onions, peeled and finely chopped
½ teaspoon hot red pepper flakes	1 teaspoon salt
1 teaspoon ground cumin	3 pounds boneless, skinless chicken
1 teaspoon ground coriander	thighs, diced
4 cloves	4 medium tomatoes, cut into ½-inch
4 cardamom pods, lightly crushed	dice
1 tablespoon minced garlic	2 tablespoons tomato paste, diluted
1 tablespoon minced ginger	in ½ cup water
¼ cup peanut oil	3 tablespoons chopped cilantro
1 cinnamon stick	leaves

1. Soak apricots overnight in 2 cups cold water, or cover with 2 cups hot water and soak until swollen and softened, 2 to 3 hours.

2. Prepare masala: In a small bowl, combine hot pepper flakes, cumin, coriander,

cloves, cardamom, garlic and ginger. Add ¼ cup water, and stir to make a paste. Set aside.

3. In a large sauté pan over medium heat, heat oil and cinnamon stick. Add onions and salt, and sauté until onions begin to soften, 2 to 3 minutes. Add masala, stir. Add chicken, and stir for about 5 minutes. Add apricots and their soaking liquid, diced tomatoes and diluted tomato paste.

4. Cover and simmer until chicken is cooked through, about 30 minutes. Check cooking liquid about halfway through; if chicken is covered with liquid, remove cover for remainder of cooking. Transfer to a large bowl, sprinkle with cilantro and serve hot.

YIELD: 6 SERVINGS   *Nigella Lawson*

CHICKEN-STUFFED FIGS, ONIONS AND EGGPLANTS IN TAMARIND SAUCE

(Adapted from Moshe Basson)

A signature dish from Moshe Basson, one of Israel's leading chefs. Like most of the menu that was served at Eucalyptus, a Jerusalem restaurant that has closed, and that is now served at Carmei Ha'ir, his new Jerusalem restaurant, this dish draws heavily on ingredients mentioned in the Old Testament.

12 medium onions, peeled
3 tablespoons olive oil
2 skinless, boneless chicken breasts
½ teaspoon ground cardamom
¼ teaspoon ground cloves
1 teaspoon salt
½ teaspoon white pepper

3 teaspoons tamarind concentrate (see Note)
2 dried or fresh figs, diced, plus 10 fresh whole figs for stuffing
3 tablespoons brown sugar
10 small Italian eggplants

1. Dice 2 onions, and place them in a large skillet with 2 tablespoons olive oil. Sauté over medium-high heat for 5 minutes.

2. Using a meat grinder or a food processor fitted with a steel blade, grind or pulse chicken until finely diced. Add chicken, cardamom, cloves and salt and pepper to skillet, and continue cooking over low heat until chicken is lightly browned. Adjust seasonings and remove from heat.

3. Mix tamarind concentrate with 4 cups hot water in a large saucepan, and bring to boil. Add 2 diced figs along with brown sugar. Reduce heat, cover, and simmer for 5 minutes.

4. Core remaining onions from bottoms up, leaving tops intact, removing all but a few inside layers. Stuff them ¾ of the way full with chicken mixture. Close hole at bottom of onion with a small piece of onion from core. Place stuffed onions in pot with tamarind sauce. Cover pot, and bring to boil. Reduce heat, and simmer for 30 minutes.

5. Meanwhile, in a large skillet, brown eggplants on all sides in remaining tablespoon of olive oil. Remove from heat, and allow to cool for 5 minutes. Make a slit in one side of each eggplant about 1 inch deep and 2 inches long. Carefully open, and scoop out seeds, making a pocket large enough to hold about ¼ cup chicken mixture. Stuff eggplants, and add them to onions in pot. Cook covered for 30 minutes more.

6. Open whole figs from bottoms up, and remove seeds. Stuff with 1 tablespoon chicken filling. Add figs to pot with onions and eggplants, and simmer for 10 minutes. Serve one stuffed fig, one eggplant and one onion to each person, with sauce drizzled over all three.

NOTE: Tamarind concentrate is sold in Middle Eastern and Indian markets and some supermarkets. Or, see "Selected Sources for Ingredients," page 352.

YIELD: 10 SERVINGS ⟞ *Joan Nathan*

A MEAL IN ITSELF

CHICKEN POT-AU-FEU

2 teaspoons olive oil

1 chicken, about 3 pounds, cut into serving pieces

6 cups chicken broth, homemade or low-sodium canned

1 teaspoon coriander seeds, crushed

2 cloves garlic, peeled and thinly sliced

1 medium-size onion, peeled and quartered

4 small carrots, peeled and cut into 2-inch lengths

8 small new potatoes, halved

4 leeks, white and light green parts only, washed and cut into 2-inch pieces

1 teaspoon salt, plus more to taste

Freshly ground pepper to taste

2 teaspoons chopped Italian parsley

1. Heat the olive oil in a large, wide pot over medium-high heat. Add the chicken and sear until browned, about 4 minutes per side. Remove from the pot and set aside. Place the chicken broth, coriander seeds and garlic in the pot and bring to the boil. Add the chicken, lower the heat, partially cover and simmer for 20 minutes.

2. Add the onion, carrots, potatoes, leeks and 1 teaspoon of salt, partially cover and simmer until the chicken and vegetables are tender, about 30 minutes. Season with additional salt and pepper if needed. Divide the chicken and vegetables among 4 large bowls, ladle the broth over them, sprinkle with parsley and serve.

YIELD: 4 SERVINGS ⟿ *Molly O'Neill*

CHICKEN AND VEGETABLES
IN CORIANDER BROTH

Whole coriander seed is coriander at its mildest. It has a slightly citrus flavor and imparts a subtle perfume when simmered uncracked. It can be used, as it is in this broth for poaching, to create a deep, dark, mysterious background of flavor.

2 quarts chicken broth, homemade or low-sodium canned

1 tablespoon coriander seeds

1 tablespoon olive oil

1 3½-pound chicken, cut into serving pieces

½ pound peeled baby carrots (about 1½ cups)

3 medium leeks, white and light green parts only, washed well,
   halved crosswise and julienned

2 teaspoons kosher salt, plus more to taste

Freshly ground pepper to taste

2 baking potatoes, peeled and cut into 1-inch chunks

1 tablespoon gin

1. Bring the broth and coriander seeds to a boil in a large soup pot. Lower heat and simmer for 1 hour.

2. Meanwhile, heat the oil in a large skillet over medium heat. Working in batches, add the chicken to the skillet and brown. Transfer to the soup pot. Add the carrots and leeks. Season with 2 teaspoons of salt and pepper.

3. Cover pot and bring to a boil. Lower heat and simmer for 25 minutes. Add the potatoes and simmer until chicken and vegetables are tender, about 15 minutes longer. Stir in gin and season with additional salt and pepper if needed. Divide among 4 soup plates and serve immediately.

YIELD: 4 SERVINGS ↜ *Molly O'Neill*

ERIC RIPERT'S
CHICKEN BOUILLABAISSE

Eric Ripert, the chef and owner of Le Bernadin, a four-star restaurant in Manhattan, prepared this dish for his staff. "It's really a Provençal fricassee," he says. "We didn't call it a bouillabaisse in Provence, but except for the chicken and the chicken stock, it uses the same ingredients as a bouillabaisse, so you know exactly what it is. The breast meat cooks fast, so I take out those pieces first and let the rest cook longer and actually, the whole dish is better made the day before and reheated."

1 frying chicken, cut in 10 pieces
Salt and freshly ground white pepper
2 tablespoons plus ¾ cup extra-virgin olive oil
2 medium onions, thinly sliced
1 cup thinly sliced leeks, white and light green parts only
1 head garlic, peeled, all but 2 cloves sliced thin
½ fennel bulb, sliced thin
3 pinches saffron threads
¼ teaspoon cayenne pepper, or to taste
⅔ cup diced ripe tomato or diced well-drained canned tomato
1 tablespoon tomato paste
½ tablespoon flour
3½ cups chicken stock
8 small Yukon Gold potatoes
1 6-inch piece baguette
1 large egg yolk
1 6-inch strip orange peel
1 ounce Pernod or Ricard
4 branches fresh thyme

1. Dry chicken, and season with salt and pepper. Pour 2 tablespoons oil in deep sauté pan or casserole large enough to hold chicken in a single layer. Place over high heat until starting to smoke, add chicken skin-side down, and sauté until golden brown, turning to brown both sides. Remove chicken to a platter, lower heat to medium, and add onions, leeks, sliced garlic and fennel. Cook, stirring, until starting to soften.

2. Sprinkle on 2 pinches saffron and the cayenne, cook a few minutes longer, then add tomato and tomato paste. Cook a minute more, sprinkle with flour, stir, then return chicken to pan, along with any juices from the platter. Add stock, bring to a simmer, and cook 20 minutes. Remove 4 breast pieces from the pan. Continue cooking remaining chicken 15 to 20 minutes longer, until done, then remove from pan. Skim any foam from surface of sauce.

3. While chicken cooks, place potatoes in a saucepan, add salted water to cover, and boil until just tender. Drain. Peel when cool enough to handle.

4. Place remaining pinch saffron in a small dish, and pour 1 tablespoon boiling water over it. Slice piece of baguette lengthwise in 4 pieces, and toast. Rub with one garlic clove, and brush with a little oil.

5. Place egg yolk in a mixing bowl. Force remaining garlic clove through a press, and add it to yolk. Beat with a whisk. Strain in water from steeping saffron, and beat. Slowly drizzle in remaining olive oil, beating vigorously, until mixture thickens to mayonnaise consistency. Season with salt and pepper, and refrigerate until serving time.

6. Add orange peel, Pernod and thyme to sauté pan, cook 5 minutes, then remove orange peel and thyme. Season sauce with salt and cayenne to taste. Add potatoes and chicken to pan. Reheat.

7. Serve chicken and potatoes in warm soup plates with sauce. Spread some of the garlic-saffron mayonnaise (aioli) on toasted baguette slices, and place one alongside each serving. (Reserve remaining aioli for another use.) Serve at once.

YIELD: 4 SERVINGS ⌐ *Florence Fabricant*

JACQUES PEPIN'S
CHICKEN RAGOUT MEME

This chicken ragout reminds chef Pepin of his mother's cooking; in fact, this combination of ingredients is very close to the type of food he ate as a child growing up in France. Although, unlike his mother, he removes the skin from the chicken legs for this recipe, like her he adds some salt pork, sometimes called cured pork or sweet "pickle." This type of meat is called lard in France, hence the name lardons for the small pieces often added to stews and other dishes. French lard is similar to what the Italians call pancetta, and both of these versions of unsmoked bacon are usually leaner than the salt pork found in markets in this country. Look for a slab with as much meat on it as possible, then cut it into half-inch pieces; blanch the pieces (lardons) to remove most of the salt, and sauté to enhance the flavor.

1 tablespoon canola or safflower oil
6 chicken legs (about 3¼ pounds), skin removed
1 6-ounce piece salt pork, as lean as possible
4½ cups water
1 bunch scallions, cleaned and cut into ½-inch dice (1 cup)
1 onion (8 ounces), peeled and coarsely chopped (2 cups)
1 tablespoon all-purpose flour
3 large cloves garlic, peeled and crushed
1 teaspoon dried thyme leaves
3 bay leaves
¾ teaspoon salt
1½ pounds small red potatoes (10 to 12)
¼ teaspoon Tabasco sauce (optional)

1. Heat the oil in a large, sturdy saucepan. When it is hot, add the skinless chicken legs and sauté over medium heat for 6 to 8 minutes, turning occasionally until browned on all sides.

2. Meanwhile, cut the salt pork into ½-inch pieces and place in a saucepan with 2 cups of the water. Bring to a boil and boil for 1 minute. Drain in a sieve and rinse under cold water.

3. When chicken is well browned, transfer it to a plate and add salt-pork pieces to the drippings in the pan used to cook the chicken. Cook the salt pork, partly covered (to prevent splattering) over medium heat, for 5 minutes, until the pieces are brown and crisp. Add scallions and onions, mix well and cook for 5 minutes over medium heat, stirring occasionally. Then add flour, mix well and continue browning mixture over medium heat for 1 minute, stirring occasionally.

4. Add remaining 2½ cups of water along with garlic, thyme, bay leaves and salt and bring to a boil, stirring occasionally. Add potatoes and chicken legs, bring mixture back to a boil and boil gently, covered, over low heat for 30 minutes. Add Tabasco sauce, if desired, stir and serve.

YIELD: 6 SERVINGS *Jacques Pepin*

LE CIRQUE'S SPRING CHICKEN WITH LIME AND CILANTRO

(Adapted from Sottha Khunn, Le Cirque, New York City)

THE BROTH

1 3½- to 4-pound chicken

3 quarts chicken broth, homemade or low-sodium canned

2 large pieces lime peel

1 tablespoon coriander seed, crushed

4 stalks lemongrass, thinly sliced, or 2 tablespoons grated ginger

1 bay leaf

1 clove garlic

4 stems fresh mint leaves, minced

6 stems cilantro, minced

4 whole black peppercorns

¼ teaspoon dried chili pepper

½ teaspoon salt

THE CILANTRO PESTO

1 cup cilantro leaves

½ cup mint leaves

½ cup basil leaves

2 tablespoons olive oil

½ teaspoon salt

1 teaspoon pepper

THE GARNISH

1 pound ¼-inch-wide fresh Chinese egg noodles

1 leek, rinsed, thinly sliced crosswise

1 medium carrot, peeled and diced

½ celery stalk, rinsed and diced

1 cup cilantro leaves

1 cup fresh mint leaves

1 lime, quartered

1. To make the broth, put the chicken in a stockpot. Add the remaining ingredients and bring to a boil. Lower the heat and simmer for 30 to 35 minutes.

2. Meanwhile, make the cilantro pesto: Put the cilantro, mint, basil and olive oil in a blender and puree until smooth. Season with salt and pepper. Set aside.

3. Bring a large pot of salted water to a boil. Add the noodles. Cook for 2 minutes. Drain and rinse under cold running water. Set aside.

4. Carefully lift the chicken out of the broth. Set broth aside. Remove skin and shred the meat. Set aside. Strain the broth through a sieve lined with cheesecloth into a clean saucepan. Season to taste.

5. Bring broth to a boil. Add the shredded chicken, leek, carrot and celery. Lower heat and simmer until the meat is warmed, about 5 minutes. Divide noodles into 4 bowls. Ladle the soup into the bowls. Add a dollop of pesto, garnish with cilantro and mint leaves, and place a wedge of lime on each.

YIELD: 4 SERVINGS *Molly O'Neill*

COUNTRY CAPTAIN

½ cup currants

1 cup warm chicken stock

4 strips bacon

1 5-pound chicken cut into 8 pieces, or 4 whole chicken breasts (with skin and bones attached), 12 to 14 ounces each

⅓ cup all-purpose flour, seasoned with ¼ teaspoon salt and ⅛ teaspoon black pepper

2 ribs celery, finely chopped

2 medium yellow onions, peeled and finely chopped

1 medium green bell pepper, seeded and finely chopped

2 cloves garlic, peeled and minced

2 cups fresh or drained canned tomatoes, peeled, cored and chopped

1 tablespoon hot curry powder

2 teaspoons dark brown sugar

½ teaspoon salt

½ teaspoon dried thyme leaves

½ teaspoon ground mace

½ teaspoon ground black pepper

¼ teaspoon ground white pepper

½ cup slivered almonds, toasted

1 teaspoon finely chopped parsley

Steamed white long-grain rice

1. In a small bowl, cover currants with warm chicken stock. Set aside.

2. Fry the bacon in a nonstick skillet over medium heat until crisp, drain on paper towels, crumble and reserve. Drain all but 3 tablespoons bacon grease from pan.

3. Heat grease in the skillet over medium heat. Dredge chicken in seasoned flour. Shake off excess and cook in grease until tender, about 30 minutes, turning pieces frequently for uniform browning.

4. Preheat oven to 325 degrees. Remove chicken to a bowl. Add celery, onions, bell pepper and garlic to drippings in pan. Sauté vegetables, about 5 minutes. Strain stock from currants and add stock to skillet along with the tomatoes, curry, brown sugar, salt, thyme, mace and pepper.

5. Stir tomato mixture, bring to boil and reduce heat to low. Cover and simmer for about 10 minutes.

6. Place chicken pieces in a large shallow baking dish, cover with tomato mixture and bake for 30 minutes. Sprinkle with reserved currants, almonds, parsley and the crumbled bacon and return to oven for 10 to 15 minutes more. Serve hot with steamed rice.

YIELD: 6 TO 8 SERVINGS *Julia Reed*

TRADITIONAL CHICKEN PAPRIKA WITH DUMPLINGS

(Adapted from Rosie Jakab)

In 1999, Rosie Jakab, a Romanian in her 90s who was still cooking the food she loved at a home for the elderly where she lived, was the subject of Nightline *on ABC News. The program was part of an oral-history project to document what remains of Jewish life in Central and Eastern Europe, including an interactive archive of recipes—of which this is one—gathered in Jewish population centers in thirteen countries.*

FOR THE CHICKEN

1 3-pound chicken

¼ cup olive oil

1 teaspoon salt

1 large onion, chopped fine

1 tablespoon mild paprika

¼ teaspoon hot paprika

1 cup chicken stock

1 tablespoon tomato paste

FOR THE DUMPLINGS

6 to 8 tablespoons flour

2 large eggs

¼ teaspoon salt

4 cups chicken stock or water

2 tablespoons parsley, chopped

1. Heat oven to 400 degrees.

2. Cut chicken into 8 pieces and pat dry with paper towels. Heat oil in a Dutch oven or a heavy frying pan that can go into oven. Sauté chicken over medium-high heat until pieces are golden brown, about 10 minutes. Remove chicken with a slotted spoon, and sprinkle with salt.

3. Place onion in same pan, sauté until soft. Remove pan from heat, and let cool for 2 minutes. Stir in mild and hot paprikas.

4. Return chicken to pan on top of onions. In a small saucepan, heat chicken stock, and stir in tomato paste. Bring to a boil, stirring until tomato paste dissolves. Pour over chicken.

5. Place pan, uncovered, in middle of oven for around 30 minutes. Turn chicken every 10 minutes or so. Sauce will thicken.

6. To make dumplings, mix flour with eggs and salt until a thick dough forms. In a saucepan, bring 4 cups of stock to a boil. Drop dumpling dough by half teaspoons into stock, simmering for about 4 minutes. Dumplings are done when plumped up and firm. Drain, and stir them into chicken mixture during the last 5 minutes of cooking. Sprinkle with parsley, and serve.

YIELD: 4 TO 6 SERVINGS   *Joan Nathan*

MARION CUNNINGHAM'S
POPOVERED CHICKEN

Since 1979, when she undertook the revision of The Fanny Farmer Cookbook, *which was first published in 1896, Marion Cunningham has never wavered in her devotion to simple American cooking. This recipe, she says, "is perfect for people who flunk dumplings."*

2 legs, 2 thighs and breast cut into 4 pieces from 3-pound chicken
3 tablespoons flour
Salt and pepper to taste
2 tablespoons shortening

THE BATTER
2 cups flour
1 teaspoon salt
5 large eggs
2 cups milk
2 tablespoons melted unsalted butter

THE GRAVY
2 tablespoons unsalted butter
2 tablespoons flour
1 cup homemade chicken stock
1 cup light cream
Salt and pepper to taste

1. Preheat oven to 425 degrees.
2. Wipe pieces of chicken dry.
3. Mix 3 tablespoons flour, salt and pepper and put on plate or wax paper. Lightly coat each piece of chicken with flour.
4. Melt 2 tablespoons shortening in skillet. When very hot add chicken pieces and brown on all sides. Remove to paper towels and pat free of excess oil.
5. Grease 14-by-9½-by-3-inch-deep (3-quart) baking dish. Place in oven while mixing popover batter.
6. In large bowl mix 2 cups flour with salt. Make well in center of flour and drop eggs into well. Beat eggs lightly, barely incorporating flour.

7. Add milk and melted butter and beat only until batter is well blended. Pour batter into very hot baking dish. Place pieces of browned chicken on top. Place dish back in oven and bake about 30 minutes; reduce heat to 325 degrees and bake 10 minutes more or until batter is golden brown.

8. While chicken is baking, make gravy. Melt 2 tablespoons butter in heavy skillet. Stir in 2 tablespoons flour. Cook for several minutes over medium heat, stirring constantly. Slowly add chicken stock and continue to stir until sauce is thickened. Add cream, stirring, and continue to cook for 3 minutes longer. Season with salt and pepper and serve.

YIELD: 4 SERVINGS

CASSEROLE OF BABY CHICKEN, BACON AND PEARL ONIONS

Baby chickens, or poussins, can be ordered from your butcher. Cornish hens, which usually weigh about 1¼ pounds, are an excellent substitute.

4 baby chickens, about 1 pound each
Salt and freshly ground black pepper
2 tablespoons unsalted butter
1 tablespoon vegetable oil
¼ pound slab bacon, in ½-inch dice
12 ounces pearl onions, peeled
1 tablespoon brown sugar
1 tablespoon flour
1 cup dry Riesling
1 pound fingerling or small yellow potatoes, sliced ¼-inch thick
3 cloves garlic, sliced
1 tablespoon chopped parsley

1. Dry the chickens and season them inside and out with salt and pepper.

2. Heat the butter and oil in a large oven-proof casserole or Dutch oven capable of holding 6 to 7 quarts. Add the chickens and sauté on all sides over medium heat until they are nicely browned. It is best not to crowd the chickens so you may not be able to do them all at the same time.

3. Remove the chickens from the casserole, add the bacon and sauté until it is browned. Remove the bacon from the casserole and pour off the fat, reserving 2 tablespoons of it in a small dish and discarding the rest.

4. Preheat oven to 375 degrees.

5. Add the onions and brown sugar to the casserole and sauté over medium heat until they start to caramelize but have not cooked through. Sprinkle with the flour, stir them around, then pour in the wine. Cook, stirring, to deglaze the casserole. Season with salt and pepper.

6. Return the chickens to the casserole, scatter the bacon over them, cover the casserole and put in the oven until the chickens are cooked through, about 45 minutes, basting once or twice during cooking.

7. While the chickens are cooking, put the reserved fat in a nonstick skillet and heat it. Add the potatoes and garlic and sauté, stirring, until the potatoes are tender and lightly browned, about 15 minutes. Season to taste with salt and pepper. Stir in the parsley. Set aside until the chickens are finished.

8. When the chickens have finished cooking, scatter the potato mixture over them, cover the casserole and return it to the oven for 5 minutes, then serve.

YIELD: 4 SERVINGS   *Florence Fabricant*

HOMINY GRILL'S
CAROLINA CHICKEN BOG

Ease of preparation is a marker of chicken bog, a rich and peppery one-pot stew that hails from the coastal plains of the Carolinas. The name derives from the way in which the pieces of chicken sit in the pot, like hummocks in a bog. Recipes for bog are as various as the 146 counties of North and South Carolina. This one features just about every part of the bird and mixed sausage—at least a pound or two of breakfast links, kielbasa and Italian sausage. There is no need to do any prepara-tion work before starting to cook. Instead, start by browning whatever needs to be browned. While that is happening, prepare the ingredients for the rest of the recipe—steps that can be taken care of once you have already begun cooking.

(Adapted from Robert Stehling, Hominy Grill, Charleston, S.C.)

3 tablespoons bacon fat, or neutral oil like corn or canola

¾ pound minced chicken gizzards and hearts

Salt and pepper

2 medium green bell peppers, diced

2 medium red bell peppers, diced

4 medium-to-large white onions, diced

4 celery ribs, trimmed and diced

2 tablespoons minced garlic

1 cup dry red wine

1 35-ounce can tomatoes, with liquid, chopped

6 tablespoons unsalted butter

4 tablespoons flour

1 pound mixed sausages and cured meat, like kielbasa, Italian sausage,
     breakfast links, chorizo, diced ham or bacon

2 cups chicken stock

1 branch thyme

¼ teaspoon red pepper flakes, or to taste

2 bay leaves

1 pound chopped chicken meat, preferably from thigh

8 chicken livers, trimmed and cut in half

1 tablespoon apple cider vinegar

½ cup Dijon mustard

Cooked white rice for serving

1. Put fat or oil in a deep skillet or large casserole over medium-high heat. A minute later, add gizzards and hearts and cook until quite brown and sticking to pan, at least 3 minutes. Stir once, sprinkle with salt and pepper, then brown other side. Add peppers, onions, celery and garlic and cook, stirring occasionally, until vegetables are soft, about 10 minutes. Add red wine and tomatoes, bring to a boil, and adjust heat so mixture simmers; cook for about 10 minutes.

2. Meanwhile, melt 4 tablespoons butter in a small skillet or saucepan over medium heat. Add flour and stir until smooth. Cook, stirring occasionally, until mixture turns quite brown, about 10 minutes. Add this roux to simmering stew; cook 5 minutes.

3. Add meats, stock, thyme, red pepper flakes and bay leaves; cook at a lively simmer, stirring occasionally, for about 40 minutes. Add chicken meat and cook another 15 minutes or more (this can sit on stove, simmering, for hours; add a little water or stock if it threatens to dry out).

4. Heat remaining butter in an 8- or 10-inch nonstick skillet over medium-high heat. When butter foam subsides, add livers, 1 or 2 at a time, and cook until quite brown on one side; sprinkle with salt and pepper as they cook. Turn and brown on other side.

5. Stir vinegar and mustard into stew. Add livers and stir. Serve over white rice.

YIELD: AT LEAST 8 SERVINGS ⟿ *Mark Bittman and Sam Sifton*

JASON EPSTEIN'S CHICKEN POTPIE

Jason Epstein made an elegant change in his re-creation of his grandmother's recipe for chicken potpie. As he wrote, "My grandmother's chicken potpie was a family favorite, but I didn't like her crust, which, no matter how shiny on top, was gummy underneath. When I began to make my own chicken pies, I saw that an obvious way to avoid this was to bake a puff-pastry crust separately and serve it in a wedge, like a gaufrette, atop the contents of the pie."

3 tablespoons vegetable oil

4 8-ounce skinless and boneless chicken breast halves, cut into 1-inch cubes

8 tablespoons unsalted butter, plus extra for greasing parchment

20 pearl onions, blanched and peeled

3 carrots, cut in ½-inch rounds

1 celery heart, cut in ½-inch dice

20 button mushroom caps or ½ pound porcini mushrooms, stems cut off, cut into 1-inch pieces

4 cups strong homemade chicken stock or 5 cups of organic chicken broth
   from a carton, reduced to 4, plus extra if needed
½ cup all-purpose flour
1½ cups half-and-half or heavy cream
1 sprig fresh rosemary, leaves finely chopped, plus extra for garnish
1 tablespoon chopped thyme leaves
1 tablespoon chopped Italian parsley
3 tablespoons dry sherry
Salt and freshly ground black pepper to taste
3 tablespoons lemon juice
1 pound homemade puff pastry (or Dufour brand ready-made)
Egg wash (1 large egg yolk beaten with 2 teaspoons heavy cream)

1. In a Dutch oven, heat oil over medium heat and sauté the chicken, in batches, until lightly golden but not cooked through. Set aside.

2. In the same, cleaned pan, melt 2 tablespoons butter. Sauté the onions until golden brown, about 5 minutes. Remove to bowl with the chicken. Repeat with carrots and celery and then mushrooms. In a separate pan, heat stock to boiling.

3. Clean Dutch oven again. Melt remaining butter over medium heat. Whisk in flour and cook until pale gold, 2 minutes. Whisk in boiling stock, half-and-half, herbs, sherry and salt and pepper and heat to a slow boil. Reduce heat and simmer 5 minutes or until thick enough to coat a spoon. (If too thick, add more stock.) Stir in 2 tablespoons lemon juice, the chicken and vegetables. Cover with buttered parchment. (Pie can be prepared ahead to this point and refrigerated until 1 hour before cooking.)

4. Preheat oven to 425 degrees. Roll out the pastry into a square just less than ½-inch thick and, using a very sharp knife, cut a round the size of the pot. Line a rimmed baking sheet with parchment and invert the round on top. (Sprinkle the scraps with sugar, twist them into corkscrew shapes and bake them as cookies.) If using Dufour, follow package directions.

5. Brush pastry with egg wash, without letting any drip down the sides, which will prevent it from rising evenly. Prick all over with a fork. (For a flatter, denser crust, omit the wash, cover pastry with a second sheet of parchment paper and a second sheet pan on top, forming a sandwich. This keeps the puff pastry from rising and provides a crunchy, buttery pastry.)

6. Bake pastry until puffed, browned and crisp, 15 to 20 minutes. Reduce heat to 350 degrees and bake until cooked through, 15 to 20 minutes longer.

7. Reduce oven temperature to 275 degrees. Bake chicken mixture until sauce is

bubbly around edges and chicken is just cooked through, about 30 minutes. Place baking sheet with pastry in oven to reheat the last 10 minutes of cooking.

8. To serve: Remove parchment from Dutch oven and taste sauce. Adjust seasoning and stir in remaining lemon juice if needed. Slide pastry onto chicken mixture and display your pie. Back in the kitchen, cut the crust into wedges with a serrated knife. Spoon chicken onto warmed plates, stick a corner of a wedge into each serving and garnish with rosemary.

NOTE: Reheat chicken in a microwave or double boiler—it may scorch over direct heat.

YIELD: 6 SERVINGS ⟍ *Jason Epstein*

THE QUILTED GIRAFFE'S CHICKEN POTPIE WITH BISCUIT TOPPING

(Adapted from the Quilted Giraffe, New York City)

Barry Wine, the chef and owner of Manhattan's The Quilted Giraffe, a four-star restaurant, now closed, uses sweet potatoes and fennel in his unconventional version of chicken potpie and caps it with a biscuit topping.

FOR THE FILLING

8 cups chicken stock
1 tablespoon black peppercorns
4 sprigs thyme
2 sprigs rosemary
3 cloves garlic, crushed
1 bay leaf
Salt to taste

2 chicken breasts, split

4 chicken legs

4 chicken thighs

4 small carrots, peeled and chopped coarse

2 small sweet potatoes, peeled and chopped coarse

1 medium-size leek, sliced and rinsed

4 small parsnips, peeled and chopped coarse

2 ribs celery, chopped coarse

1 fennel bulb, chopped coarse

4 tablespoons unsalted butter

3 tablespoons flour

¼ teaspoon chili powder

¼ teaspoon cayenne

Soy sauce to taste

Tabasco sauce to taste

Freshly ground pepper to taste

FOR THE BISCUIT TOPPING

2½ cups flour

2½ teaspoons baking powder

½ teaspoon baking soda

½ teaspoon salt

½ cup unsalted butter, melted

⅔ cup buttermilk

1. Put the chicken stock in a large pot and add the peppercorns, thyme, rosemary, garlic, and bay leaf. Add salt if using unsalted chicken stock. Bring to a boil.

2. Add the chicken pieces and lower the heat, simmering the chicken for about 25 minutes, until it is tender and comes easily off the bone. The legs may take longer to cook than the breasts. Remove the chicken from the liquid and set aside to cool.

3. Strain the stock through a fine strainer, then return to the pot and put over high heat. When the stock is boiling, add the carrots, sweet potatoes and leek and cook for 5 minutes. Then add the parsnips, celery and fennel. Return to a full boil and cook for 1 minute.

4. Remove the vegetables by passing the stock again through a strainer. Return the stock to the pot and simmer.

5. Remove the cooled chicken from the bones, tearing it into bite-sized pieces

and discarding the skin. Put the chicken and vegetables in a large ovenproof casserole and set aside.

6. Melt the butter in a small pan. When it starts to foam, add the flour, chili powder and cayenne and cook for several minutes, stirring constantly. Then, slowly add 1 cup of the hot chicken stock. Add to the rest of the chicken stock and bring to a boil. Season with soy sauce, Tabasco sauce, pepper and salt, taking into consideration that the flavors will soften when added to the chicken and vegetables.

7. Add the sauce to the vegetables and chicken, generously covering. At this point, the casserole can be refrigerated for up to 24 hours.

8. Preheat the oven to 425 degrees. Put the casserole in the oven while you make the biscuit topping.

9. To make the topping, mix the flour, baking powder, baking soda and salt, then add melted butter. Mix with fingers. Add buttermilk, continuing to mix the ingredients by hand. Make 8 ball-shaped biscuits, then flatten slightly.

10. Remove casserole from the oven. Place the biscuits around the top of the surface of the casserole. Bake until biscuits are golden brown, about 25 minutes.

YIELD: 8 SERVINGS   *Trish Hall*

SPINACH-AND-CHICKEN RAGOUT OVER POLENTA

2 teaspoons olive oil

4 chicken legs

4 chicken thighs

3 large cloves garlic, peeled and minced

1 large onion, peeled, halved and thinly sliced

12 cups spinach leaves, washed and stemmed

1 28-ounce can plum tomatoes, drained and coarsely chopped

2 green bell peppers, roasted, stemmed, cored and cut into ½-inch squares

½ cup chicken broth, homemade or low-sodium canned

4 cups water

4 teaspoons salt

1 cup cornmeal

1 tablespoon red wine vinegar

Freshly ground pepper to taste

1. Heat 1 teaspoon of oil in a nonstick skillet over medium heat. Add the chicken and brown, about 10 minutes. Remove from the pan. Add 1 teaspoon of oil and the garlic, lower the heat to medium-low and cook, stirring constantly, for 30 seconds. Add the onion and cook, stirring frequently, until browned, about 10 minutes. Add the spinach, turning it over with tongs, adding more as it wilts.

2. When all of the spinach is wilted, stir in the tomatoes and peppers. Stir in the broth. Nestle the chicken down into the mixture and simmer until the chicken is tender, about 45 minutes.

3. Meanwhile, after about 20 minutes, place the water and 2 teaspoons of salt in a large saucepan and bring to a boil over medium heat. Add the cornmeal in a slow, stream, whisking constantly. Reduce heat, switch to a wooden spoon and stir constantly until mixture is thick, about 20 minutes.

4. Stir the vinegar into the ragout and season with 2 teaspoons of salt and pepper to taste. Divide the polenta among 4 shallow bowls and spoon the ragout over it, including a thigh and a drumstick in each portion. Serve immediately.

YIELD: 4 SERVINGS   *Molly O'Neill*

COUSCOUS WITH CHICKEN

(Adapted from *The Best of Craig Claiborne*)

Craig Claiborne considered this to be one of the best recipes for couscous, made with chicken instead of the more traditional lamb.

½ cup dried chickpeas
2 tablespoons butter
1 2½-pound chicken, cut into serving pieces
½ teaspoon ground cumin
1 tablespoon finely grated fresh ginger
½ teaspoon ground turmeric
¼ teaspoon saffron threads, optional
2 teaspoons finely chopped garlic
Salt and freshly ground pepper
1 leek, trimmed, rinsed and cut into small cubes, about ¾ cup
1 cup tomatoes cut into quarters
6 very small white onions, quartered
4 cups chicken broth
2 celery ribs, trimmed and cut into 1½-inch lengths, optional
3 small carrots, peeled, trimmed and cut into 1-inch lengths
1 red or green sweet pepper, cored, seeded and cut into 2-inch cubes
3 very small turnips, cut into quarters
2 small zucchini, trimmed and cut into 1-inch cubes
Couscous (see recipe, page 301)
Hot pepper sauce (see recipe, page 301)

1. Soak the chickpeas for at least 6 hours in water to cover. Drain and put in fresh water to cover about 2 inches above the peas. Boil for 10 minutes and skim off any foam that collects on the surface. Lower heat and simmer partly covered for about 1 hour, or until tender. Drain.

2. Heat the butter over low heat in a casserole and add the chicken. Turn the pieces in the butter and sprinkle with the cumin, ginger, turmeric, saffron if used, garlic, salt and a generous grinding of pepper. Cook, stirring, until the chicken starts to lose its raw color.

3. Add the leek, tomatoes, onions and chicken broth and bring to a boil. Simmer for 20 minutes.

4. Add the celery, if used, carrots and sweet pepper and continue cooking for about 5 minutes. Add the zucchini and drained chickpeas and cook for 5 minutes.

5. Press a sieve into the broth and scoop out 3 cups of broth for the couscous.

6. To serve, spoon a generous amount of couscous into individual soup bowls. Serve the chicken and vegetables on top. Ladle a generous amount of broth over each serving. Take a spoonful of the hot broth and add as much hot sauce as you desire. Stir to dissolve. Spoon this over each serving.

YIELD: 6 SERVINGS

COUSCOUS

1½ cups quick-cooking couscous (see Note)
3 cups strained liquid from the couscous with chicken

1. Put the couscous in a saucepan. Pour the hot broth over it. Cook over low heat, stirring, for about 2 minutes. Cover and remove from the heat.

2. Let stand for 10 minutes, or until ready to serve. Before serving, fluff the couscous with a fork.

NOTE: Quick-cooking couscous is available in packages in supermarkets. For this recipe, do not use bulk, long-cooking couscous.

YIELD: 6 SERVINGS

HOT PEPPER SAUCE

2 tablespoons crushed hot red pepper flakes
3 tablespoons water
1 tablespoon olive oil
½ teaspoon ground coriander

1. Combine the pepper flakes and water in a small saucepan. Bring just to the boil, stirring.

2. Remove from the heat and add the oil and coriander.

NOTE: The traditional hot pepper sauce served with couscous is called harissa. It is available in stores that specialize in imported foods and many supermarkets.

YIELD: ABOUT 6 TABLESPOONS

RICK BAYLESS'S RED-CHILI-BRAISED CHICKEN WITH POTATOES AND MUSHROOMS

Rick Bayless, known for the authentic Mexican food he serves at Frontera Grill in Chicago, employs red chilies to add gusto and fire to this one-pot meal.

8 cloves garlic, unpeeled
4 medium dried ancho chilies (about 2 ounces), stemmed and seeded
8 medium dried guajillo chilies (about 2 ounces), stemmed and seeded
1½ teaspoons dried oregano, preferably Mexican
⅛ teaspoon ground cumin, preferably ground fresh
2⅔ cups chicken broth, homemade or low-sodium canned, plus more if needed
1½ tablespoons vegetable or olive oil
1 2½- to 3-pound chicken, quartered
1 medium white onion, peeled and cut across into ⅛-inch-thick slices
1 pound red-skinned potatoes (about 8 small), quartered
2 cups thinly sliced shiitake mushrooms
1 teaspoon kosher salt, plus more to taste

1. Heat a griddle or heavy skillet over medium heat. Add the unpeeled garlic and roast until softened, shaking pan, about 15 minutes (garlic will blacken in spots). Cool and peel.

2. Meanwhile, heat another skillet. Open and flatten the chilies (they may break), and toast 2 at a time, pressing them against the hot surface until they crackle and emit wisps of smoke. Flip over and toast other sides. Place in a bowl of hot water. Weight with a plate to keep the chilies submerged, and soak for 30 minutes. Drain.

3. Place the garlic, chilies, oregano, cumin and ⅔ cup of chicken broth in a food processor or blender and process until smooth, scraping and stirring. Add more broth, if needed, to puree the chilies. Press through a medium-mesh sieve and set aside. (The dish can be made ahead up to here.)

4. Heat the oil in a large, wide pot over medium-high heat. Pat the chicken dry and place in the pot in a single, uncrowded layer, in batches if necessary. Cook until browned, about 4 minutes per side. Remove from the pan and set aside.

5. Place all but 2 onion slices in the pot. Sauté until browned, about 8 minutes. Add the chili puree and cook, stirring constantly, until thickened and much darker, about 5 minutes. Stir in the remaining 2 cups of broth. Simmer for 15 minutes, stirring occasionally.

6. Stir in the potatoes and mushrooms, cover and simmer over medium-low heat for 10 minutes. Push the chicken legs into the sauce, cover partly and cook 15 minutes. Push the remaining chicken into the sauce, cover partly and cook until done, about 30 minutes longer.

7. Transfer the chicken to a warm, deep serving platter. Season the sauce and vegetables with salt. Spoon the sauce over the chicken and arrange the vegetables around it. Shape the reserved onion slices into rings and scatter over the vegetables. Serve.

YIELD: 4 SERVINGS ⌁ *Molly O'Neill*

HKATENKWAN

One-pot meals are common from one end of Africa to the other. The okra, hot pepper and peanut in this recipe are traditional ingredients in African cuisine.

1 chicken (approximately 2½ to 3 pounds), cut into pieces

1 1-inch piece of ginger

Half a medium onion, plus 8 ounces of chopped onions

4 cups water

2 tablespoons tomato paste

1 tablespoon peanut, vegetable, corn or palm oil

8 ounces chopped tomato

1 cup peanut butter

1 tablespoon salt

2 hot chilies, crushed, or 1 teaspoon cayenne pepper

1 medium eggplant (1 pound), peeled and cubed

10 ounces fresh or frozen okra (If using fresh okra, trim the stems and caps, if desired.)

1. Peel and cube the eggplant. Place in a colander and salt liberally. Allow the eggplant to drain, ridding it of its bitterness, for approximately one hour.

2. Simmer the chicken with the ginger, the half onion and 4 cups of water, for 20 minutes until partially cooked.

3. Meanwhile, in a large pot, fry the tomato paste in the oil over low heat for 5 minutes. Then add the chopped onions and chopped tomatoes and cook, stirring occasionally, until the onions are translucent.

4. Remove the partly cooked chicken pieces from the pan with a slotted spoon and put them in the large pot along with half the broth. Remove the ginger piece and the onion and reserve the remaining broth. Add the peanut butter, the tablespoon of salt and chilies. Cook for 5 minutes, stirring until the peanut butter is incorporated.

5. Rinse the eggplant and dry with a paper towel. Add it to the pot with the chicken along with the okra. Continue to slowly simmer the stew until the chicken and vegetables are very tender, about another 45 minutes.

6. If needed, add ladlesful of the reserved broth to maintain a thick stew consistency. Adjust seasonings.

NOTE: You can also serve this as a hearty soup. Just increase the amount of water in which you partially cook the chicken to 6 cups instead of 4.

YIELD: 4 TO 6 SERVINGS *Steven Barboza*

✦ EASY ✦
ISLANDER CHICKEN

(Adapted from *The New York Times Cook Book*)

⅓ cup olive oil

1 3-pound chicken, cut into pieces

¾ cup diced raw ham

1 cup sliced onions

2 cloves garlic, minced

3 medium tomatoes or 3 canned
   tomatoes, peeled and chopped

2½ cups water

2½ cups raw rice

¾ cup chopped green pepper

1 small bay leaf

2½ teaspoons salt

½ teaspoon cumin seed

⅛ teaspoon saffron threads

Strips of pimiento for garnish,
   optional

1. Heat olive oil in a Dutch oven, add chicken, ham, onions and garlic and brown the chicken on all sides.

2. Add the tomatoes, cover and simmer 20 minutes.

3. Add the remaining ingredients except the pimiento and bring to a boil. Lower the heat, cover and simmer slowly until the rice is tender, 15 to 20 minutes. Add more liquid if necessary.

4. Remove chicken. Heap the rice mixture in the center of a large platter and surround with the chicken. Garnish with strips of pimiento, if desired.

YIELD: 6 SERVINGS

ARMENIAN-STYLE CHICKEN
AND BULGUR

This Armenian-inspired dish of chicken and bulgur wheat is sparked with a flavorful combination of basil and walnuts. The chicken legs, besides being the tastiest part of the bird, are the most forgiving; it is almost impossible to ruin them by overcooking.

1 medium onion, chopped

2 tablespoons unsalted butter or vegetable oil (or more, to taste)

2 cups chicken stock or water

6 leg-thigh pieces of chicken, skinned and cut apart

1 teaspoon salt, or to taste

1 cup bulgur

½ cup broken walnut pieces

2 tablespoons dried basil

¼ teaspoon pepper

1. Sauté onion in butter in a pot until onion is wilted. Add stock, chicken pieces and salt; boil, cover and simmer over very low heat for 20 to 25 minutes.

2. Add bulgur, walnut pieces, basil and pepper; stir to mix well, cover and simmer 15 to 20 minutes, or until liquid is absorbed. Turn off heat and allow to stand 10 minutes, covered and undisturbed, in a warm place. Fluff bulgur before serving.

YIELD: 6 SERVINGS ⟅ *Robert Farrar Capon*

BARBARA KAFKA'S CHINESE CHICKEN IN THE POT (VARIATION ON SHABU SHABU)

8 cups canned chicken broth

1 ounce dried shiitake mushrooms

8 cloves garlic, smashed and peeled

1½-inch-thick slice of peeled fresh ginger, cut aross into ⅛-inch-thick slices and then into thin strips

2 bunches scallions, root ends trimmed, with white part cut into 2-inch lengths and half of the greens cut into 2-inch lengths to equal 1 cup greens

6 ounces snow pea pods, tipped and tailed

2 8-ounce cans peeled and sliced water chestnuts, drained and rinsed well under cold water

2 4-pound chickens, each cut into 8 serving pieces and skinned, with any excess visible fat removed (backs, necks and wing tips reserved for another use)

2 whole star anise or 1 heaping tablespoon star anise pieces

½ cup soy sauce

6 cups cooked white rice

1. Heat 2 cups of the broth until warm, and soak the mushrooms in the warm broth for 15 minutes. While the mushrooms are soaking, prepare the garlic, ginger, scallions, snow peas and water chestnuts, and skin the chicken, if necessary. After 15 minutes, drain the mushrooms, straining the liquid through a coffee filter, and reserve.

2. Place the chicken, the 6 remaining cups of stock, the garlic, ginger and star anise in a large, wide pot. Cover. Bring to a boil.

3. Add the mushroom liquid and soy sauce. When it returns to a moderate boil, add the scallion whites and mushrooms. Continue cooking, uncovered, at a moderate boil for 5 minutes.

4. Add the sliced water chestnuts and scallion greens, poking them down into the liquid. Place the snow peas on top. Cover, and return to a moderate boil. Uncover, and adjust the heat to remain at a moderate boil for 3 to 4 minutes, or until the snow peas are cooked thoroughly but still crunchy.

5. Remove chicken pieces to a platter with tongs. Skim the vegetables out with a slotted spoon, and scatter them over the top.

6. Serve ½ to ⅔ cup of cooked rice in bottom of each bowl. Divide the chicken and vegetables evenly among the bowls, and top each with 1 cup broth.

YIELD: 8 SERVINGS   Barbara Kafka

PAN-ROASTED SOY CHICKEN
WITH CHILIED SESAME NOODLES

FOR THE CHICKEN

1 tablespoon soy sauce
1 tablespoon vegetable oil
1 clove garlic, peeled and minced
1 scallion, minced
¼ teaspoon salt
⅛ teaspoon freshly ground black
   pepper
2 whole chicken breasts (skin on),
   removed from bone and separated
   into halves

FOR THE NOODLES

¾ cup chicken broth
⅓ cup roasted, unsalted peanuts
1 tablespoon sesame oil
1 teaspoon soy sauce, plus more to
   taste
1 teaspoon chili paste (see Note), plus
   more to taste
½ pound angel-hair pasta
2 scallions, minced

1. For the chicken, combine the soy sauce, vegetable oil, garlic, scallion, salt and black pepper in a shallow dish. Add the chicken, turn to coat on both sides and marinate in the refrigerator for 1 to 4 hours.

2. Fifteen minutes before serving, bring a pot of salted water to a boil for the noodles. Meanwhile in a separate pot, bring the chicken broth to a boil, remove from heat, and combine it in a blender with the peanuts, sesame oil, soy sauce and chili paste. Blend until smooth. Boil the pasta, drain well and toss with the sauce and scallions. Season to taste with more soy sauce and chili paste if desired.

3. Remove the chicken from the marinade, brush to remove bits of marinade and pat dry. Place a well-seasoned cast-iron skillet over medium-high heat until very hot. Add the chicken, skin-side down, and cook for 1 minute. Turn and cook for one more minute. Reduce heat to medium and continue cooking the chicken until it is firm to

the touch and cooked through, about 5 minutes more. Remove from skillet. Slice the chicken. Divide the pasta among 4 plates and top with the chicken. Serve immediately.

NOTE: Chili paste is available in many supermarkets and in specialty food stores.

YIELD: 4 SERVINGS ⁓ *Molly O'Neill*

CHICKEN WITH RICE AND CHILI-GINGER SAUCE

(Adapted from the Epicurean Kitchen)

FOR THE CHILI-GINGER SAUCE

5 fresh red chilies, or to taste
3 cloves garlic
5 pieces fresh ginger, peeled
2 tablespoons rice wine vinegar
2 tablespoons vegetable oil
4 teaspoons sugar
¾ teaspoon salt
2 tablespoons chicken stock

FOR THE CHICKEN AND RICE

1 3- to 4-pound whole chicken, excess
   fat removed
2½ teaspoons salt
5 scallions
1 thumb-size piece ginger, peeled and
   cut into 6 slices
8 cups homemade chicken stock
1 tablespoon sesame oil
1 tablespoon vegetable oil
2 cups Thai fragrant rice or jasmine
   rice, rinsed and drained
3 cloves garlic, thinly sliced
Sliced scallions for garnish

1. To make the chili-ginger sauce, combine the ingredients in a blender and pulse until smooth but not pureed. Set aside.

2. To make the chicken and rice, rub the chicken with the salt. Place the scallions and 2 pieces of the ginger in its cavity. Place the chicken in a kettle, add the

stock and bring to a boil. Simmer, uncovered, skimming off any foam, until the chicken is cooked through, 40 to 45 minutes. Remove from the heat.

3. Transfer the chicken to a platter and allow to cool slightly. Discard the scallions and ginger from the cavity of the bird and remove and discard the skin. Remove the breast meat, legs and wings. Discard the carcass. Slice the breast meat and separate the drumstick from the thigh. Return the meat to the platter, cover and keep warm.

4. Measure 4 cups of the stock the chicken cooked in, retaining the rest for another use. In a large saucepan, heat the oils over medium-high heat and add the garlic and remaining ginger slices. Cook, stirring, for 2 minutes. Add the rinsed rice and toss until coated. Add the 4 cups of stock and bring to a boil. Simmer, covered, until the liquid is absorbed and the rice is tender, about 15 minutes.

5. Transfer the rice to a serving platter. Top with the chicken, garnish with the scallions and serve immediately with the chili-ginger sauce on the side.

YIELD: 4 SERVINGS ⟟ *Molly O'Neill*

CHICKEN-AND-RICE SAMBAL

Molly O'Neill: "A paste, a concentrated goo that can be used as a shortcut in preparing long-simmered dishes, tends to be a distillation of a particular cuisine, often a melange of the aromatics and spices that begin traditional dishes. In Northern European cuisines, a pot begun with onion, carrots and celery can become a ragout or a soup. In Southern European cooking, they add garlic and chili peppers. In Asian cuisines, the flavors are more varied. An Indonesian dish would begin with a red, green or mahogany-colored sambal, rife with chilies and the essence of shrimp, poultry or beef. An Indian dish might start with a curry paste, containing curry, onions, garlic, chilies and, often, a fruit to balance the fire in the dish. These are not inviolable rules. Pastes are adaptable. Cooking with them is an add-and-taste deal. Pastes can be diluted with oil and used to marinate meat, seafood or vegetables. They can be served alone as condiments, used to season sauces or to turn a bowl of rice or noodles into a fine meal and a broth into a flavorful soup or stew. Paste can magically transform the work of weekday slapdash collagists like me into that of thoughtful cooks." (See Note.)

3 cups chicken broth, homemade or
  low-sodium canned

1 cup cold water

1 1-inch piece fresh ginger, peeled
  and coarsely chopped

1 clove garlic, peeled and smashed

1 strip lemon peel, 1 inch by ½ inch

¾ teaspoon salt

2 whole chicken breasts on the bone

1 clove garlic, peeled and chopped

1 teaspoon fresh ginger, peeled and
  chopped

1 lemon, peeled and seeded

1 tablespoon vegetable oil

1 teaspoon sambal (Thai spice
  paste), preferably sambal oelek
  (see Note)

½ teaspoon salt

3 tablespoons chicken broth,
  reserved

1½ cups basmati rice

1 cucumber, peeled, seeded and
  sliced very thin

4 sprigs fresh mint, for garnish

1. To make the chicken, combine the chicken broth, water, ginger, garlic, lemon peel and salt in a large shallow pan over high heat. Bring to a boil and add the chicken. Simmer, partly covered, until the chicken is just cooked through, 15 to 20 minutes. Remove chicken and cool. Strain the broth and set aside. When the chicken is cool enough to handle, remove and discard the skin, and bone and slice the meat into thin, even strips. Set aside.

2. To make the sauce, combine the garlic, ginger, the lemon flesh, vegetable oil, sambal, salt and 3 tablespoons of the reserved chicken broth in a blender. Puree completely. Taste, add more sambal if desired and set aside.

3. Cook the basmati rice in 3 cups of the reserved broth until tender, 15 to 20 minutes. Divide the hot rice among four bowls. Alternate slices of cucumber and chicken around the rice. Garnish each bowl with a mint sprig and serve with the sauce on the side.

NOTE: Thai and other spice pastes are available at many supermarkets and at stores specializing in Asian foods (See "Selected Sources for Ingredients," page 352.)

YIELD: 4 SERVINGS *Molly O'Neill*

PATTI LABELLE'S
CHICKEN WITH BLACK-EYED PEAS
AND YELLOW RICE

(Adapted from *Patti LaBelle's Lite Cuisine: Over 100 Dishes With To-Die-For Taste Made With To-Live-For Recipes*)

"When you're feeling good, your food is good," says Patti LaBelle. Since her diabetes was diagnosed five years ago, Miss LaBelle changed her diet to dishes like this one, with dietary exchanges approved by the American Diabetes Association.

1 tablespoon olive oil

1 small or medium red onion, chopped

2 garlic cloves, minced

1½ pounds chicken tenders, cut into bite-size pieces

1 14½-ounce can reduced-sodium chicken broth

½ teaspoon poultry seasoning

½ teaspoon ground black pepper

¼ teaspoon red pepper flakes

¼ teaspoon salt

¾ cup uncooked yellow rice (see Note)

1 15-ounce can black-eyed peas, drained

1 tablespoon chopped fresh thyme

1. In a large skillet, warm olive oil over medium heat. Add onion and cook until translucent. Add garlic and chicken tenders, and cook, stirring from time to time, until chicken begins to brown, about 7 minutes.

2. Stir in broth, poultry seasoning, black pepper, red pepper flakes and salt. Raise heat to high, and bring mixture to a boil. Mix in rice, and reduce heat to low. Cover and cook until rice is almost tender, about 10 minutes.

3. Stir in black-eyed peas and thyme, mixing well. Cover and cook until heated through, about 10 minutes.

NOTE: If you buy yellow rice with saffron that comes with a separate seasoning packet, mix the rice and seasoning in a bowl, then measure out ¾ cup.

YIELD: 4 SERVINGS   *Alex Witchel*

JACQUES PEPIN'S
SWEET-AND-SPICY CURRIED CHICKEN

Apples, bananas and sweet onions intensify the contrast with the heat of this curry. The apples retain their shape better if they are not peeled, and the skin has a nice chewy texture. Add more or less fruit, according to your own taste. You can make your own curry powder or use a commercial brand as is, if you prefer a mild flavor, or with added cumin and cayenne pepper if you like your seasonings piquant. Fresh mint is preferable, but you can substitute dried mint: crumble it over the dish during the last few minutes of cooking.

1 tablespoon unsalted butter

1 tablespoon vegetable oil

6 large chicken legs (about 4 pounds total), skin removed and legs split to
 separate the drumstick from the thigh

¾ pound onions, peeled and diced (2½ cups)

1 tablespoon flour

2 tablespoons curry powder

1 teaspoon cumin powder

¼ teaspoon cayenne pepper

1½ teaspoons freshly ground black pepper

1½ teaspoons salt

1 cup water

5 cloves garlic, peeled, crushed and coarsely chopped (1 tablespoon)

1 Granny Smith apple (about ½ pound), unpeeled and cut in half, seeded,
 and cut into 1-inch dice (about 1½ cups)

1 banana (about ½ pound), peeled and cut into ½-inch slices

1 large tomato, cut into 1-inch cubes (1 cup)

2 tablespoons shredded fresh mint or 1 teaspoon dried mint

1. Heat butter and oil in a large skillet. When hot, add chicken and sauté (in a couple of batches, if necessary, to avoid crowding) over medium to high heat for a total of 6 to 7 minutes, until brown on all sides. Transfer chicken to a large casserole or Dutch oven and discard all but 2 to 3 tablespoons of the accumulated fat in the skillet.

2. To the hot fat in the skillet add onions and sauté for 2 to 3 minutes over medium heat, stirring, then add flour, curry powder, cumin powder, cayenne pepper,

black pepper, salt and garlic and mix well with the onions. Add the water, stir, bring to a boil and pour mixture over chicken.

3. Add apple, banana and tomato, bring to a boil, cover, reduce heat and simmer gently for about 25 to 30 minutes. Sprinkle mint on top and serve immediately with brown rice.

NOTE: This dish is good reheated, but if you plan to make it ahead and reheat it at serving time, cook it only 20 minutes initially, instead of 30 minutes. By the time the dish is reheated, it will be cooked through.

YIELD: 6 SERVINGS *Jacques Pepin*

CHICKEN AND POTATO CURRY (MURGI ALOO KARI)

(Adapted from *The Varied Kitchens of India*)

2 tablespoons corn or peanut oil

½ cup chopped onion

1 teaspoon finely chopped, crushed garlic

1 teaspoon finely chopped, crushed fresh ginger

1 teaspoon ground cumin

1 teaspoon ground coriander

½ teaspoon ground turmeric

1 teaspoon salt, or to taste

1 teaspoon garam masala

1 teaspoon finely minced fresh hot green chili

2 cups water

2 bay leaves

1 3-pound chicken, excess fat removed, cut into serving pieces

1 pound potatoes, peeled and cut in ½-inch cubes

1 cup chopped ripe tomatoes

1 tablespoon fresh lemon juice

1. Heat the oil in a heavy 4-quart saucepan. Add the onion, garlic and ginger and sauté over medium heat until the onion starts to brown. Add the cumin, coriander, turmeric, salt, garam masala and chili. Cook, stirring, about 2 minutes. Add the water and bay leaves.

2. Bring to a boil, stirring rapidly with a wooden spoon to amalgamate and smooth the ingredients. Add the chicken and potatoes, lower heat to medium and cook at a steady simmer for 20 minutes. Be sure there is enough liquid that the ingredients are just covered.

3. Add the tomatoes. Continue cooking 15 to 20 minutes longer, until the chicken and potatoes are done and the sauce has reduced and thickened somewhat. Add the lemon juice. Taste the sauce, and add more salt if necessary. Serve.

YIELD: 6 SERVINGS *Florence Fabricant*

CHICKEN AND RICE CASSEROLE, INDIAN-STYLE

(Adapted from *The Best of Craig Claiborne*)

2 pounds skinned, boneless chicken
  breasts
1½ cups peanut, vegetable or corn
  oil
Salt to taste
¼ teaspoon paprika
4 cups thinly sliced onions
3 cups short-grain rice
¾ cup raisins
1 tablespoon crushed cumin seeds

6 bay leaves
6 whole cloves
½ teaspoon slivered garlic
¼ cup thick yogurt (see following
  instructions)
1 teaspoon crushed cardamom seeds
4¼ cups chicken stock (see recipe,
  page 317)
½ teaspoon kewra (see Note),
  optional

1. The chicken should be cut into flat pieces, each about 3 inches square.

2. Heat ½ cup of the oil in a casserole and cook the chicken pieces sprinkled with the salt and paprika until they lose their raw look. Set aside.

3. Heat the remaining cup of oil in a heavy casserole and cook the onions, stirring, until golden brown, about 20 minutes.

4. Wash the rice well and cover with cold water. Let stand for 30 minutes.

5. Cover the raisins with cold water and let stand.

6. Place the casserole with the onions on low heat. Add the cumin seeds, bay leaves, whole cloves, garlic slivers and drained raisins. Cook, stirring for 3 minutes. Add the yogurt and salt to taste.

7. Drain the rice and add it to the casserole along with the chicken pieces and any liquid that may have accumulated. Add the crushed cardamom seeds and chicken stock. Sprinkle with kewra, if desired. Cover and cook for 15 minutes.

8. Meanwhile, preheat the oven to 250 degrees.

9. Do not uncover and do not stir, but pick up the casserole firmly and with both hands toss to redistribute the chicken and the rice. Or, if the casserole is too heavy and seems unwieldy, uncover it and gently stir the rice with a rubber spatula to redistribute it.

10. Place the casserole in the oven and bake for 30 minutes.

11. It is preferable to scoop the rice mixture from the casserole to a rice dish with a saucer so that the rice grains do not become sticky.

NOTE: Kewra is a white spirit that smells vaguely and pleasantly like nasturtiums. It is available in bottles in Indian stores or see "Selected Sources for Ingredients," page 352.

YIELD: 8 TO 12 SERVINGS

THICK YOGURT

Line a bowl with cheesecloth. Empty the contents of 1 pint of plain commercial yogurt into the cheesecloth. Bring up the edges of the cheesecloth and tie with a long string. Suspend the cheesecloth bag with the string over the bowl. Let stand for about 2 hours.

INDIAN-STYLE CHICKEN STOCK

The bones of a 3-pound chicken
Water to cover
Salt to taste
2 cinnamon sticks, each about 1½ inches
4 crushed brown cardamom pods

Combine all the ingredients in a saucepan. Bring to a boil and cook, uncovered, for about 45 minutes. Strain.

YIELD: ABOUT 5 CUPS

✤ EASY ✤
MARK BITTMAN'S CHICKEN BIRIYANI

Biriyani is the Indian equivalent of arroz con pollo or paella. Mark Bittman:"The smell should beguile you: chicken, butter and spices should dominate, followed by the subtle aroma of basmati rice. The dish must be made carefully, but it is not difficult. The chicken is not browned, which actually makes it easier than many similar preparations. One key is to use butter, not oil or margarine, and good spices: cardamom in the pod, whole cloves, a cinnamon stick and real saffron. (It is red and costs about $35 an ounce, but is worth it.) Good coarse salt does not hurt either, and the better the chicken, the happier you will be when you bite into it. It is also important to leave the lid on as much as possible. You want to make sure the chicken cooks fairly quickly and that the aroma remains in the pot."

4 tablespoons unsalted butter

1 large onion, chopped

Coarse salt and ground black pepper

1 large pinch saffron

10 whole cardamom pods (see Note)

5 cloves

1 3-inch cinnamon stick

1 tablespoon minced fresh ginger

1½ cups basmati rice

3 cups chicken stock

1 3- to 4-pound chicken, cut up and
    trimmed of excess fat; skin removed
    if desired

¼ cup slivered, blanched almonds,
    optional

1. Put 2 tablespoons butter in a deep skillet or casserole that can be covered. Turn heat to medium-high. Add onion and some salt and pepper. Cook, stirring occasionally, until onion softens, 5 to 10 minutes. Add spices, and cook, stirring, another minute.

2. Add rice and cook, stirring, until ingredients are well combined, 2 or 3 minutes. Add stock, chicken and more salt and pepper, and bring to a boil. Cover and simmer.

3. Cook undisturbed for about 25 minutes. When chicken and rice are tender and liquid is absorbed, turn heat off. If either chicken or rice is not quite done, add no more than ½ cup boiling water, and cook until done.

4. Melt remaining butter in a small skillet over medium heat. Add almonds (or simply melt butter), and brown lightly. Pour mixture over biriyani, and sprinkle with a bit more salt. Let rest 2 or 3 minutes. Take pot to table, and serve.

NOTE: Cardamom seeds can be eaten, but cloves should be removed after cooking.

YIELD: 4 SERVINGS ⌣ *Mark Bittman*

LEMON CHICKEN WITH RICE AND SCALLIONS

3 teaspoons olive oil

1 chicken, about 3 pounds, cut into serving pieces and skinned

2 teaspoons salt, plus more to taste

Freshly ground pepper to taste

2 small cloves garlic, peeled and minced

8 scallions, trimmed and thinly sliced

3½ cups chicken broth, homemade or low-sodium canned

2 cups short-grain rice

½ cup white wine

1 lemon, thinly sliced

¼ cup chopped fresh mint

¼ cup chopped Italian parsley

1. Heat 2 teaspoons of olive oil in an ovenproof paella pan or large, deep skillet over medium-high heat. Add the chicken and sear until browned, about 4 minutes per side. Remove from the skillet and season with ½ teaspoon of salt and pepper to taste. Lower the heat to medium. Add the remaining olive oil, the garlic and the scallions and cook, stirring, until softened, about 1 minute.

2. Preheat oven to 350 degrees. Bring the broth to a boil in a medium-size saucepan. Add the rice to the garlic and scallions and stir for 30 seconds. Add the broth, wine and 1½ teaspoons of salt. Turn the heat to low and simmer slowly, stirring frequently, until most, but not all, of the liquid is absorbed, about 15 minutes. Push the lemon slices down into the rice and lay the chicken over it. Bake, uncovered, until the liquid is absorbed, about 20 minutes.

3. Remove the pan from the oven and cover with a kitchen towel. Let stand for 10 minutes. Season the rice with additional salt if needed and pepper to taste. Top with the mint and parsley. Divide among 4 plates and serve immediately.

YIELD: 4 SERVINGS ∽ *Molly O'Neill*

✤ EASY ✤
ARROZ CON POLLO

(Adapted from *The New York Times Cook Book*)

1 4-pound chicken, cut into serving pieces
1¼ teaspoons salt
½ teaspoon pepper
⅛ teaspoon paprika
¼ cup olive oil
1 clove garlic, minced
1 medium onion, chopped
2 cups rich chicken stock
3½ cups canned tomatoes
¼ teaspoon powdered saffron
1 bay leaf
½ teaspoon dried oregano
2 cups raw rice
1 package frozen peas or artichoke hearts, defrosted
3 pimientos, cut in pieces

1. Preheat oven to 350 degrees.

2. Season the chicken with 1 teaspoon of the salt, the pepper and paprika. In a skillet, heat the oil, add the chicken and brown on all sides. Remove to a baking dish.

3. To the skillet add the garlic and onions and sauté until the onion is tender. Add the chicken stock and heat while scraping loose the brown particles. Add the tomatoes and their liquid, seasonings and remaining salt. Bring to a boil and pour over the chicken. Add the rice and stir. Cover tightly.

4. Bake 25 minutes. Uncover and toss the rice. Stir in the peas, arrange the pimientos on top, cover and cook 10 minutes longer.

YIELD: 6 TO 8 SERVINGS

JEAN DALRYMPLE'S
ARROZ CON POLLO WITH CHORIZO

(Adapted from *Cooking with Herbs & Spices*)

½ cup unsalted butter

6 tablespoons olive or other oil

4 cloves garlic, or to taste, minced

2 3-pound chickens, disjointed

Salt and freshly ground black pepper to taste

3 cups long-grain rice

8 cups chicken stock

1 chorizo or 1 pepperoni, cut into ½-inch pieces

1 tablespoon saffron, or to taste

2 cups large fresh or frozen lima beans

2 cans pimientos

3 cups hot cooked peas

1. Preheat the oven to 350 degrees.

2. Melt the butter in a flameproof casserole. Add the oil and garlic and sauté the chicken in it until golden brown. Season with salt and pepper. Remove the chicken and keep it warm.

3. Add the rice to the casserole and stir it in the fat until golden. Add the stock and stir well. Add the chorizo, saffron and lima beans. Return the chicken to the casserole and stir thoroughly.

4. Cover the casserole with aluminum foil and bake until the chicken is tender and the liquid has been absorbed by the rice, about 45 minutes. Serve garnished with pimientos and green peas.

YIELD: 6 TO 8 SERVINGS

CHICKEN AND SPANISH RICE CASSEROLE

(Adapted from *The Best of Craig Claiborne*)

A basic chicken and Spanish rice casserole is a traditionally American dish. Craig Claiborne's version is a bit more elaborate and flavorful in its seasonings and in the use of cubed zucchini as well as green peppers.

1 2½-pound chicken, cut into serving pieces
Salt and freshly ground pepper to taste
2 tablespoons olive oil
1 cup finely chopped onion
2 teaspoons finely minced garlic
1¼ cups cubed green peppers
1½ cups cubed zucchini
1½ cups fresh or canned cubed tomatoes
1 cup rice
1 cup fresh or canned chicken broth
1 bay leaf
½ teaspoon dried thyme

1. Sprinkle the chicken pieces with salt and a generous grinding of pepper.

2. Heat the oil in a deep, heavy skillet or casserole and add the chicken pieces skin-side down. Cook over high heat until golden brown on one side. Turn and cook until golden brown on the other side.

3. Add the onion and garlic and stir to blend. When the onion wilts, scatter the green peppers and zucchini over all. Add the tomatoes, rice, chicken broth, bay leaf and thyme. Add pepper to taste. Cover closely and cook for 20 minutes. Uncover and cook for 5 minutes longer.

YIELD: 4 SERVINGS

PAELLA

(Adapted from *The New York Times International Cook Book*)

¼ pound salt pork, diced

2 cloves garlic, finely chopped

½ teaspoon dried thyme

Salt

1 tablespoon red wine vinegar

¼ cup olive oil

½ teaspoon ground coriander

1 2½ pound chicken, cut into serving pieces

1 pound raw medium shrimp, shelled and deveined

1 2-pound lobster, cut into serving pieces

2 chorizos (Spanish sausages) or hot Italian sausages

¾ cup chopped onion

1 teaspoon whole saffron or ¼ teaspoon powdered saffron

2 tablespoons capers

⅓ cup chopped fresh or canned tomatoes

½ cup dry white wine

2½ cups uncooked rice

3½ cups chicken stock approximately

Freshly ground pepper to taste

20 mussels, well scrubbed (optional)

20 small clams, well rinsed

1 package frozen artichoke hearts, partly defrosted

½ cup freshly cooked or frozen peas

1 4-ounce can pimientos

1 teaspoon anise liqueur, such as Pernod or Ricard

Lemon wedges

1. In a heavy 4-quart ovenproof skillet, casserole, or paella pan, sauté the pork until the fat is rendered and the pork bits are brown. Remove the pork and reserve.

2. Chop the garlic with the thyme and 1 teaspoon salt. Scrape into a bowl, then add the vinegar, oil and coriander. Coat the chicken pieces with the mixture and allow to stand at least 30 minutes before cooking.

3. Meanwhile, in the pork fat remaining in the pan, sauté the shrimp quickly until bright pink; remove and reserve. Do the same with the lobster.

4. Fry the chorizos in the same pan until cooked, about 20 minutes. Slice and reserve.

5. Brown the coated chicken pieces in the fat remaining in the pan. Sprinkle with the onion, saffron, capers, and tomatoes.

6. Return the pork pieces to the pan. Add the wine, rice, and chicken stock. Season with salt and pepper to taste. Cover and simmer gently about 15 minutes.

7. Meanwhile, steam the mussels and the clams in ¼ cup water until they open, about 5 minutes. Discard any that do not open.

8. Preheat the oven to 350 degrees.

9. Add the shrimp, lobster, artichoke hearts and peas to the chicken and rice. Cook, uncovered, 5–10 minutes. If all the liquid has been absorbed, add the liquid from the mussels and clams or more chicken stock. The rice should be moist, but there should be no excess moisture.

10. Add the pimientos, liqueur, and reserved chorizos. Garnish with the mussels and clams, cover, and place in the oven to reheat. (If the dish is to be kept warm for as long as 30 minutes, reduce the oven heat to 200 degrees.) Serve with lemon wedges.

YIELD: 8 TO 10 SERVINGS

OAXACAN TAMALES

(Adapted from Hilda Jaimes)

Immigrant cooks in New York City without the wherewithal to open a restaurant serve quick, cheap and delicious tastes of home from makeshift stands at the curbside. Some are so good that they have developed wider reputations, particularly among a segment of the culinary cognoscenti for whom the difficulty in finding a meal only adds to its appeal. Such a cook is Hilda Jaimes, who sells great, oversized Oaxacan tamales, made from her grandmother's recipe, out of a cooler in front of Taco Bell on 116th Street in Manhattant. The masa—cornmeal dough tinted with chilies and infused with an artichoke-like flavor from deep green banana leaves—conceals a stewy center of chicken and aromatic spices, known as guajillos.

1 1-pound package of banana leaves (see Note)

3½ to 4 pounds bone-in chicken breasts, skin removed

5 cloves garlic, peeled and halved

1 medium onion, peeled and halved

4 ounces dried guajillo peppers, stemmed and seeded

1 large tomato, quartered

1 teaspoon cumin seed

1 teaspoon black peppercorns

1 teaspoon coriander seeds

1 tablespoon oregano

8 cloves

2 tablespoons corn oil

3 bay leaves

Salt and freshly ground black pepper

1 cup fresh lard

7½ cups instant corn masa mix

1. Trim fibrous edges from banana leaves, and cut into 14-inch-long rectangles. Soak in warm water until ready to use. (At least 20 will be needed.)

2. Put chicken, 3 garlic cloves and onion in a medium stockpot, cover with cold water, and bring to boil over high heat. Skim off foam, reduce heat to medium, and cook for 20 minutes. Put chicken in a bowl to cool; strain and reserve 4 cups broth.

3. Put 1 cup cold water in a blender. Toast guajillos in a large, dry pan over medium heat for 1 minute, pressing down with a spatula to soften each side. Submerge peppers in blender. Add remaining garlic, tomato, cumin, peppercorns, coriander, oregano and cloves. Blend until smooth, about 2 minutes.

4. Combine oil, guajillo sauce, bay leaves, 2 tablespoons salt, some black pepper and reserved broth in a large Dutch oven, and place over high heat to boil. Reduce to medium-low and simmer for 20 minutes.

5. While sauce is simmering, shred chicken into bite-size strands with your fingers; set aside. Melt lard in a small saucepan over low heat and cool to room temperature. After sauce has simmered for 15 minutes, remove 1 cup and set aside to cool.

6. In a large mixing bowl, whisk 3 cups cold water into 2 cups masa to form a loose paste. Whisk paste into simmering sauce, switch to a spoon, and stir until sauce has thickened, about three minutes. Stir in chicken and remove from heat. Season to taste.

7. In a large mixing bowl, combine reserved guajillo sauce, 1 cup cold water, 2 tablespoons salt, and 5½ cups masa. Mix masa between your fingers, adding lard and 1½ to 2 cups more water. Continue mixing; dough is ready when it no longer sticks to your hands.

8. Drain banana leaves and dry with paper towels; discard leaves with sizable tears. Place a leaf shiny-side down on a sturdy work surface. Roll ⅓- to ½-cup masa dough into a ball, flatten it in the leaf's center, and spread it thinly with the palm of your hand to cover all but 2-inch perimeter. Add more masa, if necessary. Add ⅓- to ½-cup filling (it will be soupy), then fold tamale into a rectangular package: top edge of leaf to the bottom edge of masa; bottom edge leaf to top of tamale; right and left sides overlapping in the center. Turn over and stack until ready to steam. (Tamales may be frozen now: thaw for two hours before steaming.)

9. Fill stockpot with two inches of water, line pot or steamer insert with leaf, carefully stack tamales, and cover tightly. Steam for 40 minutes; tamales are ready when leaves easily pull away from masa.

NOTE: Banana leaves are sold at Asian and Mexican markets.

YIELD: ABOUT 20 LARGE TAMALES (ABOUT 6 INCHES LONG) ⌒ *Dana Bowen*

POZOLE

(Adapted from *The New York Times International Cook Book*)

Pozole, a Mexican dish that can be served as a soup or a main course, is usually made with pork or a combination of pork and chicken. For this variation we use chicken only.

THE SOUP

2 dried ancho chilies
2 dried pasilla chilies
3 3½-pound chicken breasts with bone and skin
2 quarts rich chicken stock

1 whole onion, peeled

2 large garlic cloves, peeled

1 bay leaf

2 sprigs fresh thyme, or ½ teaspoon dried

Salt

1¾ cups water

1 tablespoon peanut, vegetable or corn oil

2 16-ounce cans whole hominy, available where Latin American and Puerto
   Rican foods are sold

THE GARNISHES

Toasted tortillas or corn chips

1 small head iceberg lettuce, shredded and coarsely chopped

8 radishes, thinly sliced

3 tablespoons crushed oregano leaves

Hot powdered pepper or cayenne pepper

12 lemon or lime wedges

Coarsely chopped fresh cilantro

1 avocado, peeled and cubed

1. Place the ancho and pasilla chilies in a bowl and add water to cover. Soak several hours, turning occasionally, until slightly softened.

2. Put the chicken breasts in a kettle with chicken stock to cover. Add the onion, 1 clove of garlic, bay leaf, thyme and salt to taste. Bring to a boil and simmer, skimming the surface to remove the scum and foam. Simmer for 20 minutes, or until the chicken is cooked. Remove the chicken and allow to cool. Let the remaining ingredients continue to simmer.

3. Meanwhile, drain the chilies. Remove and discard the stems. Split the chilies in half and remove and discard the seeds. Slice away and discard the inside veins. Put the chilies in a saucepan and add 1 ½ cups cold water. Bring to the boil and cook, stirring down occasionally, until the chilies are tender. Pour the chilies and their cooking liquid into the container of a food processor or electric blender. Add the remaining clove of garlic and blend to a fine puree. Heat the oil in a saucepan and add the puree, stirring. Add salt to taste. Rinse out the processor container with the remaining ¼ cup of water and add it to the saucepan. Cook briefly, stirring.

4. When the chicken is cool enough to handle, pull away and discard the skin and bone. Cut the meat into 2-inch pieces.

5. Discard the thyme, bay leaf, garlic and onion from the simmering soup. Add the chicken and the pureed chili mixture. Drain 1 can of hominy and add it. Do not drain the remaining can of hominy, but add the hominy and liquid to the soup. Continue cooking for 30 minutes, skimming the surface to remove the scum and fat. (The finished soup may be cooked to this point and reheated just before serving.)

6. Serve the soup boiling hot in very hot bowls. Serve the corn chips and other garnishes on the side. The garnishes can be added to the soup according to each guest's whim and appetite.

YIELD: 4 TO 6 SERVINGS

CHEF PAUL'S CHICKEN GUMBO

Paul Prudhomme: "Louisiana cooking is old French cooking that traveled from Nova Scotia when my ancestors migrated to Louisiana. I learned how to cook gumbo when I was a child in the kitchen, helping my mother. It has a nutty, brown flavor that is familiar to so many people, even those from other parts of the world. I always seem to meet someone who says, 'That's how my grandmother used to cook.' This is a dish that doesn't require that much effort. . . . You carefully prepare your roux, combine it with the other ingredients and seasonings and let it cook for hours on the back burner. . . . The long cook time helps the flavors develop into a delicious gumbo."

SEASONING MIX

1 tablespoon plus 2 teaspoons Chef Paul Prudhomme's Poultry Magic®
 or Meat Magic® or Magic Barbecue Seasoning® or Fajita Mix® (see Note)
or
1 tablespoon plus 2 teaspoons of home-made seasoning blend of the following,
 mixed together:
  1½ teaspoons salt
  1 teaspoon ground red pepper, preferably cayenne

¾ teaspoon black pepper

½ teaspoon white pepper

½ teaspoon onion powder

½ teaspoon garlic powder

2 bay leaves, crumbled

1 3- to 4-pound chicken, cut up

1 cup finely chopped onions

1 cup finely chopped green bell peppers

¾ cup finely chopped celery

1¼ cups all-purpose flour

Vegetable oil for deep frying

About 7 cups chicken stock or water

1 teaspoon minced garlic

Hot cook rice (preferably converted)

1. Remove excess fat from the chicken pieces. Rub approximately 2 teaspoons of the Magic seasoning blend of your choice or the home-made seasoning blend on each piece, making sure all sides are evenly covered. Let stand at room temperature for 30 minutes.

2. Meanwhile, in a medium-size bowl combine the onions, bell peppers and celery, set aside. Thoroughly combine the flour with 1 tablespoon of the Magic seasoning blend of your choice or the home-made seasoning blend in a paper or plastic bag. Add the chicken and shake until pieces are well coated. Reserve ½ cup of the flour.

3. In a large skillet (preferably not a nonstick type) heat 1½ inches oil until very hot (375 degrees to 400 degrees). Fry the chicken pieces until crust is brown on both sides, about 5 to 8 minutes per side; drain on paper towels. Carefully pour the hot oil into a glass measuring cup, leaving as many of the browned particles in the pan as possible. Scrape the pan bottom with a metal whisk to loosen any stuck particles, then return ½ cup of hot oil to the pan. Place pan over high heat. Using a long handled metal whisk, gradually stir in the reserved ½ cup flour. Cook, whisking constantly, until roux is dark red-brown to black, about 3½ to 4 minutes, being careful not to let it scorch or splash on your skin. Remove from heat and immediately add the reserved vegetable mixture, stirring constantly until the roux stops getting darker. Return pan to low heat and cook until vegetables are soft, about 5 minutes, stirring constantly and scraping the pan bottom well. Set aside.

4. Place the stock in a 5½-quart saucepan or large Dutch oven. Bring to a boil. Add the roux mixture by spoonfuls to the boiling stock, stirring until dissolved be-

tween additions. Add the chicken pieces and return mixture to a boil, stirring and scraping pan bottom often. Reduce heat to a simmer and stir in the garlic. Simmer uncovered until chicken is tender, about 1½ to 2 hours, stirring occasionally and more often toward the end of cooking time.

5. When the gumbo is almost cooked, adjust the seasoning if desired with an additional amount of Magic seasoning blend of your choice or the homemade seasoning blend to taste. Garnish with green onions and chopped parsley and serve immediately.

NOTE: See "Selected Sources for Ingredients," page 352.

YIELD: 6 MAIN-DISH OR 10 APPETIZER SERVINGS. ⌁ *Craig Claiborne*

FRIED CHICKEN AND ANDOUILLE-FILE GUMBO

½ cup vegetable oil

1 4-pound chicken, cut up, at room temperature

½ cup all-purpose flour

¾ pound spicy andouille or chorizo sausage, cut into ½-inch slices

¼ pound tasso ham, with or without spicy rind, or plain cooked ham, diced

1 large onion, peeled and chopped

1 green bell pepper, seeded and chopped

3 stalks celery, diced

6 scallions, green and white portions, sliced

3 cloves garlic, peeled and minced

⅔ cup chopped Italian parsley

2 teaspoons dried thyme

2 large bay leaves

1½ to 2 quarts water

Kosher salt and freshly ground pepper to taste

Cayenne pepper or Tabasco sauce to taste

2 tablespoons file powder

2 cups white rice

1. Heat the oil in a heavy 5-quart pot over medium heat. Add the chicken and brown on all sides. Remove chicken and set aside.

2. Make a roux by blending the flour into the oil in the pot and stirring constantly with a long-handled spoon until the mixture is a deep coffee brown. Add the sausage, ham, onion, green pepper and celery. Sauté, stirring, for about 10 minutes. Add the browned chicken, scallions, garlic, parsley, thyme, bay leaves and enough water to cover, stirring to incorporate the roux into the liquid.

3. Stir in salt and pepper and simmer the soup slowly, partly covered, until the chicken is tender, about 1 hour. If you are using the very spicy rind of tasso ham, you will probably not need cayenne or Tabasco. Otherwise, add either toward the end of cooking.

4. Take out the chicken and set aside just until cool enough to handle. Pull off the skin and bones and return the chicken to the soup in large pieces. Adjust seasoning if needed. The soup can be prepared in advance up to this point and stored, covered, in the refrigerator for 2 days. Skim fat from soup.

5. Bring the soup to a simmer. Five minutes before serving, remove from heat and stir in the file powder. Cover and let stand for about 5 minutes. Do not boil the soup after the file has been added. Mound rice in soup plates and ladle the gumbo over.

YIELD: 6 TO 8 FIRST-COURSE SERVINGS,
OR 4 OR 5 MAIN-COURSE SERVINGS ⤙ *Molly O'Neill*

CAJUN JAMBALAYA

(Adapted from *The New York Times Heritage Cook Book*)

1 3-pound chicken, cut into serving pieces
Salt and freshly ground black pepper
2 tablespoons bacon drippings or shortening
2 tablespoons flour
1 pound smoked sausage or smoked country ham, diced
2 onions, chopped
1 green pepper, diced
3 cups peeled and diced fresh or canned, drained tomatoes
1 clove garlic, finely chopped
2 cups shelled and deveined shrimp (about 1¼ pounds)
3 cups water
½ teaspoon dried thyme
½ teaspoon Tabasco sauce, or to taste
2 cups uncooked rice
¼ cup chopped parsley
⅓ cup finely chopped scallions, including green part

1. Season the chicken with salt and pepper and brown on all sides in the drippings or shortening in a heavy skillet. Remove chicken.

2. Sprinkle the flour over fat remaining in the skillet and cook, stirring, until roux turns light brown. Do not allow to burn.

3. Add the sausage or ham, the chicken, onions, green pepper, tomatoes, garlic and shrimp and cook, stirring, about 10 minutes.

4. Add the water, 1½ teaspoons salt, the thyme, Tabasco sauce, ½ teaspoon pepper and the rice. Bring to a boil and then cover and let simmer about 30 minutes, or until the rice is tender. Stir in the parsley and scallions. Cook 5 minutes longer.

YIELD: 8 SERVINGS

CHICKEN FAJITA SALAD

This salad can be served with warm flour tortillas on the side, or it can be spooned onto the tortilla and eaten fajita style.

3 large garlic cloves, chopped
¼ cup chopped onion
2 tablespoons chili powder or more, to taste
Salt
4 tablespoons extra-virgin olive oil
5 tablespoons fresh lime juice
1½ pounds skinless and boneless chicken breast
4 large ripe tomatoes, diced
1 medium red onion, diced
1 small red bell pepper, cored, seeded and diced
½ fresh jalapeño pepper, cored and minced
1 ripe Haas avocado (black pebbly skin)
3 cups cooked kidney or pinto beans
2 tablespoons chopped cilantro
16 soft flour tortillas
Quick Mango Salsa, optional (see recipe, page 334)

1. Combine the garlic, onion, 2 tablespoons chili powder and a generous pinch of salt in a blender or food processor. Add 2 tablespoons of the olive oil and 1 tablespoon of the lime juice and process until smooth.

2. Taste for seasoning and add additional chili powder and salt, if desired. Rub this mixture on the chicken breasts, place on a plate or in a shallow dish, cover with plastic wrap and allow to marinate in a refrigerator for 2 hours, turning once.

3. Combine the tomatoes, red onion, bell pepper and jalapeño pepper in a large salad bowl.

4. Peel, pit and dice the avocado. Mix it with the remaining 4 tablespoons of lime juice and gently fold into the mixture in the salad bowl. Fold in the beans, the cilantro and the remaining 2 tablespoons of olive oil. Check the mixture for seasoning, adding additional salt and chili powder if desired.

5. Preheat oven to 250 degrees. Wrap the tortillas in foil and place them in the oven to warm.

6. Preheat a grill or broiler. Grill or broil the marinated chicken until lightly seared on the outside and cooked through, 10 to 12 minutes. Cut the chicken at an angle into slices about a half-inch thick. Add them to the salad mixture, toss lightly and serve with warm flour tortillas and Quick Mango Salsa, if desired.

YIELD: 6 TO 8 SERVINGS *Florence Fabricant*

QUICK MANGO SALSA

2 large mangoes, moderately ripe
½ cup finely chopped scallions
½ cup minced cilantro
¼ cup fresh lime juice
Freshly ground black pepper to taste
Tabasco or other hot pepper sauce to taste

1. Cut the mangoes in thick sections horizontally, cutting as close to the pits as possible. Trim off the skin, then dice the flesh, removing as much of the flesh as possible clinging to the pits. Do this over a dish to capture any juice.

2. Place the diced mangoes and juice in a bowl and fold in the remaining ingredients. Refrigerate until ready to serve.

YIELD: 6 TO 8 SERVINGS

WARM CHICKEN AND SPINACH SALAD

(Adapted from *Cafe Boulud Cookbook*)

⅔ cup plus 3 tablespoons extra-virgin olive oil
4 bone-in chicken breasts, skin removed, cut into small strips
Coarse sea salt and freshly ground white pepper
6 baby artichokes, trimmed and quartered

1 clove garlic, peeled and crushed

1 sprig thyme

1 tablespoon water

2 medium shallots, peeled, trimmed, diced, rinsed and dried

1/4 cup sherry vinegar

2 tablespoons snipped basil leaves

1 tablespoon tarragon leaves, chopped fine

4 plum tomatoes, peeled, seeded and cut into thin strips

8 cups baby spinach, well washed and dried

1. Center a rack in the oven and preheat the oven to 400 degrees.

2. Warm two tablespoons of the olive oil in a large, ovenproof sauté pan or skillet over medium-high heat. Season the chicken with salt and pepper, and when the oil is hot, slip the breasts, skin-side (or what would have been skin side) down into the pan. Sear the chicken on one side until golden, 3 to 4 minutes, then turn it over and give the other side equal treatment. Turn the breasts again and slide the pan into the oven. Roast the chicken until it is cooked through, about 12 to 14 minutes.

3. Meanwhile, warm a tablespoon of the olive oil in a sauté pan or skillet over medium-high heat. Add the strips of chicken skin and cook until they start to color lightly. Add the artichokes, garlic and thyme, season with salt and pepper, cover, and cook for 3 minutes. Lift the lid and stir in the water. Cover the pan and cook for another 3 to 4 minutes, until artichokes are tender. Discard the garlic and thyme. Remove the pan from the heat and keep warm.

4. When the chicken is cooked, transfer it to a cutting board and put the pan over medium heat. Add the shallots to the pan and cook, stirring, until they soften, about 2 minutes. Pour in the vinegar and scrape up whatever little bits of meat may have adhered to the pan. Reduce the vinegar by half, then whisk in the remaining two-thirds-cup of olive oil and the herbs. This is the dressing for your salad. Remove the pan from the heat, correct seasoning and stir in the tomatoes.

5. Put the spinach in a large bowl and season to taste with salt and pepper. Slice the chicken breasts and put the strips, along with the artichokes and pieces of chicken skin, in the bowl. Toss the salad with the warm chicken pan juices and serve immediately.

YIELD: 4 SERVINGS ⟋ *Moira Hodgson*

LARRY FORGIONE'S
BUFFALO-STYLE CHICKEN SALAD

(Adapted from An American Place, New York City)

Larry Forgione, the chef and owner of An American Place in Manhattan, created this main course salad by combining Buffalo chicken wings and its traditional accompaniments of celery sticks and blue cheese dressing with field greens and baby lettuces. "The integrity is there," Forgione says. "It tastes exactly like Buffalo chicken wings. We stay true to the street version, but do it as if you were making it for yourself."

THE DRESSING

3 tablespoons Maytag blue cheese
   (or other aged blue cheese)
1 tablespoon hot water
3 tablespoons mayonnaise
3 tablespoons sour cream
Freshly ground pepper
A few drops Tabasco sauce

THE CHICKEN

8 chicken thighs, boned and skinned
Salt and freshly ground pepper
2 to 2½ cups peanut or vegetable
   oil, for frying
2 tablespoons unsalted butter,
   softened
2 teaspoons freshly squeezed lemon
   juice

2 teaspoons chopped parsley
½ teaspoon Tabasco sauce
¼ teaspoon cayenne pepper, or to
   taste

THE SALAD

8 cups assorted lettuces and greens
   (like arugula, bibb, red leaf,
   endive, romaine and chicory
   hearts), washed and dried
½ tablespoon wine vinegar
1 tablespoon olive oil
Salt and freshly ground pepper
6 inner celery stalks, trimmed and
   cut in thin strips
2 ripe tomatoes, cored, seeded and
   diced
½ cup pale celery leaves

1. To make the dressing, crumble the blue cheese into a small bowl. Add hot water and mash to a coarse paste. Add mayonnaise, sour cream, pepper and Tabasco sauce, stirring until smooth. Cover and refrigerate until needed.

2. For the chicken, pat the pieces dry and cut each thigh in 4 lengthwise strips. Sprinkle with salt and pepper. Meanwhile, heat the oil in a fryer or deep, wide skillet to a depth of about ¾ inch. Bring oil to a temperature of 375 degrees (test with a ther-

mometer, or drop in a piece of bread, which should sizzle and begin to brown as soon as it hits the oil). Add the chicken pieces and fry, turning them with 2 forks or long-handled tongs, about 5 minutes, or until crisp and lightly golden.

3. Remove the chicken from the fat with a slotted spoon or skimmer, and drain briefly on paper towels. Immediately transfer to a bowl and toss with the butter, lemon juice, parsley, Tabasco sauce and cayenne.

4. To make the salad, toss the lettuces with vinegar, olive oil and a light sprinkling of salt and pepper. Arrange on 4 large plates. Arrange 8 chicken pieces and the celery strips over each salad. Sprinkle with diced tomatoes and celery leaves; drizzle with some of the blue cheese dressing. Serve; pass the dressing separately.

YIELD: 4 SERVINGS ⤳ *Richard Sax*

PANZANELLA WITH GRILLED CHICKEN

This classic tomato-bread salad can be made up to two days ahead and should be served cold. Topped with the warm chicken, it makes a lovely lunch.

THE CHICKEN

½ cup fresh lemon juice

¼ cup olive oil

4 cloves garlic, peeled and coarsely chopped

1 teaspoon freshly ground black pepper, plus more to taste

1½ pounds boneless, skinless chicken breasts

Salt, to taste

½ cup fresh basil leaves, cut across into thin strips

THE SALAD

8 cups crustless bread cubes (1 inch) from good, firm country-style bread

About 1¼ cups water

9 large tomatoes, cored and cut into medium dice

1 large red onion, peeled and cut into small dice

4 large cloves garlic, peeled and minced

1 cup chopped Italian parsley

1½ tablespoons chopped fresh rosemary

3 tablespoons extra-virgin olive oil

1½ tablespoons red wine vinegar

1 tablespoon salt

Freshly ground black pepper to taste

1. To make the chicken, combine the lemon juice, olive oil, garlic and pepper in a large, shallow dish. Add the chicken and coat on both sides. Marinate in the refrigerator at least 2 hours.

2. To make the salad, toss the bread with just enough water to moisten it completely. Let stand for 10 minutes. Squeeze out the excess water and place in a bowl. Toss with the tomatoes, onion, garlic, parsley and rosemary. Mix in the olive oil, vinegar, salt and pepper. Store in the refrigerator for 1 hour.

3. Start a charcoal grill. Grill the chicken until just cooked through, about 3 to 4 minutes per side. Season with salt and pepper to taste. Slice the chicken on the diagonal into thin strips.

4. Divide the salad among 6 plates. Fan the chicken over the salad and garnish with the basil. Serve immediately.

YIELD: 6 SERVINGS   *Molly O'Neill*

LE COLONIAL'S VIETNAMESE CHICKEN AND VERMICELLI SALAD (BUM GA NUONG)

(Adapted from Le Colonial, New York City)

This refreshing salad of grilled chicken tossed with rice vermicelli in a chili vinaigrette flavored with fresh lime juice, is the creation of Viet Tran, the Vietnamese chef of Le Colonial in Manhattan. It is light but highly spiced, combining interesting contrasts of texture and flavor in traditional ingredients like fresh mint, coriander, cucumber, bean sprouts and iceberg lettuce, which adds crunch. The salad can be prepared ahead of time and put together at the last minute, which makes it great for summer entertaining.

2 whole chicken breasts, split to make 4 pieces
2 cloves garlic, finely chopped
2 shallots, finely chopped
Coarse salt and freshly ground pepper to taste

1 tablespoon vegetable oil

½ cup dry rice vermicelli (available in Asian grocery stores)

1 small head of iceberg lettuce, shredded

2 cucumbers, sliced

¼ cup fresh mint, chopped

¼ cup unsalted roasted peanuts, chopped

FOR THE CHILI-LIME VINAIGRETTE

½ cup water

Juice of 1 lime

4 tablespoons Vietnamese fish sauce

1 tablespoon sugar

1 clove garlic, chopped

1 tablespoon chopped red chili pepper

2 tablespoons vegetable or olive oil

1. Marinate the chicken breasts in the garlic, shallots, salt, pepper and the vegetable oil for 20 to 60 minutes.

2. Bring 3 quarts of water to a boil. Add the rice vermicelli and cook 3 to 4 minutes, or until it is almost soft. Strain in a colander and set aside.

3. Grill the chicken on both sides until done. Cut into bite-size pieces.

4. In each of 4 bowls, divide the lettuce and cucumbers. Top with the vermicelli. Arrange the chicken on top of the vermicelli.

5. Combine the ingredients for the chili vinaigrette and mix together thoroughly. Pour 3 to 4 tablespoons of the chili vinaigrette on each salad. Sprinkle with fresh mint and peanuts and serve.

YIELD: 4 SERVINGS *Moira Hodgson*

CHICKEN BREAST SALAD WITH WARM CURRY DRESSING

The curry dressing can be made in advance. Mix mustard, curry powder, balsamic vinegar, chopped scallions, olive oil, salt, pepper and herbs of your choice. While the chicken is cooking, warm the curry dressing over a low flame. When the chicken is ready, lay it over greens and pour on the dressing.

> 4 skinless boneless chicken breast halves, about 1¼ pounds
> 2 teaspoons olive oil
> 2 tablespoons fresh lemon juice
> 2 tablespoons chopped fresh rosemary or 1 teaspoon dried
> 2 teaspoons finely chopped garlic
> Salt and freshly ground pepper to taste
> 1 head radicchio, about ¼ pound, core removed, rinsed and dried
> 2 heads bibb lettuce, core removed, rinsed and dried
> ¼ pound arugula, cut into manageable pieces, rinsed and dried
> Warm Curry Dressing (see recipe, page 341)
> ¼ cup coarsely chopped fresh basil or chervil

1. If chicken breasts are connected, separate halves and cut away membrane or fat. Place oil in mixing bowl with lemon juice, rosemary, garlic, salt and pepper. Stir well. Add chicken pieces and turn them in the marinade to coat well. Cover and set aside until ready to cook. (If marinating for a long period, refrigerate them.)

2. Preheat a charcoal grill or broiler.

3. Put the chicken pieces on the grill or the broiler rack. Cover grill or close broiler. Cook 2 to 3 minutes, turning pieces. Continue cooking until done, about 3 to 5 minutes on the grill, possibly longer under the broiler.

4. Remove pieces. Slice each breast on the bias about ¼-inch thick.

5. In a large mixing bowl add the radicchio, bibb lettuce and arugula. Toss well. Add half the warm dressing, and toss again. Place the sliced chicken over the salad and sprinkle with the remaining dressing and basil.

YIELD: 4 SERVINGS

WARM CURRY DRESSING

2 teaspoons Dijon mustard
1 teaspoon curry powder
2 tablespoons balsamic vinegar
¼ cup chopped scallions
⅓ cup olive or vegetable oil
Salt and freshly ground pepper to taste
¼ cup coarsely chopped fresh basil or chervil

Place the mustard, curry powder, vinegar and scallions in a saucepan. Blend well over low heat with a wire whisk. Add the oil, blending well. Remove from the heat and add salt, pepper and basil. Keep warm.

YIELD: ABOUT 1 CUP *Pierre Franey*

ROAST CHICKEN SALAD WITH BEETS AND FETA CHEESE

4 large beets
2 whole chicken breasts, bone in, skin on
Coarse sea salt and freshly ground pepper to taste
3 cloves garlic, in their skins
1 teaspoon Dijon mustard
¼ cup balsamic vinegar
½ cup olive oil
1 bunch watercress, washed and trimmed (see Note)
1 small red onion, sliced
About 16 cherry tomatoes, cut in half
¼ pound kalamata olives, pitted
¼ pound feta cheese, crumbled

1. Preheat the oven to 450 degrees. Roast the beets in their skins until they are tender (about 45 minutes). Season the chicken breasts with salt and pepper and roast for about 35 minutes, or until they are done. Put the garlic cloves on a baking dish and roast for 20 minutes.

2. When the beets are cool enough to handle, peel and slice them. Remove the meat from the bones and cut the chicken into half-inch slices.

3. Peel the skins off the garlic and mash the cloves into a paste. Add the mustard and vinegar and mix well. Gradually add the olive oil to make a smooth emulsion. Season to taste with salt and pepper.

4. In a large bowl, combine the watercress, red onion, tomatoes and olives. Add the dressing and toss well.

5. Divide the salad among 4 plates, top with chicken and feta cheese and serve.

NOTE: Arugula can be used instead of watercress. This salad should be served at room temperature, not cold from the refrigerator.

YIELD: 4 SERVINGS ⟅ *Moria Hodgson*

WARM CHICKEN SALAD WITH GREEN BEANS

On a warm, lazy evening, this poached chicken salad may be the way to go. The sliced meat is laid on lettuces sprinkled with radishes, mint and beans and dressed with a tangy yogurt infused with cumin, tarragon and Aleppo pepper.

Kosher salt

1 clove garlic

4 chicken thighs and 2 chicken breasts, skin on

2 teaspoons red wine vinegar

3 tablespoons orange juice

1 tablespoon Dijon mustard

1 tablespoon chopped tarragon

1 teaspoon ground cumin

Pinch Aleppo pepper

3 tablespoons extra-virgin olive oil, more for greens

¼ cup whole milk yogurt

1 romaine heart in 2-inch pieces

2 handfuls red leaf lettuce

20 mint leaves

8 icicle radishes, thinly sliced

½ pound green beans, blanched

1. Fill a large pan with water and season with salt. Add garlic; bring to boil. Place chicken in water and simmer gently until cooked through, 20 minutes. Transfer to plate.

2. In a small bowl, whisk together vinegar, orange juice, mustard, tarragon, cumin and pepper. Season with salt. Gradually whisk in olive oil until smooth, then whisk in yogurt.

3. In a large shallow bowl, toss romaine, red leaf, mint, radishes and beans. Sprinkle with oil and salt, and toss once more. While chicken is warm, remove skin; cut breasts into ⅛-inch slices. Pull meat from thighs.

4. Arrange chicken over greens and spoon dressing on top. Serve.

YIELD: 4 SERVINGS *Amanda Hesser*

APPENDIX

CLASSES OF CHICKENS

Chickens are classified primarily by the size, weight and age of the bird when processed. Chickens are produced to meet specific requirements of the customer, which can be a retail outlet, fast-food chain or institutional buyer, among others.

Poultry: Domesticated fowl raised for meat and/or eggs.

Broiler: A chicken raised for its meat, as distinguished from a "layer," which is a chicken that lays eggs for the table.

Poussin: Less than 24 days of age and about 1 pound or less.

Cornish Game Hens: Less than 30 days of age and about 2 pounds.

Fast-Food-Size Broiler: 2 pounds 4 ounces to 3 pounds 2 ounces (mostly 2 pounds 6 ounces to 2 pounds 14 ounces); usually cut up, without necks and giblets, may have tail and leaf fat removed, less than 42 days of age.

3's and Up: 3 to 4¾ pounds, usually with neck and giblets for retail grocery; whole, cut-up, parts, 40 to 45 days of age. Typical retail size.

Roaster: 5 to 8 pounds, less than 10 weeks of age (usually 55 to 60 days of age).

Broilers for Deboning: 5 to 6 pounds, males usually 47 to 56 days of age. Deboned for nuggets, patties, strips and similar boneless products; most often sold without neck and giblets.

Capon: Surgically desexed male broilers weighting 7 to 9 pounds, about 14 to 15 weeks of age. Plump and tender. Capons were once common but are now a specialty item.

Heavy Hens: Spent breeder hens that are no longer commercially productive for laying hatching eggs, usually 5 to 5½ pounds, about 15 months of age, used for cooked, diced or pulled meat. Also sold at retail as "stewing hens." Because of their greater age, stewing hens have more flavor than broilers but are considerably less tender.

All weights are r.t.c. (ready-to-cook or eviscerated/dressed weight basis).

CHICKEN TERMS

Hormone-Free: No artificial or added hormones are allowed by the U.S. government in the production of chickens in the United States, so any chicken or chicken product could be advertised as *hormone free*. The term is largely a marketing concept. Steroids are similarly banned.

Free Range: In theory, the term *free range* indicates a production unit where chickens are allowed to forage in an outdoor area in search of insects and other types of "range" food. However, there is no official federal government definition of *free range*, and the U.S. Department of Agriculture approves label claims on a case-by-case basis. The USDA generally permits the term to be used if access to the outside of the chicken house is available for some part of the day, whether or not the chicken choose to go outside. Experience shows that most chickens will stay close to water and chicken feed, which is usually located within the house. As one "free range" producer told *Consumer Reports* magazine: "It's not the chickens' nature that if you give them a 15-acre pasture they're going to gallop and jump and roll over." *Consumer Reports* observed 50 chickens in the sunshine outside the production house, while 5,000 remained inside. Most blind taste tests find "free range" chickens comparable in taste to conventionally raised chickens.

Natural: Under USDA regulations, a "natural" product has no added ingredients and is minimally processed, just enough to get it ready to be cooked. Most ready-to-cook chicken can be labeled *natural* if processors choose to do so.

Organic: The concept of "organic" production generally prohibits the use of pesticides and manufactured fertilizers, although "natural" fertilizers such as animal manure may be used on crops. "Organically produced" chicken must be fed a diet of organically produced feeds and receive no medication.

The U.S. Department of Agriculture published a rule in December 2000 that defines organic production and prohibits the use of the term *organic* on the packaging of any food product not produced in accordance with the rule. Under the rule, which went into effect on October 21, 2002, poultry labeled *organic* has to be raised in qualifying conditions from the second day of life; can be vaccinated but not medicated; has to be given feed made from organic ingredients that can include vitamins and minerals but not poultry or mammalian byproducts or antibiotic growth promotants; and has to be given suitable "access to the outdoors," including shade, shelter, exercise areas, fresh air and direct sunlight, and may be "temporarily confined" only for reasons of health, safety, the animal's stage of production, or protection of soil or water quality.

"Farm-Raised": This term, when used on restaurant menus and the like, usually refers to chickens raised on a local farm. However, all chickens are raised on farms, so it could refer to any chicken.

BUYING, HANDLING, STORING AND PREPARING CHICKEN

Chicken has become America's favorite food choice. Buying, handling, storing and preparing chicken properly will help make chicken more enjoyable and maintain top quality. Good food preparation and safety practices will ensure a meal that family and friends can take pleasure in.

Buying Chicken: The amount of fresh chicken to purchase at the supermarket depends on the number of persons to be served, the size of the servings, the yield of cooked meat, the method of preparation, and whether or not leftovers are desired. As a general rule of thumb, plan on 4 to 8 ounces of raw, bone-in, skin-on chicken for each adult. For raw boneless, skinless meat, plan on using about 4 ounces per adult. In general, one whole chicken weighing about 3½ pounds with neck and giblets serves four and yields slightly over 3 cups of cooked, diced chicken meat without skin and bone, and ½ cup of meat from the neck and giblets.

On a price-per-pound basis, leg quarters are the least expensive. However, if time constraints and individual preferences are important, buying chicken parts to suit specific needs is a wise choice. If only breast or only leg meat is desired or if a recipe calls for specific parts, choose the parts package that best meets the need.

Consumer color preference in chicken varies in different sections of the country. Skin color ranges from white to deep yellow, depending on the chicken's diet. Color does not indicate a difference in nutritional value, flavor, tenderness or fat content.

Remember to check the "Sell By" date on the chicken package label. This date indicates the last day the product should be offered for sale, although it will maintain its high quality if properly refrigerated or cooked within a few days after the posted "Sell By" date.

Handling Raw Chicken: Each package of fresh chicken carries a USDA-mandated safe food handling and cooking message. This message reads as follows:

"This product was prepared from inspected and passed meat and/or poultry. Some food products may contain bacteria that would cause illness if the product is mishandled or cooked improperly. For your protection, follow these safe-handling instructions. Keep refrigerated or frozen. Thaw in refrigerator or microwave. Keep raw meat and poultry separate from other foods. Wash working surfaces (including cutting boards), utensils and hands after touching raw meat or poultry. Cook thoroughly. Keep hot foods hot. Refrigerate leftovers immediately or discard."

Chicken, like all fresh meats, is perishable and should be handled with care to maintain top quality. To maximize food quality and safety, grocery shop last before you go directly home. Never leave chicken in the car and refrigerate immediately on reaching home to help maintain the highest quality. Never leave the chicken on a countertop at room temperature. Packaged fresh chicken can be refrigerated in original wrappings in the coldest part of the refrigerator for 1 or 2 days. If rinsing whole chicken or parts in cold running water is a personal preference, rewrap it for storage before cooking and always remember to clean sink and countertops thoroughly afterward.

Storing Chicken: If chicken parts are wrapped separately in foil or other freezer wrap before freezing, it is easier to select just the right number and kind of parts for a single meal. Plastic sandwich bags are also good for holding a single chicken part. Individual parts can then be gathered together in a larger plastic freezer bag or wrapped in heavy-duty foil and labeled before freezing. Be sure to press air out of the package before sealing. Individual quick frozen (IQF) product is available in essentially all markets and offers the convenience of selecting individual parts that are not frozen to other parts. Resealable plastic bags are most often used as IQF packaging.

It is not recommended that either cooked or uncooked chicken be refrozen in a home freezer once it has been thawed. However, if the previously frozen product, either cooked or uncooked, is refrozen within 2 hours of being at room temperature or no longer than 2 days in a refrigerator in a thawed state, it can be refrozen. Depending on how the product was handled and stored, there may be a certain loss in flavor and quality.

Preparing Chicken: Chicken can be thawed safely in the refrigerator (not on the countertop) or in cold water. It takes approximately 24 hours to thaw a 4 pound chicken in the refrigerator, and 3 to 9 hours for cut-up parts. If chicken is to be thawed in cold water, place the chicken in its original wrap or in a watertight plastic bag and immerse in cold water; the water should be changed often. It takes at least 2 hours to thaw a whole chicken.

For quick thawing of the chicken (raw or cooked), use the microwave. Thawing time varies according to the form in which the chicken is frozen (i.e. whole or parts, number of parts frozen together). Use defrost or medium-low setting. Microwave 2 minutes; let stand 2 minutes. Repeat as needed. Turn chicken and separate parts as it thaws, taking care that it does not begin to cook. Be sure chicken is covered to reduce splattering.

Different recipes may call for various cooking temperatures. Follow the instructions and always cook chicken well done, not medium or rare. In general, for bone-in parts and whole carcass chickens, an oven roasting temperature of 375 degrees Fahrenheit will give an even doneness and a favorable yield. Occasionally certain cooks prefer an even higher temperature, such as 400 degrees. Internal temperature should reach 180 degrees for whole carcass chicken with bone in; 170 degrees for bone-in parts; and 160 degrees for boneless parts. Coarsely and finely ground chicken with or without added ingredients should reach at least 165 degrees. If a poultry carcass or part is stuffed, the stuffing temperature must reach 165 degrees.

Using a meat thermometer is recommended as the most accurate indicator for doneness. To check visually for doneness without using a thermometer, pierce the chicken with a fork; juices should run clear (not pink) when the fork is inserted and should come out with ease when the chicken is done. The marinade in which the chicken has been standing should not be used to baste raw chicken or be served with cooked chicken. Uncooked chicken should be frozen if it will not be used within 2 days.

When barbecuing chicken outdoors, keep it refrigerated until ready to cook. Do not place cooked chicken on same plate used to carry raw chicken to grill. Microwave cooking can be used in conjunction with barbecuing/grilling. Follow cookbook instructions. The usual recommended procedure is to raise the temperature of the chicken in microwave until juices are flowing from meat and then transfer to the grill to complete the cooking process. Microwaving can be done while the charcoal briquettes become fully ignited and turn white in color.

When roasting a whole, uncut chicken in the oven, allow about 30 minutes per pound of cooking time. The temperature of the oven should be about 350 degrees but can be set for 400 degrees for the first 30 minutes to help speed the cooking process. Thus, an unfrozen, fully thawed whole chicken weighing about 4 pounds without the neck and giblets in the body cavity will take about 2 hours of cooking time (30 minutes per pound times 4 pounds). Stuffing a 4-pound chicken with traditional bread-based ingredients will add an additional 30 minutes or so to the total cooking time. The key point to remember is to have the stuffing reach a temperature of 165 degrees.

Always wash countertops, cutting boards, knives and other utensils used in preparing raw chicken before they come in contact with other raw or cooked foods. Hot soapy water works well for this type of cleaning. Remember, too, that clean hands also reduce the possibility of cross-contamination.

Cooked Chicken: Cooked chicken should never be left at room temperature for more than 2 hours.

If not eaten immediately, it should be kept either hot (between 140 and 165 degrees) or refrigerated at 40 degrees or less. Cooked chicken should be prepared for freezing the same way as uncooked chicken except when it is made with sauce or gravy. Then it is best to pack in a rigid container with a secure, tight-fitting lid. Keep frozen until time to thaw or cook. If the chicken is stuffed, remove the stuffing to a separate container before refrigerating or freezing.

Cooked, cut-up chicken is at its best quality refrigerated for no longer than 2 days; whole cooked chicken, an additional day. If leftovers are to be reheated, cover them to retain moisture and to ensure that the chicken is heated all the way through. Bring gravies to a rolling boil before serving.

If the cooked chicken is to be transported to a picnic or other out-of-home dining site, place the chicken in an insulated container or ice chest until ready to eat. Keep the chicken below 40 degrees or above 140 degrees.

Storing Chicken at Home: If properly packaged, these recommended storage times will keep chicken in top quality.

	Refrigerator 40 degrees	Freezer 0 degrees
Fresh Raw Chicken		
Whole Chicken	1–2 days	1 year
Chicken Parts	1–2 days	9 months
Giblets	1–2 days	3–4 months
Ground Chicken	1–2 days	3–4 months
Cooked Chicken and Leftovers		
Fried Chicken	3–4 days	4 months
Whole Roasted Chicken	3–4 days	4 months
Cooked Chicken Dishes	3–4 days	4–6 months
Chicken Parts (Plain)	3–4 days	4 months
Parts with Gravy, Broth	1–2 days	6 months
Chicken Nuggets, Patties	1–2 days	1–3 months

NOTE: Commercially frozen chicken will maintain top quality in home freezer for up to one year.

SELECTED SOURCES FOR INGREDIENTS

Adriana's Caravan, (800) 316-0820. *www.adrianascaravan.com*

Chef Paul Prudhomme's Magic Seasoning Blends, (800) 457-2857. *www.chefpaul.com*

The CMC Company, (800) 262-2780.

Dean & DeLuca 560 Broadway, New York, N.Y. (212) 431-1691. *www.deandeluca.com*

Ethnic Grocer 1090 Industrial Dr., Suite 5, Bensenville, IL 60106. (630) 860-1733.
    www.ethnicgrocer.com

Greater Galilee Gourmet, Inc. Santa Monica, CA (800) 290-1391.

Kalustyan, 123 Lexington Avenue, New York, NY 10016; (212) 685-3416. *www.kalustyans.com*

Kalpana Indian and International Groceries, 2528 Broadway, New York, NY (212) 663-4190.

The Oriental Pantry, (800) 828-0368.

Sahadi Importing Company, 187 Atlantic Avenue (Court Street), Brooklyn, NY; (718) 624-4550.
    www.sahadis.com/

Shallah's Middle Eastern Importing Company, 290 White Street, Danbury, CT 06810; (203) 743-
    4181.

The Spice House, 1941 Central Avenue, Evanston, IL 60201; (847) 328-3711. *www.thespicehouse.
    com*

Sultan's Delight, P.O. Box 090302, Brooklyn, NY 11209; (800) 852-5046.
    www.sultansdelight.com

Surfas Restaurant and Supply, 8825 National Boulevard, Culver City, CA 90232; (310) 559-4770.
    www.surfasonline.com

BIBLIOGRAPHY

Agatson, Arthur. *The South Beach Diet Cookbook*. San Francisco: Rodale Books, 2003.

Algar, Alyla. *Classical Turkish Cooking*. New York: HarperCollins, 1991.

Anderson, Pam. *How to Cook Without a Book*. New York: Broadway Books, 2000.

Bach, Ngo, and Gloria Zimmerman. *The Classic Cuisine of Vietnam*. New York: New American Library, 1979.

Barr, Beryl, and Barbara Turner Sachs. *The Artists' and Writers' Cookbook*. Sausalito, Calif.: Contact Editions, 1961.

Becker, Marion Rombauer, et al. *The New Joy of Cooking*. New York: Scribner (Simon & Schuster, Inc.), 1997.

Behr, Edward. *The Art of Eating* (magazine). Peacham, Vt.

Bhumichitr, Vatcharin. *The Taste of Thailand*. New York: Anetheum, 1988.

———. *Vatch's Southeast Asian Cookbook*. New York: St. Martin's Press, 1998.

Bittman, Mark. *The Minimalist Cooks at Home*. New York: Broadway Books, 2000.

———. *The Minimalist Cooks Dinner*. New York: Broadway Books, 2001.

———. *The Minimalist Entertains*. New York: Broadway Books, 2003.

Boulud, Daniel. *Café Boulud Cookbook*. New York: Scribners, 1999.

Chapman, Emalee. *Fifteen Minute Meals*. San Francisco: 101 Productions, 1988.

Claiborne, Craig. *The Best of Craig Claiborne*. New York: Times Books, 1999.

———. *Cooking with Herbs & Spices*. New York: Harper & Row, 1970.

———. *Craig Claiborne's Gourmet Diet*. New York: Times Books, 1980.

———. *The New York Times Cook Book*. New York: Harper & Row, 1990.

———. *The New York Times International Cook Book*. New York: Harper & Row, 1971.

———. *The New York Times Menu Cook Book*. New York: Harper & Row, 1966.

Colwin, Laurie. *More Home Cooking*. New York: HarperCollins, 1990.

Dunlop, Fuchsia. *Land of Plenty*. New York: Norton, 2003.

Glass, Peggy K. *The Home Cooking Sampler*. Upper Saddle River, N.J.: Prentice-Hall, 1989.

Glazer, Phyllis, and Miriyam Glazer. *The Essential Book of Jewish Festival Cooking*. New York: Harper-Collins, 2004.

Greaves, Ellen, and Wayne Nish. *Simple Menus for the Bento Box*. New York: William Morrow/Harper/Collins, 1998.

Hay, Donna. *Off the Shelf*. New York: William Morrow/HarperCollins, 2001.

Hewitt, Jean. *The New York Times Heritage Cook Book*. New York: G. P. Putnam's Sons, 1972.

———. *The New York Times Large Type Cook Book*. New York: G. P. Putnam's Sons, 1972.

Hom, Ken. *The Taste of China*. New York: Simon & Schuster, 1990.

Jaffrey, Madhur. *Indian Cooking*. Hauppauge, N.Y.: Barron's Educational Series, 1983.

Kafka, Barbara. *Roasting: A Simple Art*. New York: William Morrow/HarperCollins, 1995.

Kaimal, Maya. *Savoring the Spice Coast of India*. New York: HarperCollins, 2000.

Kamman, Madeleine. *The New Making of a Cook*. New York: William Morrow/HarperCollins, 1997.

Kasper, Lynne Rosetto. *The Splendid Table*. New York: William Morrow/HarperCollins, 1992.

Kendall, Sadie. *The Crème Fraîche Cookbook*. Atascadera, Calif.: Ridgeview Publishing, 1989.

LaBelle, Patti, and Laura Randolph Lancaster. *Patti LaBelle's Lite Cuisine*. New York: Gotham Books, 2003.

Malouf, Waldy, and Molly Finn. *The Hudson River Valley Cookbook*. Reading, Mass.: Addison-Wesley, 1995.

Marks, Copeland. *The Varied Kitchens of India*. New York: M. Evans, 1986.

McDermott, Nancie. *Real Thai*. New York: Chronicle, 1992.

Medearis, Angela. *The African-American Kitchen*. New York: E. P. Dutton, 1994.

Meyer, Danny and Michael Romano. *The Union Square Café Cookbook*. New York: HarperCollins, 1994.

Raichlen, Steven. *The Barbecue Bible*. New York: Workman, 1998.

———. *Beer Can Chicken*. New York: Workman, 2002.

———. *How to Grill*. New York: Workman, 2001.

———. *Raichlen's Indoor Grilling*. New York: Workman, 2004.

Richard, Michel. *Home Cooking with a French Accent*. New York: William Morrow/HarperCollins, 1993.

Rodgers, Judy. *The Zuni Café Cookbook*. New York: Norton, 2002.

Rosen, Marvin, et al. *Welcome to Junior's*. New York: Morrow/HarperCollins, 1999.

Routhier, Nicole. *The Foods of Vietnam*. New York: Stewart, Tabori & Chang, 1989.

Samuelsson, Marcus. *Aquavit and the New Scandinavian Cuisine*. New York: Houghton Mifflin, 2003.

Scotto Sisters and Gilles Pudlowski. *France: The Beautiful Cookbook*. New York: HarperCollins, 1989.

Solomon, Lois, and Anita Reitman. *The Calico Pantry Cookbook*. New York: Simon & Schuster, 1980.

Stern, Jane, and Michael Stern. *American Gourmet*. New York: HarperCollins, 1991.

Tsuji, Shizuo. *Japanese Cooking: A Simple Art*. Tokyo: Kodansha International, 1986.

Vongerichten, Jean-Georges, and Mark Bittman. *Jean-Georges: Cooking at Home with a Four-Star Chef*. New York: Broadway Books, 1998.

Waltuck, David, and Melicia Phillips. *Staff Meals from Chanterelle*. New York: Workman, 2000.

BYLINES

Apple, R. W., Jr.
Barboza, Steven
Bittman, Mark
Boulud, Daniel
Bowen, Dana
Burros, Marian
Calta, Marialisa
Capon, Robert Farrar
Chira, Susan
Claiborne, Craig
Colicchio, Tom
Ducasse, Alain
Epstein, Jason
Fabricant, Florence
Ferretti, Fred
Fitzpatrick, Jean Grasso
Flaste, Richard

Franey, Pierre
Fussell, B. H.
Gugino, Sam
Hall, Trish
Hamlin, Suzanne
Hesser, Amanda
Hewitt, Jean
Hodgson, Moira
Hom, Ken
Idone, Christopher
Jenkins, Nancy Harmon
Kafka, Barbara
Kaiser, Emily
Kleiman, Dena
Lawson, Nigella
Lee, Matt
Lee, Ted

Leimbach, Dulcie
Miller, Bryan
Nathan, Joan
O'Neill, Molly
Owens, Mitchell
Pepin, Jacques
Raichlen, Steven
Reed, Julia
Rentschler, Kay
Reynolds, Jonathan
Samuelsson, Marcus
Sax, Richard
Sheraton, Mimi
Sifton, Sam
Viladas, Pilar
Wells, Patricia
Witchel, Alex

INDEX